CW01338249

THE COST OF LIFE

Recovering from an epidemic of addiction, anxiety, depression, and obesity.

DONNA ROSS

Copyright © 2022 Donna Ross

All rights reserved. No part of this book may be reproduced or used in any manner without written permission of the copyright owner.

One day you will tell your story of how you overcame what you went through, and it will be someone else's survival guide.

CONTENT WARNING:

This book contains material that may be traumatising to some readers.

Dr. Stephen Pereira. Thank you for helping me find my peace.

I dedicate this book to you.

DEDICATIONS

In sharing this personal account of my life, I must express my gratitude to the health and medical profession. Without your help, I wouldn't be alive to share my knowledge, experience, strength and hope. I dedicate this book to you.

With special thanks to:-

Dr Stephen Pereira, Dr Rasmita Ori, James Moore, Miss Sovra Whitcroft, Professor Arun Ranganathan, Dr Bruce Lipton, Dr Joe Dispenza, Professor Piet Haers, Professor Simon Shorvon, Professor Ernest Schilders, Professor Nima Heidari, Professor Mike Loosemore, Professor John Dickinson, Professor Greg Whyte, Professor Mike Mcmahon, Professor Marcos Sforza, Professor Mauro Tarallo, Lesley Chorn, Jefferey Rink, Janine Dobson, K Samantha Matern, Mr Mike Bowen, Dr Lynda Greathead, Dr Richard Kaczmarski, Dr Angus Kennedy, Dr Akbar de Medici, Mr Alex Shorrt, Colleen Derango, Dr Nerina Wilkinson, Dr Mattheos Fraidakis, Dr Jasmine Piran, Dr Jas Singh, Dr Mark Bowes, Dr Howard Gluckman, Richard Higgins, Dr M Venter, Dr Gerard Hall, Mr Sean Curry, Mr Lloyd Williams, Mr Brian Cohen, Mr Luke Jones, Dr John Outhwaite, Dr Dean Halfpenny, Dr Sean White, Dr Glynn Towlerton, Dr Dharindar Bhullar, Dr Jessica Briscoe, Mr Charles East, Mr Naresh Joshi, Mr Alistair Windsor, Dr Peter

Hawker, Mr Hugh Cable, Dr Elaine Ross, Dr Pyry Peltola, Krina Panchal, David Wales, Darren Chin, Toni Russo, Dr Anna Pallecaros, Jim Pate, Pedro Philippou, Dr Rebecca Robinson, Chris Allen, Mike Naylor, Ciaran Keen, Dr Simone Tomaz, Dr Karen Gerber, Vijay Rana, Wayne Farrell, Mr S Khan.

BUPA Global, BUPA UK, Novo Nordisk, Motiva, NHS, Nuffield, Spire, BMI, Netcare, Healthcare America, The Althea Practice, The Institute of Sport, Exercise and health, The Centre for Health and Human Performance, One Welbeck, The London Clinic, The Princess Grace Hospital, The Harley St Clinic, The Wellington Hospital, The Hospital of St John and St Elizabeth. University College Hospital, Chelsea and Westminster Hospital, St Thomas's Hospital, Warwick Hospital, The Queen Elizabeth Hospital, Birmingham City Hospital.

CONTENTS

INTRODUCTION

My name is Donna Ross, I am 49 years old and for over twenty-five years, I have been on the front lines of the health and beauty industry, obesity treatment clinics and a plastic surgery empire.

I created the largest weight loss surgery company in Europe. My family and I owned the first hospital in the world built specifically for weight loss and cosmetic surgery. I have worked with many celebrities and influential people that came to me for help. My life appeared very glamourous and I had everything anyone would wish for.

I was becoming increasingly disillusioned with the weight loss and beauty industry. I felt I wasn't making a difference to the lives of the people who were coming to me for help. At the same time my own demons were slowly catching up with me. I was also living a lie, which my family and many people within the industry, benefited from covering up. When I couldn't live a lie anymore, I walked away from the businesses and my life as I knew it.

Over the next ten years I would mentally, physically and cosmetically deconstruct and reconstruct my mind and body. During this time, I gained invaluable knowledge into how to change our inherited patterns of behaviour, so we may live promising and healthy lives for ourselves and our children.

I came from a poor working-class family to build my way up to be the face of the weight loss surgery industry. The media hailed me as the 'cosmetic surgery boss' or 'Donna Ross the Boss', to many people my life seemed perfect. I was living the dream - what millions of people around the world fantasise about. I had sports cars, fabulous homes, expensive jewellery and more designer shoes, bags and clothes, than I could ever wear. I travelled the world first class and stayed in luxury hotels and exotic places. I dated athletes and models. I was surrounded by 'hot' men and fabulous people. The reality was I was living a nightmare and I often wished I was dead.

I bring you my story of healing from addictions and dysfunctional behaviour. I am a survivor of sexual abuse and domestic violence. Throughout my long journey to a place of peace, I have recovered from eating disorders, obesity and many other addictive behaviours. I have suffered such severe anxiety and depression that I thought the only way to stop the pain was to take my own life. Throughout this book I wish to share my personal experiences of how I found my way to a place of peace. Through my story I would like to offer the knowledge I gained on my journey.

Over the last two years we have been in the grip of a global pandemic. We are beginning to see the long-term effects of living in this traumatic environment. We have found ourselves living lives for which we were never prepared. We could not conceptualise what removing our freedom of choice would do to us. We've had to sit with emotions we had spent years trying to avoid.

Questions have been raised throughout the pandemic, what is the economic loss compared to the numbers of lives lost? What is the cost of life? I understand the real cost is the systemic sadness, misery and despair people are living with all around the world. This can feel like the slowest, most painful death of all, unimaginable and at times, worse than any acute illness. When we evaluate the trauma, addictions and dysfunctional behaviours that have risen from this pandemic, perhaps the very word, 'cost' might be worth re-evaluating?

Alcohol sales have soared during lockdown, and unfortunately so have toxic patterns in relationships, including domestic violence. It is understandable that people turn to drugs, food and sex to numb and disassociate from the fear, anxiety and boredom of lockdown. Alongside the rising trends of alcohol misuse, we have seen a huge increase in the use of online pornography, gambling and shopping. Activities that were once sought outside of our homes are now living within them, virtually.

The compulsive use of social media to escape our painful realities is at epidemic levels. Many people have sought medical help from their doctors. We are seeing the use of medical crutches such as medication for anxiety, depression and pain being prescribed at unimaginable levels. People are spending hours constantly looking at themselves during online meetings. Subsequently the demand for cosmetic enhancement procedures has hugely increased. We find ourselves seeking superficial solutions to emotional problems.

What lies beneath these behaviours is often a much deeper wound. How then do we get to the source of these dysfunctional behaviours and heal ourselves.

To many, the environment of the pandemic to is one of trauma. Trauma is defined as 'a deeply distressing or disturbing experience'. While many of us have managed to escape relatively unscathed, we have been living in a sustained environment of fear. Fear is defined as 'an unpleasant emotion caused by the threat of danger, pain or harm'. We have feared death for both ourselves and our loved ones, we have feared losing our jobs, businesses, homes, cars and our freedom. Many people around the world have faced starvation.

A stress response to fear or trauma can manifest itself in ways we wouldn't immediately associate with trauma. This response is likely to show itself in dysfunctional behaviours, anger, rage, pain, sleep disturbances, anxiety, depression, illness and in the most extreme cases, suicide or murder. Not all coping strategies are destructive, some can even appear healthy. The commonality is the source of these strategies and that is often a place of fear, emotional and physical pain.

For many years I had been using coping strategies that appeared healthy or were considered 'acceptable'. When they eventually stopped working, I started to use other behaviours that would become very destructive. I was also consumed with chronic health issues. Doctors were struggling to find solutions to my growing health problems. I set upon a mission to find answers to my rapidly deteriorating health. I wasn't sure how I was going to find a solution to my mounting problems. I knew, without a doubt, that I'd be dead if I didn't. I also had to find a way to stop dragging my past life issues everywhere with me.

My work life was like Groundhog Day. For fifteen years I'd worked with thousands of patients who wanted to lose weight or change their appearance. It was quite clear there were far bigger issues that lay beneath their desires. I was seeing huge numbers of patients sabotaging their own weight loss surgery. The Cosmetic surgery patients would keep coming back for more and more treatments and they ended up looking worse, not better.

I decided I wanted a change of career. I decided to do something where I could help people make a real difference to their lives. I focused my new vocation to helping others change their behaviour. During my studies, one of my tutors discussed the theory of epigenetics and a scientist named Dr Bruce Lipton. I'd even never heard of epigenetics, but my interest was sparked.

I researched Dr Lipton and found out he was presenting his data and findings, at a conference in London. I went along to meet Dr Lipton and to my surprise I ended up spending three days at the conference. I listened to speakers who presented astonishing information and theories. These people thought in ways I couldn't understand. I met Dr Lipton, Dr Joe Dispenza and Greg Brayden- known as *'the three amigos'*. I had no idea how lucky I'd been to spend time with these brilliant minds. This meeting would be the basis of a complete change in my thinking.

Dr Lipton talked about inherited blueprints and how DNA was fixed at only 3-5%. I had always been told and believed DNA was fixed and you inherited your parents' combined genetics. I would learn that you do inherit their genetics, but by changing your thinking, you can change your DNA. This knowledge blew my mind, for forty years, the basis of my beliefs was incorrect.

My family are, what I would now describe as, extremely toxic. Back then I thought we were all just a bit crazy. When listening to Dr Lipton, I would come to understand that the way I was raised and the environment I lived in was having a profound impact on me. I would finally understand why my geographical moves from place to place, home to home and country to country never worked long term. My environment was in my mind, manifesting in my thoughts. I discovered that to change my thinking was as easy as making the decision and as hard as reversing generations of programming.

When I understood that 95-97% of my DNA could be changed by my thinking, I also understood that my illnesses were potentially mapped in my mind. These illnesses had taken me to death's door and destroyed my immune system. After years of treatment to suppress my immune system, I was left with little immunity. I lived with the constant worry that a virus or infection could kill me.

At 17 years old, I was confined to a wheelchair due to my rheumatoid arthritis. I was told I could be paralysed from the neck down and had to have three spinal surgeries. I was scheduled for surgery to have my colon removed, so severe was my Crohn's disease. My body had become overwhelmed with numerous critical health issues. I had no idea that I could and would heal myself of every single chronic illness. I would be an example of how humans could not only heal from, but completely reverse all chronic illness, as if it had never even existed. All I would be left with were the scars across my body from over thirty operations.

When I learned more about epigenetics, it allowed me to pull everything I was learning together. Suddenly everything made sense, I now understood the dynamics of my blueprint. Once I knew that my blueprint could be changed, I wanted to learn how that blueprint had been created. Over the next few years, I would learn everything I could about trauma and how it impacted the mind and body.

My blueprint was a toxic blueprint of generational trauma and abuse. The thinking and behaviours that had unconsciously been passed down to me, were destructive. What I came to understand was that my family of origin believed what they had been told and shown, just as their parents had done before them. One dysfunctional generation unknowingly passing toxic knowledge onto the next generation.

The gift of this awareness would not only lead me to a place of healing, but also to a place of forgiveness. I found a fire and drive inside me that I had no idea existed. What drove me to find a solution was the love for my son. I was determined to change my blueprint, so in turn he could change his. The generations that followed would then be able to live completely different lives.

I would come to understand that the knowledge I was gaining had to be shared. The environment of the global pandemic, although absolutely devastating, has facilitated this book. I began to believe that all I have been through and all that I have learned would be of use to others. When I understood this, I realised that I couldn't not tell my story, no matter what it cost me.

The information in this book has been a long time coming. There are parts that will shock you. There are terrible crimes that have been committed and gone unpunished. The price I have paid to find my freedom and tell my story was immense. It cost me my immediate family, my extended family, most of my friends, my businesses, my homes and all my money. It cost me my life as I knew it.

I hope this book will inspire you to believe that you can change every aspect of your life and reach heights that you never dreamed were possible.

Following the pandemic, we can change our lives for the better. We can take the positive out of the most emotionally and financially devastating circumstances. To all those that read my story, I hope it helps you find hope where you think there's none, answers to questions that can't be found and the most priceless thing of all, peace of mind.

Your life need never be the same again.

CHAPTER ONE

WHERE IT ALL BEGAN

BEGINNING

A POINT IN TIME OR SPACE WHEN SOMETHING BEGINS

There is something so cold about a blueprint - so accusatory about a fingerprint. Family, I believed, were the people who are meant to love and take care of you. Intrinsically perhaps, most of us must believe this because life simply prepares us to hope for it. So often, the mechanism of how our lives develop, is referential to those in the past. Those we have never met or remain as reminders in photograph albums. Photographs often carry a sense of another's pain passed down somewhere along a long lineage of others, along with their myths and truths.

I came into the world at 7:30am on Friday 26th January 1973. I was a big baby. My father said I looked like the Christmas turkey next to the other babies in the hospital nursery. My mother, Judith Dawn Smith, was dropped off at the hospital the night before I was born by her father Doug. My mother was left to suffer the agony of contractions alone. She was sixteen years old and no more than a child herself. I can only imagine the fear my mother must have felt, suffering labour pains with not one member of her family there to take care of her. It was not simply the feeling of being abandoned, but a large dose of shame and guilt. These are all deeply negative feelings when welcoming a new life. I would carry these negative feelings into my own life, and they lived with me like ghosts.

This was to be my blueprint. I was born into an environment of shame, guilt and fear, with a lack of nurturing or warmth. Most of all, I wasn't really wanted. A baby draws on all resources, including emotional ones, such as stability, love and warmth. When these are scarce from the beginning, this will negatively 'rock the baby's cradle' and fracture their understanding of a secure place in the world. I developed a dysfunctional attachment style from birth. I was anxious, avoidant and fearful. I never felt safe or secure in the world and I suffered a chronic fear of abandonment.

On the day I was born I felt the hit of my first drug, oxytocin, known as the 'love drug'. I would spend my life searching for this drug, doing anything I could to get hold of this drug, I even tried to buy this drug. I would look for this drug in the most destructive places and this would lead me on to have very dysfunctional relationships. This drug was love. My first addiction was to love, and it would become my most chronic addiction – the one that would take me to the doors of death. It took me almost fifty years to feel safe in the world and to experience a healthy relationship and pure love.

My mother named me Donna, after the most beautiful girl at her school. I was Donna Michelle McNerlin and from the day I was born, beauty and image were enforced upon me. It would become my world, my business, my life and what my family and I would become known for.

My mother was also obsessed with her weight during the pregnancy. She was full of shame and didn't want to gain weight and look pregnant. She kept her pregnancy weight card for thirty years to show how thin she was when pregnant. She would compare her weight throughout her life against the weight she was at nine months pregnant. Weight, from the time I was being carried in my mother's womb, was an issue. What I weighed was to torment me throughout my life and what I weighed, just like image and beauty, had been ingrained into my DNA.

My father Stephen John McNerlin was eighteen years old at the time I was born. He did not want a child. His parent's Jean and Joe wanted my mother to have an abortion because they felt having a child at such a young age was completely wrong. My mother and her family refused their offer to pay for an abortion. My father became so distraught by the prospect of having a child and being forced to get married, that he attempted suicide.

Once the period of no return had passed and everyone knew I was coming, there was some excitement. Unfortunately, for my father, this did mean marriage. It was the seventies and in working class England if you got a girl pregnant you married her. There was no discussion. Doug, however, was obstructive, but finally he gave his permission so my parents could marry. He could have given his permission many months before and saved my mother much of the shame and embarrassment she felt as an unmarried woman with a child. My mother would be free to marry when she was seventeen and Doug knew this, so to maintain his control, he gave his permission just before the power was taken from him. Doug was a bully who beat my mother with a belt for coming home a few minutes late while she was pregnant with me. Doug was vicious with his tongue and with his punishments. My grandmother, Janet, did exactly as he said, when he said it. My mother grew up with a bullying father who was physically and mentally abusive. This was her role model for a man. It would also become my role model for some of the men I would choose in my life.

Doug was a chronic hypochondriac and his illnesses, and subsequent inability to work, were the reason he moved the family from Wolverhampton (a very industrial town in the Black Country) to Smethwick (then 'white' working-class area four miles from the centre of Birmingham. The Black Country gained its name from the black soot that came from all the foundries and forges in the area during the mid-nineteenth century and the use of iron. The Black County produced the anchor and chain for SS Titanic. This area was home to the politician Enoch Powell. Doug thought Enoch Powell was a visionary although today, he is widely considered a racist of the highest order. Enoch Powell's "*rivers of blood*" speech was inflammatory, but totally in line with the attitudes of my family. My family environment was extremely racist. For example, women who mixed with men of colour, were called *wog bait*, a horrific term coined from gollywogs which is a black toy that is now banned. I never understood this concept or how people can feel this way. My childhood friends were a mix of colours, my father's closest friends were of Caribbean origin, yet no way was I allowed to date someone of colour.

My mother had been so happy in Wolverhampton. The family had a lovely home with a garden. She enjoyed school and had lots of friends. When she was fifteen, the family moved to Smethwick and she had to start all over again. She was at such a vulnerable period in her life. My mother missed the spacious home and the friends she had left in Wolverhampton and longed to return to the life she had before. The family of seven were now living in a cramped terraced house. Money was scarce and sometimes there wasn't enough food to feed the family. Today we are aware that when children or teenagers suffer a move of homes, schools or countries, they can be so disrupted that they change who they are to fit in. The sense of security in a child's development can often be a marker for a better or worse life. This is how I believe my mother became prey to my father.

As money was so scarce, my mother found a Saturday job in the local sweet shop. My father had a job in the nearby butchers until his father, (a chronic alcoholic) turned up drunk. My father was so embarrassed he never went back to work in the butchers again. He visited the sweet shop where my mother worked and asked her to go out with him. My mother loved the attention. She was blonde, pretty and innocent. My mother maintains that she did not have sex to get pregnant with me. She never said how or what she did to get pregnant, just that she didn't have sex. Years later, I would laugh with one of my doctors who said, "there's only one woman who I've heard of that got pregnant without having sex." My mother was no Virgin Mary, but that's what I would come to learn denial can do to protect us from our shame.

My father also had a very difficult childhood. His mother, Jean Cowdel, was Irish Catholic and his father, Joseph McNerlin, was Irish Protestant. My grandmother (who I called Nanny Mac) was feisty and defiant. She had lived through World War II, rationing, bombings and loss. She was not going to be told what to do. At this time, a Protestant and Catholic marrying was virtually forbidden, but she did not care and married him.

Nanny Mac was told she should not have children. She contracted scarlet fever as a child and advised that this meant possible complications in childbirth. The risks of childbirth were far too high, but she wouldn't listen to the doctors and became pregnant with my father. While giving birth, she suffered a stroke. The whole of her left side was paralysed, and the family were told she was not going to survive. Flowers were ordered for her coffin, such was the surety of her death. She fought hard and survived. Over the next forty years she would continue to fight chronic and life-threatening illness and numerous heart surgeries. Both my father and I also almost died through illness and injury. We both survived unimaginable odds. Through Nanny Mac, we had an amazing example of sheer defiance, resilience and survival.

Following the stroke, Nanny Mac had gone from a feisty young woman who wouldn't be told what she could do, to being totally reliant on others. She walked with a permanent limp and dragged her left leg. Even after intensive rehabilitation she was still severely paralysed down her left side. My father had a chronic alcoholic as a father, a disabled mother who he lived in fear his whole life would die. He was the runt of the litter. Money and food were scarce, and he would be the last to receive anything. I cannot imagine what life was like for my father, being passed around homes, no stability, fearing and never knowing what would happen next.

On top of the chaos of his childhood, he suffered a life-threatening illness- meningococcal meningitis-and was never expected to live. He survived the illness, but it meant that his extremely naughty behaviour was often excused. He was so naughty that Nanny Mac would beat him so badly that her sisters would threaten to call the 'cruelty man,' as they called child welfare services in those days. My father was given material things to keep him quiet when, I believe, he just wanted love and attention and his behaviour was a dysfunctional way to get it.

My father would do the most devious things. He would unwrap the *Quality Street* sweet tin that was brought for Christmas, eat everything he wanted, and then re-seal the tin. When Christmas came and the tin was opened, the best sweets had been eaten. He wanted a guitar one Christmas, but didn't receive it. He threw such a tantrum that he was taken to the store on Boxing Day (26th December) and they bought him the guitar he wanted. His parents went away for one weekend, so he took a motorbike to the top of the stairs, rode it down the stairs, through the front garden and into the street. He always found a way to get what he wanted, and he did what he wanted. This behaviour was covered up by my grandmother or other family members. They would justify this behaviour as after-effects of the meningitis. I grew up thinking my father was a megalomaniac and that it was completely normal, and this was because of the meningitis. When unravelling my life and childhood, I learned that another term related to megalomania is psychopathy.

There was dysfunction on both sides of my family tree. On my father's side, I had an alcoholic, gambling grandfather and a kleptomaniac great grandmother. One of Nanny Mac's brothers was a paedophile, who went to prison for raping his own children. There was also womanising, addictions and mental illness.

On my mother's side, was the abusive, bullying father and a brother who had an affair with his mother-in-law, among many other women. Another was severely alcoholic and beat his partner endlessly; another is a thief who sold information about my parents and the youngest brother claimed benefits because of illness, yet for years worked on homes for cash, lifting slabs and building extensions. He would then turn up for his assessments on crutches.

Sadly, my chaotic childhood and the dysfunctional people in it were completely normal to me. Another normal was memory of my childhood which I now understand was fragmented. I had memory around specific places and parts of my childhood. I also remembered bizarre information, but I had no idea how I knew this information. I didn't understand as a child why I had very specific and vivid memories then nothing.

Some memories seemed happy whilst some made no sense at all. One of the memories was at Nanny Mac's caravan in Woolacombe Bay in Devon. I would go there at weekends and spend lots of summer holidays there. We had to travel across Exmoor and Porlock Hill to get to the caravan. The bends and the edges of the road, which I thought the car would go over, scared me and I can remember screaming, but I considered the memory happy. I can also remember Grandad Mac taking me to the shops while running errands for Nanny Mac. Grandad Mac was a gambler and would always be sneaking to the betting shop. While he was placing bets, I was left outside; I wasn't even five years old. I couldn't even see where he was because the windows were covered. Grandad Mac gave me ice cream and sweets and told me not to tell anyone where we had been or what he'd been doing. Although I was scared standing outside alone, I believe because of the ice cream and sweets, I considered the memory happy. I spent some of my early childhood years at Nanny Mac's flat in Brand Hall in Oldbury. She moved to the flat from the brewery house in Smethwick. I remembered the flat was near the orphanage on Perry Hill. I had no idea why I had this vivid memory. I remember visiting my cousins' homes on Nanny Mac's side of the family. I was an only child, so I loved playing with the other children. Nanny Mac took me to visit her brother, Uncle Fred. From an early age I knew that he had gone to prison for sexually abusing his own children. I could not understand how I not only knew such a thing, but I also understood what this meant. It was completely normal to go to Uncle Fred's house and play with the children. Uncle Fred looked just like Jimmy Savile, the paedophile, and was also a real character and 'appeared' great with kids.

I had memory of being in my grandfather's big truck with him and his best friend Peter Morris. They were drayman who delivered barrels of beer to pubs. They were both alcoholics, back then it was accepted that's just the way they were. As a child of three or four years old, they took me out in their delivery trucks, delivering beer while drunk and then hide me under their feet in the truck. They also took me into the brewery canteen where beer was served free as a perk of the job. I was a small child in a brewery full of drunken men and no one seemed to think there was an issue with this.

I also remember sleeping at the home of Peter Morris and his wife Jean. I often stayed after nights out at Mitchell and Butler's Working Men's Club. Their house was only five minutes' drive from the club, while my grandparent's flat was twenty minutes away. Grandad Mac refused to give anyone his keys and would drive home drunk. I still remember his car swerving from side to side in front of me while I was in the car behind. Everyone in the car would be screaming because they thought he was going to hit another car, a lamp post or a person. As a child I was petrified. The arguments outside the club, trying to get the keys from him, his snarling face and mouth spitting out abuse to anyone that dared take his keys away. My father had the same snarl and growl when he was raging angry.

I would come to understand and make sense of these memories, but it would be another forty years before I did.

In some areas, life appeared to be getting better. My parents' hard work was starting to pay off. Nanny and Grandfather Mac helped my parents save the deposit to buy a house in a nice working-class area called Bearwood, a suburb of Birmingham. The property needed renovation, so my father worked on the property while my mother worked at her job so our family had an income. My mother came home at night, prepared dinner and cleaned the house. She worked very hard and did her utmost to be a good employee, wife and mother. My father lacked focus and concentration and he got things done when he felt like it. Not having a proper job and renovating the house meant he had lots of time on his hands for other women.

I was a cute child. I looked like Shirley Temple, with big ringlets and a beautiful face. I was the first child and grandchild, so everyone adored me. Everywhere I went, people said how pretty I was and wanted to touch my hair. I would pull away from them unless I was getting something, then I was all smiles and charm. There was a TV show called *Just William* with a character called Violet Elizabeth Bott. The character was the lisping, spoiled daughter of a nouveau riche millionaire. She had ringlets and said, "I will scream and scream until I'm sick, and I can." This was her way of getting what she wanted. I think I modelled myself on Violet Elizabeth, who knew exactly how to get what she wanted. l looked just like her. I've still got a bit of a lisp and curls when I don't straighten my hair. I sadly learned, at a very young age, how to use what I had and how I looked to get what I wanted.

I used to skip along like the happiest child ever, all smiles and singing, *"the good ship lollipop"* ,just like Shirley Temple when I was getting something I wanted. When I wasn't, I would stamp and scream, then lie on the floor and roll around. Initially, people thought it was the terrible twos, but it continued until I was around six years old. One night, I found a pair of scissors and I cut off the front of my ringlets when everyone was asleep. Nanny Mac was hysterical the next morning. She cried and took me to the hairdressers to try and fix the golden child. Another time, I poured hot soup all over my chest and was taken to hospital with third degree burns. My skin was red and blistered, the pain was horrific, and I constantly had to have the dressings changed. There was another physical issue where my arms would keep coming 'out of their sockets'. Nanny and Grandad Mac would swing me while playing and I would have to be taken to the emergency department. I was constantly ending up in a hospital.

After renovating our home, my father decided to buy, renovate and sell properties. He started renovating small, terraced houses in Bearwood, where we now lived. Sadly, as my father became more successful, life didn't get better. It got worse. He would go out with his friends on his Thursday night ritual and meet women. My parents continually argued, although my father was the adulterer, he was jealous and full of rage if any man gave my mother attention. That rage would be directed at my mother in a physically violent way. I can remember after a family wedding she looked so beautiful in a white dress. In a jealous rage, he hit her so hard across her head with a brush that blood covered her face and the white dress. There was nonstop arguing and fights about him having sex with other women or attention that she got from other men, which she could not help. They stood at either ends of the lounge and threw ornaments at each other until every ornament in the lounge was smashed. They used to shout and scream, and then be kissing, making up and in bed together. I was so frightened. I was a scared child who knew something was not right, but it happened repeatedly. I thought this was what being married was meant to be. Once my mother left my father and took me to her parents' house, but was sent away being told, "You made your bed, lie in it." So, we did. I was to live my life in a family full of domestic abuse, physical abuse, sexual abuse, mental abuse and financial abuse. I was to be used in every single way possible.

I looked forward to starting school so that I would be away from the home. I started Abbey Infant School at five years old. I can't really remember much about infant or junior school. I was a daydreamer and looked out of the class window into the playground. I remember a church that was at the corner of the road. I'm not sure why or how I ended up going to Warley Woods Methodist church. I just know I drove my parents crazy to let me go to Sunday school. I can remember the first Sunday and all the other children in the classroom. I was consumed with stories of Jesus and his disciples. I would read the children's Bible every day and I loved the stories. I would pray on my knees with my hands together resting on my bed at night. I loved Sunday school. People were kind and happy, and there was no shouting or violence. I lived for those Sundays. I can remember walking from the classroom up into the big old church. The vicar preaching, the singing – I was in heaven. It was my escape from the horrors of my world. Over the next two years, I drove my parents crazy. I wanted them to let me be christened and they finally agreed. I had a floor length, flowery dress; my hair now was big girl curls, not ringlets, and it was the happiest day of my life. I have a picture of me with the biggest smile on my face. I believed, now I was christened, God was going to save me from my life like all the miracles in the Bible. I prayed every night for a miracle, but nothing changed. So, I kept on praying.

The miracle I prayed for as a child never came, but miracles happened to me many times over many years. These miracles would challenge medical beliefs and some of the most eminent medical minds in the world. Before the miracles came, I would visit hell over and over and over. Then and only then was I ready to face my own demons. I would face the devil within me head on. What I didn't understand as a child, was that I was destined to live a miraculous life. God would eventually guide me to be blessed by one of his most eminent representatives on Earth, and I would come to understand what my life journey and destiny was about.

Just after I was christened, I started Abbey Junior School, which was also across the road from the church. I met my best friend, Joanne, and we became inseparable. We were a pair of tomboys running around together. Joanne had short hair and I wanted short hair too. I was so glad to be rid of those curls and people touching me and my hair all the time. I thought if I looked like a boy, no one would want to touch me.

My father often took and collected me from school as my mother worked office hours. Nanny Mac now lived one street away from my school. As my parents had made money from their property business, they had helped my grandparents buy their own home and move closer to us. In the working-class area where I lived, everyone knew everyone and watched out for each other's children. We played out in the summertime, sometimes until eleven o'clock at night. It all looked so idyllic, running around with my friends, a seemingly carefree childhood existence. The reality was so different. Everyone knew about my father's affairs and all my friends' parents gossiped about my father and his women. I was so embarrassed. Once we came back from a holiday while my father stayed home. On our return my mother found out that he'd been having sex with one of her friends. As usual the arguments ensued and then they were in bed together making up. After, the friend would come over to the house and it was as if nothing had happened.

I had no safe space or place that I could go to other than my beloved Sunday school. Joanne knew how sad I was, and she said she would help me run away. We would regularly pack our bags, get on our bikes and 'run away'. We didn't get far before we came home. That was the reality of my childhood, I just wanted to run and get away from the noise, the abuse, the chaos. Running to escape would become a constant theme and another dysfunctional coping strategy in my life. I would run and I would be 'out', and then I would be pulled back or I would come back. That was until my life depended on me walking away and never coming back.

My parents' property business was now making money and they wanted to expand. All the people that were now involved in the businesses were family members or people they introduced to it. Everyone was family, or knew family, and it was all controlled by my father. He was known as a tyrant and once fired someone for eating a Mars bar that he had left in his van. While he was a tyrant, he had vision and could see opportunities where others couldn't. He was willing to take risks. My mother was the stable, sensible, extremely hard working one. My father started using felt slates on the properties he developed, so he set up a felt slate business. He built a large shed in the garden of our terraced house and Mother's brother (Roy) and Jean Morris's son (Andrew), worked with machines to cut out the shapes from felt.

While the machines clunked away, I rode around the garden on our Great Dane dog, Mistra. I pretended he was my pony, and we were rich. I used a tall lampstand as a microphone and danced around the garden in my black leotard, singing and pretending I was a superstar, and everybody loved me. I would escape to my fantasy land and dream of a place far away from home, just like Dorothy in *The Wizard of Oz*. I would imagine clicking my heels and then I would be out of there and everyone would see me for who I was, a star. I could be anyone I wanted in fantasy land. I would sometimes be Violet Elizabeth, with my rich fabulous family, getting everything I dreamed of. I had no idea I was using fantasy to cope with the horrors of my life. Today fantasy is treated as an addiction, my first dysfunctional coping strategy was fantasy.

Despite the chaos, I placed my father on a pedestal and continued to adore him. Nanny Mac doted on me and gave me everything. My mother was pushed aside by them, and by me. I don't know when my mother began to resent me but, looking back, I have gained some understanding of why she did. I was the beloved first child and grandchild, and despite all the chaos and embarrassment, my father was a god in my eyes. I looked like my father, he taught me to think like him, he told me from a very young age when all these women were around him, "you are not like them, you are like me". I considered all women, like my mother and the women he had around him, as weak, needy and stupid. I wasn't weak like them I was strong like him. I hated them because they got his attention and took him away from me. I wanted all the attention. I wanted my father all to myself, just me and my father and we could rule the world. My mother's resentment grew, as the 'hold' I had over my father became stronger. My mother started to use me against my father and do anything she could to turn me against him.

As the businesses grew, my parents started to buy houses outside of the local area. They bought a house on Haden Hill Road in Halesowen and there my father met Terry who was also a builder. My mother would tell me, "Terry's wife is a prostitute, and your father has sex with her". My father once said he was going to the newsagents and didn't come back for days. He called my mother to tell her he was on his way to Hamburg with Terry. My mother told me that my father was going to Germany with Terry to have sex at clubs; I was eight years old. My father went on a holiday to Majorca with Mitchell's and Butlers Social Club. Family friends and relatives, including Nanny and Grandad Mac also went on the holiday. My mother told me about the women he was having sex with while in Majorca and how he locked out the man he was sharing his room with all night because he was having sex. My mother would constantly drive me around in her car scouring the streets looking for my father at bars or other women's homes. The more my mother used me and told me things to turn me against my father, the closer the bond to him became.

My parents also bought two abandoned cottages next to a farm. They had belonged to the farmer. The cottages were on the edge of the Forest of Dean, near Ross-on-Wye. The extended family would come down from Birmingham and they went canoeing on the River Wye at Symonds Yat. The adults drank at the Crown Pub in the village. The children went to the local maze to play. I used to walk from one cottage up to the other, or out into the farmer's fields. I was allowed to walk alone to the shop which was a half hour walk away along busy roads with lorries shooting past, and no one seemed to care. Life at home was horrible. My father was often at the cottages working, or with other women. The cottages just seemed like a great excuse for my father and other family members to get away from home, work, drink and be with women. My mother told me that Terry's wife worked in a massage parlour, and she had sex with lots of men. She told me that my father was at the cottages with Terry, his wife and other people having sex. I longed for my father to come home, but when he did it was constant fighting. The novelty for people visiting the cottages had worn off and I was so lonely. I had no one to talk to or play with. I can remember walking along those busy roads and the trucks were flying past me. I used to think if I stepped out just a little, the truck would kill me. This was the first time I can remember thinking about killing myself. I was just nine years old.

I was so lonely I prayed for a sibling, but my father was clear about only wanting me. My mother was being pushed aside and the other women were becoming a real problem and threat. I think my mother realised she could be on her way out. My mother 'discovered' she was pregnant. She told me that my father had taken her to a clinic to have an abortion, but she refused. My sister would be another unwanted child that would be born into a chaotic abusive family. However, I was going to have the sibling I wanted. Even now I cannot find the words to express my joy. I thought I will be lonely in this family no more.

The chaos, however, continued. After yet another argument and fight with my father, my mother took me and we escaped to Nanny Mac's. My father followed and was in one of his usual psychotic rages. Nanny Mac would not let him in the house because he would most likely smash the contents to pieces or attack my mother. This was a tree lined street in Harborne – a beautiful area of Birmingham. My father took a sledgehammer from the boot of his car and smashed the new family car to pieces. He wrote off the car. Shockingly, no one came out of their homes or called the police. Nothing happened. We all went home and yet again carried on as if nothing had happened.

The arrival of my sister seemed to calm the family environment for a while. I was in love with my sister. I would rush into her bedroom every morning and get her out of her cot. One morning she wriggled, and, to my horror, I dropped her and she was taken to hospital. That lunchtime, my school headmaster came to sit with me and asked me what had happened. I'm not sure if it was because of all my childhood injuries that my family were being watched. As ever, no one came to help or asked anymore questions.

Of course, it wasn't long before the chaos started again. Suddenly Terry disappeared and everyone was told he had 'ripped my father off'. No one ripped my father off and got away with it, but Terry seemed to have. At the same time, there was a desperate rush to finish the renovations and sell the cottages. We were now going to return to Birmingham as a family. I was about to start senior school and instead of my Nanny Mac looking after me, I was sent to my mother's parents (the Smiths) for some of the summer. What happened that summer at their home, with a Smith family member, would be the first clear memory I had of sexual abuse.

As a young child I had been given a diary with a lock on it. I was a child and I believed no one could get into my diary. My mother did and she read what I had been writing every night about my life. I got the beating of a lifetime for what I had written. What I learned was another dysfunctional coping strategy, I learned to keep everything that was happening and had happened to me inside my mind. I had learned three dysfunctional strategies that I unconsciously developed to cope with, what I would come to learn, was trauma. I learned to escape into fantasy to numb the pain I was in, I learned to lock details of traumatic events in my mind, and I learned to dissociate from my horrific reality. I was also learning to bond with abusive people to survive. How did I cope with the violence and chaos of my environment? I identified with the ruler, my father. I had no opinions of my own. My opinions were my father's and my views were my father's. I would learn to think like him, watch him, and copy the way he behaved with people, in business, in his personal life, in every aspect of his life. I was a young girl becoming exactly like her father.

My family were moving into a beautiful new home, I was going to senior school, I had a sibling. My parents' businesses were doing well, and the money was flowing. I thought life was going to get better. It didn't. It was about to take on a whole new level of horror.

The strategies I was using weren't enough to numb the pain, so I found new ones. I was eleven years old when I entered my thirty-year battle with eating disorders.

MY NEW DRUG WAS FOOD, THE MOST WIDELY ABUSED DRUG IN THE WORLD.

WHAT CAN THE READER TAKE FROM THIS CHAPTER?

Our behaviours and our thinking are often the blueprint of our childhoods.

Our primary attachments to our parents or caregivers set the blueprint for our interactions with other humans.

Nature and nurture are passed down to us from multiple generations, not just our parents.

Addictions can be developed in very subtle ways and in early childhood.

Our minds will develop multiple strategies to protect us from emotional and physical pain.

You can never truly know what is happening in other people's homes, lives or minds.

CHAPTER TWO

BINGEING, DIETING, STARVING

FOOD

ANY NUTRITIOUS, SUBSTANCE THAT PEOPLE EAT OR DRINK IN ORDER TO MAINTAIN LIFE AND GROWTH

The new family home was on Lightwoods Hill which was one of the finest roads in Bearwood. It was a lovely three-bedroom, semi-detached house with a garage. There were two big bedrooms – one at the front with a large bay window, one at the back that overlooked the garden, and a box room. My room overlooked the garden. I had a big double bed, a sofa and two huge wardrobes. I was in heaven. Ever since I was a small child, my bedroom had become my place of escape, a place to be alone and get away from all the noise and chaos of the family. The more items I could have in my bedroom to be self-sufficient, the better. I never wanted to leave my own little sanctuary.

The house needed renovation, so we went back to periods of living with bare floorboards or half a bathroom fitted and a kitchen with only a sink and a single unit with a cooker. A large building was also constructed at the top of the garden for the felt slate business. This building also stored equipment for the growing property business.

My sister was now eighteen months old, and I was becoming her babysitter for my mother. My mother had found a new way to punish me for the attention I received, and that was to treat me like Cinderella. I cleaned the house top to bottom every Saturday. The carpet had to be vacuumed perfectly throughout the week and in lines. I was on constant call to look after my sister and my life, or what I was doing, didn't matter. I was at my mother's beck and call. Nothing had really changed with my father. The women were still around, the arguments and the chaos continued, and he was still the centre of my universe.

My father was completely obsessed with his image. Since his early twenties, he had been losing his hair. His hair loss had become such a huge problem and the focus of his life. Before hair loss became the big issue, he was obsessed with his big nose. There was always something regarding how he looked on which to focus. He would sit all day long just putting his hands through his hair to see how much was falling out. There were tantrums regarding how he looked, and he would blow dry or style his hair in the correct way to cover up his hair loss. His grandfather had become completely bald in his twenties and my father was petrified of having no hair.

My father was an amazing researcher. He found a doctor in Harley Street (the famous medical district of London) who was conducting trials for a hair loss drug. To be part of this trial was extremely expensive and you didn't know if you got the placebo or the actual drug. My father went to see him in London and wanted to start using whatever was available to keep his hair. It was a huge amount of money for my family to pay. The other issue was that my father was still a young man and might want more children. The doctors had no definitive idea what the side effects could be. This was a great opportunity for my mother. She convinced my father that this would be his last chance to have any more children and that he wanted to have a son. My father agreed to have another child before he started his hair loss treatment.

A major driver for my mother wanting another child was because of the permanent woman in my father's life- Diane Hartland. Diane was an upgrade on his former women, no doubt attracted by the Porsche. She was a former librarian and now worked at Central Television in the media library. She worked in TV and that was very glamourous and attractive to my father. My mother knew this woman was going to be a problem and feared she could possibly be the end to their marriage.

While the dramas continued at home, I was excited to be starting high school. In September 1984, I became a student at Bristnall Hall High School. It was a state-run school in Oldbury on the edge of the Black Country. There was a mix of students, and the racial and socio-economic demographic of the students was very different to that of my junior school. Every day I would catch the number 448 bus across the road from our new house and it would drop me back right outside.

Since I was a small child, I had bitten my nails halfway down my finger and nothing would stop me. I would bite nail and skin. I had also weirdly started pulling my eyebrows out at the ends. What I was developing would cripple my life for years to come and sometimes make me unable to leave the house. I started having to wash myself in a very specific way. This bizarre new washing routine would take me up to two hours every morning. I would get in the bath and scrub with a scrubbing brush from my toenails up, in a set routine. If I missed any part of the routine, I would have to start again.

My hair shampoo and conditioner had to be applied at the right time in my set routine or again, I would have to start from the beginning. I would start washing myself by sitting on the seat in the corner bath and finish off in the shower. We had one bathroom in a house with four people. I was screamed at, shouted at, hit and the bathroom door was nearly banged off its hinges for being in the bathroom so long, but I couldn't move unless the routine was finished.

After I had finished washing my body, I brushed my teeth. I had another routine for my teeth. I would brush as hard as I could and if I missed any point of the routine, I would have to start again from the beginning. My gums constantly bled because I brushed them so hard. I had to have a particular toothbrush and toothpaste and I took them to school with me. At school I would make excuses to go to the bathroom during class, because I had to wash my hands and face. My life was ruled by my washing routine, I couldn't leave the house without the routine being carried out, which meant I was constantly late for everything.

I was often late for school because of my washing routine, and this got me into trouble. Academically I was a good all-rounder, nothing remarkable. My reports would say I had difficulty concentrating or noted my 'erratic behaviour'. I can remember looking at the blackboard and seeing what was on it, but I was unable to take anything in. I was physically in the classroom, but it was as if I wasn't there. I would look out the window into the playground and I felt numb, like I was in a glassy bubble. I found concentration extremely difficult unless something really caught my interest.

David Ross caught my interest. David was a year older than me, and all the girls chased after him. David chased after me. He loved my curly hair, and we would just chat and flirt in the playground at breaks or lunchtime. He only had eyes for me, and I for him, and we became inseparable. I was still going to church and praying, but nothing was changing. I decided David was going to be my new god and he was the one that was now going to save me. My father was my first god, and I still worshipped him. Jesus was my second God, but I was giving up on him. Like so many of us do, I was about to create a lifelong pattern of thinking that another person was going to save me. Over the next thirty-five years I made man after man my new god in the hope that this one was going to save me. I believed, one day, my knight in shining armour would come and sweep me off my feet.

At home, Diane had become a presence, not just in my father's life, but in our family's. I can remember the first time I was taken by my parents to visit her house. Diane had a little house on a new estate in Oldbury. I remember we had some chilli con carne and I got hit in the eye by a part that flew off the garden strimmer. I knew something was completely strange about this situation. My parents and Diane went on a skiing holiday together. Everyone knew, and it was so embarrassing. I think my mother would have done absolutely anything to keep hold of my father and my father used that to his advantage.

My father started his hair loss treatment with the Harley Street doctor, and he also carried out some more research himself. He wasn't going to take the chance he was having a placebo and he wanted the real drug. He researched the drug minoxidil, found a friendly pharmacist to mix the drug for him and used it on himself. That was how one of the world's largest hair loss medical groups was formed. That company would one day go all the way to the Hollywood A-listers.

My father soon realised the amount of money that could be made in hair loss treatments and drugs. He found doctors to prescribe the drugs and his pharmacist, Angela, mixed the potions he wanted. He advertised and set up a company called the Edgbaston Medical Group and found a little office in Edgbaston, the most affluent area in Birmingham. The cash rolled in. We had bags of cash stored in my parent's wardrobe. It was happy days for me. If I wanted something, I would go and get some cash from the wardrobe. This new found wealth meant my parents now had an elevated sense of status among their family and friends. I was left to babysit my sister and clean house. With no regular family meals, I could, and did, eat what I wanted.

As a child, I had always had a very 1970s working class meal structure. Certain meals on certain days, at the same time. Up until then, my weight had been completely normal, and I had no weight or food issues at all. As my parents were out working and building their new business, I was home alone, and had to fend for myself and my sister. I snacked. I would eat a small *KitKat* bar from a six pack and then have another and another until the six pack was gone. It felt good. I would go upstairs and take cash if I wanted chocolate bars or other goodies, so no one knew what I was really eating. At first, the sweet eating didn't really affect my weight, then it crept up slightly. Even if my weight had gone up, my parents were too busy to notice or care. My father was chasing the business and my mother was chasing him.

With my parents working crazy hours, I had more time to spend with David. David was my world. I loved him more than words could express. He was my saviour, my light during all this darkness, and my anchor. We spent every minute of every hour together. My sister would tag along, but we were absolutely devoted to each other. David had come from a working-class background like me. His father was a brewer, and his mother had a small café in the market in Smethwick, the area we had both spent our early childhoods. Unlike my parents, David's were the most wonderful people you could meet. Going to David's house and spending time with his family was heaven. They were a loving family. David's father doted on his mother and called her, "the duchess". He was the complete opposite of my father. They giggled, they laughed and were kind to each other. I not only loved David, but I also loved all his family too.

David had a Saturday job working on a fruit and vegetable stall and his mother gave me a job working at her café. I loved working at the market with David and his family. When my parents started to make money, they wanted me to give up my job. Me working in a café didn't suit their new image. The fact that I loved my job didn't matter and, as usual, I did what my parents wanted.

I grew up in the most sexualised home. I had been sexualised from an early age and sex was my version of normal. Sadly, I knew nothing about contraception.

David and I had sex at a young age, and I fell pregnant quickly. I can remember the panic David and I felt when we found out. We were still children and didn't know what to do. I had to tell my parents, but there was no way I could tell my father. I waited until my father went on his usual Thursday night out and I told my mother. I was in floods of tears because the shame and guilt were killing me. I begged my mother not to tell my father, which course she did. An abortion was the only option. I agreed and did as I was told. I was taken to a private doctor to avoid the abortion being on my medical notes, and then to a clinic. The pain I felt after the procedure was the worst pain ever. I thought it would never stop and this must be God's punishment.

I was told not to see David again, which I ignored. David was the only good thing I had in my life, and I wasn't losing him. Sadly, the shame of my early pregnancy was used against me for thirty years. Even on the last day I spoke to my mother, in August 2015, she used the teenage pregnancy card. People may wonder why I want to discuss this. I ate on my shame and guilt, and those secrets kept me sick. As I've learned, shame does die on exposure and along with it I was able to drop all the emotional pain I'd been carrying with it for years. Both my siblings had teenage pregnancies, but I was the only one my mother used it to shame.

How did I cope with my shame and guilt? I used food. I binged and I starved. How did I make myself stronger to fight off my abusers? I ate to become bigger. How did I make myself less attractive to my abusers? I ate to get fat. How did I gain control over my abusers? I starved myself to become thin and more attractive. My thirty-year battle with weight and food had just started, and in the years to follow it would almost kill me.

I went to bed thinking about food and I woke thinking about food. If I didn't start eating in the morning, I was better throughout the day. At night, all bets were off. I couldn't stop eating. I ate mainly sweet items, but I would eat anything. On my starvation days I would eat an apple and drink water. I could not imagine one day in my life when food wouldn't consume my thoughts. It would take me almost thirty years to relieve my obsession with food and my weight.

My father had now grown his hair business and wanted to diversify into other areas. This included skin products, lotions, topical creams, and prescription diet pills. He applied for, and received, a pharmaceutical specials licence, which meant he now had the capacity to buy the most highly regulated drugs such as opiates. He set up a company called Central Pharmaceuticals and another company called Bio Medical.

The non-prescription products and creams were mixed by Grandad Smith in an industrial food mixer. David was allowed back into the family, and he would fill the bottles of minoxidil. This became his new Saturday and holiday job. My family weren't happy with David seeing me and working on the fruit and veg stall, not now they had their newfound elevated status.

Exactly as before with the property business, my father controlled everything, and he used the family to be his worker bees. Everything and everyone were controlled by my father. Diane gave up her job to come and work at the company and so did her sister Leila. All my mother's brothers and their wives worked at the company. Many of our cousins were also involved.

With so much power, my father started to mix his own medical products, not just for himself, but for people buying the products. He became an uncontrollable monster, who thought he was beyond the law. My father illegally mixing prescription products would eventually lead to someone's death. The pharmaceutical company also supplied prescription diet pills. They are now banned drugs because they were prescription amphetamine. We had diet pills and diuretics at home, next to the cornflakes.

The rollercoaster home life had taken an unexpected turn. My father wanted to leave my mother to be with

Diane. One night my mother woke me out of my sleep to tell me Diane had come over to our house to discuss the situation and that my father and Diane had gone for a walk. My mother told me I needed to go and speak to them. This was the start of years of my mother winding me up into a rage with Diane or my father's other women.

At three o'clock in the morning, I ran up Lightwoods Hill barefoot, in my pyjamas, screaming at Diane and my father. I was just thirteen years old. It didn't stop there, another time I had to go with my father to take Diane to the emergency department because she had taken an overdose. She found out she was pregnant, and my father had kicked her in her tummy because she refused to have an abortion. I was fifteen. The drama and chaos were relentless, I started to not be able to cope.

After my abortion, my chronic need for love and approval from my parents kicked in. When I wanted something, I would work to get it or would somehow find a way to get it. I went from a very average student at the end of the third year of high school to, a student that was excelling. I had decided that I wanted to study English literature for my A levels. I needed to get to the top set in English to do the foundation work needed to be accepted. At the start of year four, I was in the fifth English set out of nine. By the end of year four, I was the third highest exam scoring student in English literature.

The school had no choice but to move me to the number one set. In one year, I'd gone from an average student to excelling in every subject I needed to progress. I realised that when I needed to, I could turn on my brain and achieve whatever I wanted. There were three caveats; It had to really interest me I had to really need it, or it would gain me love and approval. What I was developing was another dysfunctional coping strategy. I had no idea love and validation needed to come from within me first. I would spend thirty years looking for external validation and approval from others to make me feel good about myself or be happy.

My chosen career was law, and my work experience was at a law firm. The company offered me a job, but I turned the offer down for two reasons. One was that I wanted to join David at Halesowen College. He was a year older than me and was already studying for his A levels. The other reason was, I had bigger plans. I had no idea what, but I felt I was destined for something bigger.

During the final two years at school, I used food to cope with my home life and the shame and guilt of the abortion. Throughout the study period for my final exams, I ate food and gained more weight. I was now 10kg overweight. During the summer holidays, I restricted my food intake and exercised daily. I lost the weight in six weeks. At the end of the summer break, I went on my first holiday with David. I came back to receive my exam results and I achieved the eight GCSE exams required to study A levels in Economics, English and Government & Politics. In September 1989, I started Halesowen College and I was with David again. I was also five minutes from where my parents bought the house in Haden Hill Road.

I started Halesowen College looking and feeling fabulous. I'd kept my weight off over the summer holidays and was eating normally again. Something changed. For no apparent reason when I started college and went back to the area, I started to eat lots of food again. I couldn't stop. I couldn't control my eating at all. I was getting fatter. I did what I'd seen my parents do and I went to the cereal cupboard and took the pills. That's how easy it was. I became addicted to diet pills. I was using a drug to control my other drug – food. As well as the diet pills and diuretics, I started using laxatives.

I would start my week with a Sunday night laxative ready to start my diet on a Monday. The diet never lasted even with the diet pills, so I used more diet pills and more laxatives. Initially, it kept my weight down, but without even realising it, I was using a highly addictive drug. Without knowing it, I had become addicted to diet pills and my eating disorder was spiralling out of control. I was on the binge, starve, go on another diet and use another magic pill rollercoaster. I was on the roller coaster on which a multi billion dollar industry is built – the diet industry.

After everything I had been through as a child, after everything I had endured and managed to overcome, I could not escape those feelings inside me. No drug or any of my obsessive and compulsive behaviours could control the pain I was holding inside me.

All the signs of trauma and abuse had been obvious in all the behaviours I had been exhibiting since I was a child. The nail and skin biting, the pulling out of the eyebrows, the ritualistic washing and how I was using food and drugs to control my weight – these were all huge signs. The hair cutting, the scalding myself and the arms coming out of their sockets, the teenage pregnancy were all signs. I just didn't know how to read the signs, nor did the medical professionals who were treating me.

My mind and body were overloaded with trauma. They were both about to give the biggest signal they could that something was seriously wrong. At seventeen years old I was about to be thrown into the cycle of anxiety and depression. My body was to become riddled with chronic illness that would confine me to a wheelchair.

WHAT THE READER CAN TAKE FROM THIS CHAPTER?

Obsessive and compulsive behaviours are dysfunctional coping strategies.

Shame and guilt can be immensely destructive emotions.

Secrets influence your mind and body. Secrets can make you sick.

Food can be used like a drug and can have the same effects as a chemical drug.

Dysfunctional coping strategies can quickly become normal behaviour patterns.

An unstable home environment can have devastating and lifelong effects on children.

CHAPTER THREE

THROWN INTO DEPRESSION

DEPRESSION

A COMMON AND SERIOUS MEDICAL CONDITION, THAT NEGATIVELY AFFECTS THE WAY YOU FEEL, THE WAY YOU THINK, THE WAY YOU ACT

The first cracks started to appear after a holiday to Florida with David, and Nanny and Grandad Mac. Grandad Mac was about to turn sixty. With the money flowing, my parents arranged a big party and a dream holiday to America for him. David and I went too because of their health issues.

We all looked forward to the holiday, especially because none of us had been to America before. We arrived in Orlando to glorious sunshine and a fabulous hotel. Unfortunately, the four of us had been put in a room together. David and I headed straight over to the water park. They wanted to stay in the room.

David and I had a fabulous day enjoying the water park – we had an absolute ball. When we returned to the hotel room, my grandparents were in bed together. They weren't having sex or doing anything sexual, but the way they were lying and the way they looked at me is still clear in my mind to this day. Our room couldn't be changed so we continued to share. David and I slept in one double bed and my grandparents slept in the other double bed next to us. We had a fantastic time in Walt Disney World, and we all acted like big kids. It felt like the first time in my life I was allowed to be childlike and playful.

We then moved on to Fort Lauderdale. As it was USA spring break, the parties we saw were wild and everyone was having so much fun. David and I were ridiculously sensible. We should have been having fun and enjoying our student lives but, instead, we were focused on our careers, making money and getting out of our poor working-class environment. David's driver was money and mine was to get as far away from my family as possible. We were so focused on our goals that we were not enjoying our lives day to day. We focused on the future, and we were missing out on the most important thing. The now. The moment.

The final part of the vacation was to Freeport Bahamas on a cruise ship. We had a wonderful holiday and couldn't wait to return home to share our experiences. We were due back at college, so I went to the hairdressers to freshen up my hair colour. I came home from the hairdressers and told my mother that I didn't feel well. I believe I had a rash as well. Something concerned my mother and when the symptoms became more severe, I started to deteriorate quickly. My mother was advised to take me to hospital. In the emergency department at Dudley Road Hospital, I was assessed by the doctors who suspected meningitis and I was taken into isolation. I was hysterical, the doctors wanted to carry out a lumbar puncture to aid their diagnosis. This involved a needle in my back. Since age of three or four, I had been terrified of medical people wearing masks. This was a likely result of a bad experience at the dentist where I had been held down. Even Nanny Mac recalled hearing my screams as a child. Ever since that time, I would only go to the dentist when I was in so much pain that I needed a tooth extraction, and even then I would often jump out of the chair when the dentist came towards me and would not stop running until I was halfway down the street.

My parents used to bribe me with everything to get me to go to the dentist. What I would come to learn is sexual abuse survivors often don't like things in their mouths and many have dental phobias. Twenty-five years later, I would learn why I had developed a dental phobia and unravel it. In the meantime, the phobia was linked to masks and white coats, and I continued to refuse the lumbar puncture, so severe was my phobia. The doctors and my mother told me I could die if they didn't find out what was wrong with me. David begged me to agree. I refused, saying I didn't care if I died. I couldn't have them come near me with a big needle, a mask and a white coat. The doctors realised the severity of my phobia and agreed to remove all masks and white coats, and anything medical looking. I reluctantly agreed to the test. After five days in isolation and every test possible, I was allowed to go home with a diagnosis of an unidentified virus. The doctors could not find out what the issue was. I was even tested for tropical illnesses because of the recent overseas travel. I was delighted to return home mainly because I had lost 10 pounds in weight. I didn't worry about the risk to my life. This is typical with eating disorders. After five days I was still unable to walk unaided, but I was happy to be out of the hospital.

This mystery virus affected me very badly and I was away from college for too long to catch up with lost study and lectures. David was due to start university in London in the September, so I went with my mother to look at colleges in London where I could take my A levels in one year. The plan was that I would go to London with David when he took his place at the London School of Economics (LSE).

When I felt a little better, I decided to find a job until we went to London. I found a job at an insurance company in the claims department. I absolutely loved it and within six weeks I was promoted to a claims handler and was the youngest person in my department by ten years. I wanted to stay working at the company and I asked David if he would defer his place for a year. David agreed and started his professional accountancy exams and worked with the finance at my family's company.

During his economics A level, David had learned how to trade stocks and he had excelled at fantasy trading. David took the little money he had saved for university and started trading stocks and options. He was a naturally gifted trader and made money straight away. He lived off his wages from his job and reinvested his trading monies. He was focused on his professional exams, work and making money. After being so ill and reassessing my life, I was focused on shopping and going out with my friends.

I made great friends at Minster Insurance Company, and we went out for pub lunches and after work drinks. I was finally living the life of a seventeen-year-old. I also learned what had happened to the car my father had smashed to pieces in the street years before. The family name is McNerlin and it's very unusual, so I put McNerlin in the system and up popped a claim for a car that had been 'stolen', smashed to pieces and abandoned. My parents had dumped the car, that my father had smashed to pieces with a sledgehammer, away from Nanny Mac's house and called the police to report a theft. I couldn't believe it. I didn't bother saying anything to my parents. It would just be another 'so what and don't you dare say anything'.

I was having so much fun socialising with friends, spending, shopping and getting attention from men, I thought I was in heaven. I met a handsome guy who was eleven years my senior. He drove a Mercedes, had a good job and we got on well. My mother came out one night with my Aunty Barb, and the new guy was there. David was my boyfriend, yet my mother was encouraging me to start seeing the new guy for the simple reason that he was wealthy. I started seeing him as well as David. In my childhood I'd seen my father dating multiple women, so I did what was normal to me. I dated two men. The new guy wanted me to go skiing with him which meant I would have had to tell David, and I couldn't do that. I loved David so much and his heart would have been broken. I was obsessed with this guy, not for a week or two, but for years to come! I couldn't stop thinking about him, it was absolute insanity. What I would come to learn and understand is that my parents were addicts when it came to sex and love. What I was suffering from was obsessional thinking, an element of sex and love addiction. My role models, my parents, would now be classified among many other things as sex and love addicts. All this sex, obsession and chasing others, and the chaos I had seen as a child, had become part of my blueprint and I had absolutely no idea.

Unlike today, these addictions were not understood well. The obsessional thinking goes way beyond thinking about your ex-partner and feeling sad. Your thinking is compulsive and obsessive. The thoughts and actions it can induce can feel like you are going out of your mind. What I also didn't understand was that because of my dysfunctional childhood experiences, I was a co-dependent. My co-dependency was keeping me in a relationship with David. While I loved David dearly, we weren't right for each other. David was too consumed with his addiction to work and money to even notice what I was doing. He would now be considered emotionally unavailable. He couldn't talk about his feelings and that was perfect for me because it excused me from discussing mine. At this time, the understanding of co-dependency, and what causes it, was in the early stages.

I was still living at home with my parents and my home life was as chaotic as ever. The Diane circus continued, although my father had other women too. When it suited her, my mother went from hating Diane, to being her best friend. When other women came on the scene, the two of them ganged up against my father and any new women. My mother still used me as a pawn against my father and Diane. On one occasion, my father and Diane were at the Central Pharmaceutical's office in Oldbury. I can't even remember what caused this drama, but my mother wound me up again against Diane and my father. My mother drove me to the office and waited at the bottom of the stairs so she could hear what was happening. I went upstairs and I flew at Diane. My father pushed me very hard, and I fell backwards straight back down the extremely steep stairs. I lay at the bottom, unable to move. They all kept telling me to get up, but I couldn't. An ambulance was called, and a story concocted for paramedics. I was taken to Dudley Road Hospital. I had numerous scans and I was placed on a traction device for a week. I was told I could not move. The doctors discovered I had a fractured neck, however they wanted to send the scans over to Birmingham Children's Hospital for a second opinion. When the doctors came back with their final diagnosis, we were told that I did have a fractured neck but that the fracture was a childhood fracture. No one could understand how or when my neck had fractured, or how could I have fractured my neck and not been in severe pain. It would be twenty-five years before I would feel safe enough to recall how that fracture had happened.

I settled down again after my period of having fun with my friends and my little romance. David was doing well trading and I enjoyed my job, so he decided to carry on with his professional exams and not go to LSE. We found a house we wanted to buy in Bishopton Road in Bearwood. It was a lovely road next to Lightwoods Park and it was also the road Julie Walters (British actress) had lived in as a child. My parents gave us £10,000 deposit for the house. David proposed and gave me a lovely engagement ring. Both of our families were happy and excited, and a fabulous wedding was planned for two years' time. David and I were so young and inexperienced, we hadn't lived. I was recreating history, my parents' life, albeit we didn't have a child and we had money. I made very clear to David that I did not want children and that I was career focused. I'd had to raise my sister and I wanted to focus on my career and us.

There had been something lurking in the background with my health. Since I had been released from hospital with the unidentified virus, I had suffered with progressively bad diarrhoea. I was so used to having to deal with problems, I didn't let it affect me or stop me doing anything.

I found a much better job in the same industry, and I decided to take a break before starting my new position. My weight was going up again and I wanted to focus on getting my weight down and get in a routine of eating less. I started starving and excessively exercising. This time my weight wasn't moving at all and, when I exercised at the gym, I kept getting severe pain in my calf.

On the first day of my new job, as I put my heel to the floor, I had shooting pains going up my legs. I was in agony. It was a similar pain to what I'd experienced at the gym, but it was now in both legs and the pain was much worse. It was my first day in a new job, I had to go. I just focused my mind and I managed to get through the day and get home and rest. I was in severe pain, but I kept going back every day for two weeks until the point I could not walk. I was devastated. I would never return to that job because illness and depression were about to hit me like a train.

My mother took me to our family doctor. Blood tests were taken, and we waited for the results. It wasn't all the time that my mother and I were at each other's throats, or that she didn't care for me or look after me. When I really needed my mother, she would be there, often begrudgingly, but she came. The blood results came back, and my inflammatory markers were through the roof. I was referred to a rheumatologist.

I went to see the rheumatologist who diagnosed rheumatoid arthritis. I was seventeen and I was now in so much pain I had to use a wheelchair. Due to the severity and rapid escalation of the arthritis, I was admitted to hospital for lots of different tests. My medical team could not understand why the arthritis had occurred or the rapid escalation. The rheumatologist brought his team in to see me because they felt they were missing something with my case. They asked me endless questions and test after test was carried out. One of the doctors asked if I'd had any diarrhoea. I said I had ever since my unidentified virus. A colonoscopy was performed. The doctor came to see me with my mother and David, and told me I had Crohn's disease. I was seventeen, in a wheelchair, now with a diagnosis of two chronic illnesses. I needed constant care and Nanny Mac could give me that, so I moved into my grandparents' home. I loved being with her. She was kind, calm, fiercely protective, and the one person that encouraged me not to get married. Grandad Mac was indifferent. I had gone from a vibrant young woman, to one that was bedridden and chronically ill. I didn't know what depression was, but I was about to find out. I didn't want to do anything, not get out of bed or even wash. I didn't want to go anywhere because if I went out, I had to go in a wheelchair. I was on a huge number of drugs to suppress my immune system, and they had side effects. I had to attend endless doctor appointments, have weekly blood tests and, with a needle phobia, life became unbearable.

The medical team brought in dieticians who wanted to rest my colon and put me on a liquid diet. I couldn't stick to that because my eating disorders made it impossible. I felt hopeless, I was in absolute despair and thought my life was over. I thought David would leave me. Who would want to marry someone like this? My thinking was dark, all doom and gloom, and no hope in sight.

At one of my medical appointments, my mother raised the issue of my low mood. The doctor gave me tablets. I just took what he gave me in the hope I would feel better. I would later find out I'd been given highly addictive anti-depressants, anti-anxiety medication, sleeping pills and Vicodin for the pain. It took a long time for the drugs to help because, as anyone who suffers from anxiety and depression knows, when you are in such a black hole with your thinking it takes a long time to get out of it. My doctor didn't consider my family history or my medical history, so the treatment pathway I was given was completely inappropriate. I became addicted to anxiety pills, sleeping pills and pain killers.

The health issues didn't stop with the Crohn's disease and arthritis, I was having cramps in my legs so severe I would scream with the pain in my joints and muscles. I was then diagnosed with fibromyalgia. At eighteen years old, I had a clinical diagnosis of Crohn's disease, rheumatoid arthritis, fibromyalgia, depression, anxiety and sleep disorders.

At this point, I felt lost, hopeless, and full of despair. I didn't know there was another option other than to take pills, so I took all the medication the doctors gave me for all my illnesses. Auto immune diseases (including Crohn's disease and arthritis) are strongly linked to trauma. Fibromyalgia is strongly linked to trauma. Anxiety and depression are strongly linked to trauma. Sleep disorders are linked to trauma, eating disorders are linked to trauma, addictions are linked to trauma, OCD is linked to trauma. How many more signs did the medical profession need to see what was happening and had happened to me? My body and mind were screaming out for help, they were telling the medical profession my story. My body was my voice, because I couldn't speak to tell anyone what had happened to me.

David had worked hard throughout the time of my illnesses. He had continued trading, preparing the house and visiting me. David was very decent and loyal then and, without him, I don't think I would have survived my teenage years. We moved into our new home, and we loved it. We brought all the furniture and chose the décor ourselves, my mother helped as she had a real eye for interior design and my father paid for and oversaw the building work.

David and I were happy. He was taking his professional accountancy exams, trading and making money. He was also excelling in finance and financially running my parent's companies. My health really started to improve now I was no longer living with my family. I started to feel good about myself and have some hope in my life. We were due to get married in a year and the world was our oyster. We had a small circle of friends because we had grown apart from our school friends due to the illnesses and depression. I didn't want to go out with my friends in a wheelchair and they were away at university, so when I saw them, I just felt more depressed. David kept his circle very small and has never had more than two or three friends.

My mood improved and I stopped the anti-depressants, anxiety pills, sleeping pills and pain killers. I only took medication for Crohn's disease and arthritis. I had to have twice monthly blood tests because the immune suppressant drugs are aggressive and could quickly drop my white cell count. I hated having bloods taken, but I had to get used to needles. I also managed to see a dentist who was very caring and gave me Valium to start having treatment. He extracted teeth that were beyond repair and gave me fillings to the others. Finally, my medical fears and phobias were starting to improve.

I wanted to return to work, but I'd been off sick for eighteen months. I couldn't go back. No company would want to employ me with my health issues and employment record. I had so little choice. Should I return to studying, or try and find something else to do?

I did something I swore I would never do; I went to work at my parent's company. I had my own home, I didn't have to live with them anymore, yet I went back. I spent over twenty years trying to 'get out' then ended up going back.

I would go through another twenty-five years of misdiagnoses, unexplained illnesses, hospitalisations, depression, anxiety, addictions and- what would become -a hellish existence. That was until I found myself in the office of the world-renowned psychiatrist, Dr Stephen Pereira. Later, I found the first person I would trust enough to tell my truth to, a female psychiatrist named Dr Rasmita Ori. Dr Pereira and Dr Ori gently guided me to a place of peace and wholeness. What they saw happen defied even their beliefs.

WHAT THE READER CAN TAKE FROM THIS CHAPTER?

The examples we are given in childhood of intimate and sexual relationships, can manifest in us as adults.

We can often unknowingly repeat the relationship patterns of our parents or caregivers.

Many people are completely unaware they are suffering from co-dependency.

The mind can manifest in the body, what the mouth cannot speak of.

Our bodies will tell us that there is something wrong, we just need to learn how to read them.

Fears and phobias will have a root cause, many originate in childhood.

CHAPTER FOUR

THE BUILDING BLOCKS OF AN EMPIRE

EMPIRE

A GROUP OF TERRITORIES OR PEOPLE UNDER ONE RULER

My parents' companies had grown very quickly and business was booming. My father had found a loophole in the law which meant that clients ordering certain prescription drugs from the Channel Islands, would not need to see a doctor. The caveat was that the drugs needed to be dispatched from the Channel Islands. The drugs were manufactured in the UK and a group of us would deliver minoxidil (and some other drugs) to Jersey by plane. They would then be posted back the to the UK. We would pick up cheques or postal orders from the P.O. box in Jersey. The postal orders would be cashed at the post office, cheques would be banked and the cash would go into the wardrobe.

The orders got bigger and the number of products increased requiring us to fly most days. My father decided that no one would notice if the cheques and Postal Orders were sent to the Channel Islands, but the minoxidil and other prescription drugs were sent from the UK. The UK pharmaceutical company started sending the drugs direct to the patient despite this being illegal. These businesses became so busy that the operation was moved to Guernsey. A house was rented for a postal address and all wc had to do was go and pick up the cheques and postal orders. This operation went on for several years. We would have weekends away, summer holidays and shopping trips to Guernsey.

The companies were now dominating the hair loss and skin cream markets. My father has an exceptional skill: he is good at copying and refining others business ideas and models. He would copy what other businesses were doing and do it more efficiently and at a lower cost. He saw another opportunity when the UK liposculpture market started to explode. He saw what companies such as Transform Medical (owned by John Ryan) and The Bromsgrove Private Hospital (owned by John Terry) were achieving. He found a building for sale in Oldbury. He bought it and it was renovated. He turned the building (called Crown House) into a small facility to carry out liposculpture procedures. He kept all the stock for the non-prescription hair and aesthetic products in the back of the building. Crown House was in the most bizarre place to have a cosmetic surgery hospital, but people came from all over the country. The prices were good, and the sales and service were efficient.

My parents had achieved so much in the hair and aesthetic business, but they had no idea how to run a hospital or a sales system. My father head-hunted a women named Kay Franklin who had set up the sales for Transform Medical Group. Kay came on board and set up the sales network for the new company. The company was called The National Centre for Cosmetic Surgery. There was nothing national about the company because it was a small facility in an industrial area of Birmingham. The brochures made the hospital look like a fancy hospital in Mayfair. Kay recruited other salespeople including Paul Fowler who Kay had worked with at a hair loss clinic. I also joined the team and would be trained by the toughest salespeople in the medical business.

On the medical side my father head-hunted Paula from The Bromsgrove Private Hospital. Paula set up all the theatres, recruited all the medical staff and introduced surgeons she had worked with in previous roles. In recruiting Kay and Paula, my father managed to antagonise his cosmetic surgery neighbour- John Terry, and the owner of biggest cosmetic surgery provider in the UK-John Ryan. This was the start of, what the press would call, *"the cosmetic surgery wars"*.

My father had become very powerful, and he wasn't getting caught for any of his illegal activities. He thought he was invincible. From our small offices in London and Manchester, along with the main centre in Oldbury, the company was a dominant force in hair loss products, prescription drugs, aesthetic products and liposculpture. This became the building blocks of the largest weight loss surgery centre in Europe, one of the largest cosmetic, dentistry and hair transplant companies in the UK. The company would also go on to have locations in Ireland, Spain, Dubai and the USA.

I was 20 years old when I joined the company, I had no interest in any of the businesses. I wanted to work, and my parent's company seemed the most logical option. Kay Franklin got 'landed' with me, I was 10 years younger than every other salesperson. I was a confident person or so it seemed to everyone else, but inside I wasn't at all. I think so many people wear masks to hide their true selves and to hide the way they really feel about themselves. I started off with hardcore sales training with Kay. She told me straight, "you don't hit the numbers you are out!". I was so scared and nervous when seeing patients, but I didn't want to fail, and I could sell. I started to earn a lot of money. Kay would remind me 25 years later about the first day I was sent to see patients at the Manchester clinic. I had 10 patients to consult, and Kay told me "Don't bother coming back unless you book them". I came back the next day and I had booked 8 of 10 patients, which by sales conversion standards is amazing. Within 6 months I was earning £10,000 a month. This was in 1993 when I was just 20 years old.

The liposculpture company was growing rapidly with more family members coming to work as drivers to chauffeur patients around, nursing, or administration staff. David's family members were now being recruited. His aunts worked as care assistants and his cousin and her friends as administration staff. My father had a whole new pool of women to harass, some just ignored him, many had sex with him. Diane was working in the administration and my mother oversaw the administration. Those two were either friends or enemies depending on whether or not there was another woman on the scene. My mother played the victim card of, "poor me-my husband has his mistress working here and has sex with the staff, poor me". She was all about the money and she stayed for money. Diane did try to get away from my father and left to work at a police station but he stalked her until she returned. He promised her cars, homes, pay rises and holidays and she returned. Within no time, Diane was so sick she was on high doses of Valium and many other drugs for anxiety and depression. So severe was the mental impact of all the drama, Diane would fall for no reason and injure herself. Eventually, Diane was admitted to All Saints' Mental Hospital in Birmingham. Diane suffered severe mental health issues for years, but she still stayed with my father and worked in the company. My mother was more ruthless. She loved the attention brought by the 'poor Judy card'. What would be her identity if she wasn't Steve's long suffering wife?

The relationship between Kay and my father was starting to break down. Kay is a ruthless woman, She worked at the company with her husband Martin. Kay claimed my father sexually propositioned and harassed her. Kay said she put him straight. Things got heated and Kay left. Kay requested her month's pay but he refused so Kay proceeded to claim sexual harassment. My father was to find out that Kay had taken patient leads from his database and was contacting them for surgery. This was now war so he set out to destroy her. He was referred by the company solicitors to a private detective who illegally tapped Kay's home phone line. These were the days when a ladder had to be used to get up a telephone pole and phone tap from that point. My father was listening to every call made on Kay's phoneline. The company applied for, and was granted, an Anton Piller order to raid Kay's home. This order was a civil application, but the police attended. My father, David and the police raided Kay's home. The books containing the details of the patients were not found during the raid. The phone tapping continued, and the information was gained that Kay did have books containing patient details. As the police arrived, Kay had sent her nanny out of the back of the house with the information that my father sought. The young nanny was tracked down through the private detective and threatened so that she appeared in court and testified against Kay. Kay was sentenced to 28 days in prison suspended for a year. My father got away with everything. Sadly, this wouldn't be the last I saw of Kay.

The cosmetic surgery 'war' became public and very nasty. My father doesn't play to lose, nor did John Terry. He would hit back at John Terry. Sometimes he would pay journalists he knew to place a story in the press. One of the stories was about John's Terry's wife being a pornography star. Maz Mahmood (the now disgraced journalist) had an exposé stopped at the eleventh hour via an injunction by John Terry. The exposé was on the wife of the cosmetic surgery boss being a porn star. My father was now set to reignite the story. He did not care about her young son or that it was her former life, Christine was just fodder in the cosmetic surgery war.

This was also the time when celebrities started to talk about their surgeries and were paid to promote healthcare companies. A famous sports personality was paid to have and promote a new type of surgery at the clinic in Oldbury. He had an awful reaction to surgery and his face looked like a bruised balloon. The sports personality wanted to take legal action for damages over, what he felt, was botched surgery. It all got very nasty: Blood tests were taken to identify the issue. My Father told the clinical staff to include without obtaining the knowledge and consent of the individual patient. They did as they were told. The test came back positive for cocaine and of course that knowledge was used against the sports personality. It didn't matter who you were, if you dared to go against my father, he would attempt to destroy your life.

The hair loss/prescription products being sent from the UK was working well with no regulating authorities seeming to notice. No one gave it a second thought until the day the Medicines Control Agency (MCA) raided the Central Pharmaceuticals building and other locations linked to the illegal operation. The information the MCA had, and the buildings they raided, meant somebody within the inner circle had talked. The story was across the local news TV channels and in the papers. Nanny Smith was in tears after seeing this on TV because she thought my mother was going to prison. The solicitors warned my parents that prison was highly likely for someone. There was a family meeting at their large house on the Harborne hill, to choose the unlucky family member.

This would stop most people from the illegal activity but not my father. The operation was moved to a secure unit half a mile away from the hospital. David worked from there along with a couple of key people who my father knew couldn't have talked. Everything continued just as it did before, but no one knew who the informant was. Yet again, my parents were about to get away with another crime as the legal action was dropped. There was due to be a change in the law regarding how these drugs could be ordered and dispatched, so the Crown Prosecution Service (CPS) dropped the case. To others the family appeared Teflon proof. We seemed untouchable and the staff and people around the family were scared.

My father controlled by fear. On one occasion, when my parents were leaving the hospital in Oldbury, some youths were circling them on bikes. My parents went back inside the hospital and my father called some of my mother's family to come and deal with the youths. They came in a van, with baseball bats and beat the youths badly. This was across the street from the law courts and police station! Nothing-not even the law- got in the way of my father.

The sexual harassment was rife in the business and even one of David's aunts left due to sexual harassment by my father. As it was David's aunt, she was paid a fee to keep quiet and left alone. I had gone through my childhood with no one ever seeing what these people were doing. My parents had got away with so many criminal acts. At this point, I gave up hope of anyone ever stopping my family and their criminal activity, or me getting out of the hell I lived in with them.

I think people can relate to life beating you down over and over and nothing changing. The hopelessness, despair and absolute frustration. What I would call frustration, I came to learn was my anger and apocalyptic rage for what had been done to me and others. I could not believe how these people could keep getting away with so many crimes.

However, things were about to change and the businesses were to take a major blow due to a lot of bad press. The company and staff were featured on prime-time TV programmes regarding high pressure salespeople going into potential patients' homes to sell surgical procedures. This, combined with other companies coming into the hair loss market and customers being able to order products without prescription, caused a cash flow problem. My father sold the Mercedes which David had sourced for him through one of his accountancy contacts. Both of their cars had been gained illegally through an accountant who disposed of assets from liquidated companies. The contact would sell you the car at half the list price and he would be given a cash 'backhander' by the person buying the car. Life seemed to be one big scam, loophole or what felt like constant criminal activity.

My parents considered selling the hospital, but instead decided to convert more of the building into a cosmetic surgery hospital, from a liposculpture clinic. The strategy worked and the business grew from strength to strength, I now went into sales for cosmetic surgery. With Kay gone and the information and staff needed left behind, my father oversaw sales. My father wanted control over every area of the business and for everyone who worked in and outside of the company to know who he was.

My parents' companies moving into the cosmetic surgery market had taken an impact on Bromsgrove Private Hospital. John Terry and his wife Christine were having a nasty divorce and his business was suffering. Opportunity was about to come knocking on my father's door. My father received a call from Christine Terry, John's wife. She wanted to meet with my father.

Christine needed to earn money because john had stopped all her income. She needed a job. Christine told my father that John Terry had reported him to the MCA. The informant was my mother's brother. He not only gave information regarding all the illegal activity he knew about, but any business information he could find. Luckily, for my parents, what he knew was very limited as he was only a driver for the company. My mother's family had always been jealous of each other, but this would now open a can of worms within their family. The brother who was the informant was now threatening to tell his sister-in-law about her husband's affair with her mother.

Christine Terry also advised my father that Kay Franklin had stopped working at Bromsgrove Private Hospital. With Christine gone, the Terry's vicious divorce was about to be horrifically bad press for John Terry, Bromsgrove Private Hospital was for the taking and my father planned to take it from Terry.

John Terry was a man like my father. He'd served prison time rather than pay a tax bill despite having the required funds. He also had guns, and this was to be his downfall. My father started an affair with Christine and would call John while with Christine. John was raging and he called his wife Christine and threatened to kill her. This was on a phone line that my father had arranged for all calls to be recorded. The publicity killed what was left of

Bromsgrove Private Hospital and my father brought the hospital. He planned to build the most magnificent hospital for cosmetic surgery and hair transplants.

David was now making so much money trading that he had his own trading room, and he would employ, traders. David also oversaw the company finances, and became the finance man. David knew the loopholes; and the tax havens and he knew the accountants at the big firms that would give the best advice re 'tax planning'. Unfortunately for David, some of the structures that were set up in Malta were with criminals. The Maltese contact embezzled millions of pounds of surgeons' money, which caused huge problems for David and the company.

My father, in his desire to build the most magnificent hospital, kept knocking down and rebuilding parts of the hospital. The building was going millions over budget and was almost two years behind schedule. Yet again the businesses were in jeopardy. At the same time a women name Sandra Dolan came for an interview for a job in our London office. I interviewed Sandra and said absolutely no way would I employ her. She was lovely but was in no way suitable to work with me in sales. My father took a fancy to Sandra, so he ignored me and employed her. Sandra was to become the new girlfriend and my mother and Diane hated her. I found the pair hilarious. They had come together after years of sharing my father between them and other women. My mother would send my sister and her boyfriend to Sandra's house in London to find my father and harass Sandra. My father went to Orlando on business and lied that he'd taken Sandra with him. My mother asked me to call the hotel and find out if Sandra was there - she was. She asked me to go to the airport with her, as she wanted to surprise my father, when he came through with Sandra. My mother ran at my father in the middle of Heathrow airport arrivals and went crazy, shouting and hitting him. It was so embarrassing that I was hiding behind a post. My mother was going crazy in the middle of Heathrow, saying it was their 25th wedding anniversary and he'd taken another women away! My mother is completely delusional. My father sent Sandra home with the chauffeur and came back with my mother and me. The shouting and screaming in the car were horrific, I was 26 years old; this was all I had known my whole life. It was a never-ending cycle of another women, chaos and drama. I had got to get away from these people somehow, I didn't know how, but it was making me ill, my Crohn's disease and arthritis were an ongoing battle, and all this drama was causing me to continually relapse.

My parents had separate homes, my father lived in Worcestershire, my mother in Warwickshire. After Sandra came on the scene, my mother finally realised there was no marriage, and it was over and filed for divorce. They split assets but carried on working together. Diane was as bitter and resentful as ever. She'd hung around for almost 15 years waiting for her payday, and still nothing.

Sandra lived at my father's cottage at weekends. She had a young daughter Rachel, and my father was reluctant to move Sandra into his home permanently because he did not want a child living with him. Diane would call Sandra and call her the most horrific names and tell Sandra about what she had been doing with my father. This disgraceful behaviour from the women who'd been having an affair with my father while he was still married to my mother.

Over the last eight years, David and I had become close friends with the salesman Paul Fowler and his wife Caroline. The four of us would often go on holiday together. There was a summer holiday to Spain where Caroline and I had gone ahead of Paul and David. They would join us a week later and bring my brother with them. Caroline would comment on my obsessive scrubbing of my body and how bad it had become. I was scrubbing my body with a nail brush until it bled. Things were very bad between David and me and my washing rituals -which had continued for over 15 years - were escalating. I was to learn this was a very dysfunctional way of having some control over what was happening in my life.

On that holiday, we received a call that would change the course of many people's lives. We were on the beach and David received a call to say there had been a fire at my father's house. We were told that my father had been mixing his hair potions on the AGA cooker at his cottage. Heat isn't easily regulated on an AGA and the glass cylinder broke. The alcohol in the cylinder hit the heat and became a ball of flames., My father caught fire and Sandra came into the kitchen because of the screams. She also caught fire when, most likely out of fear, he put his arms around Sandra. They both ran into the garden and rolled around on the grass to put the flames out. The neighbours heard the screams and saw what was happening and called the ambulance. My father managed to make a call on his mobile. He told my mother what had happened and to get people over to the house to clean up the mess before the police arrived.

David, my brother and I, went straight to the airport. It was Alicante airport in August and all the flights were full. David said he needed to go because he had to look after the business, I said I had to go because I was next of kin and had now become head of the family and I would have to make the decisions on my father's behalf. My brother was 16 and wanted to see his father, so we chartered a jet for the three of us and flew to Birmingham airport. Some of my family were waiting for us at the private jet terminal. Customs had been briefed on the situation, and we were taken straight to the cars.

On the journey to the hospital, we were told that my father had been taken to Worcester Hospital, but that his burns were so bad that he had been taken by air ambulance to a specialist burns' unit at Selly Oak Hospital in Birmingham. Sandra was also taken to Selly Oak Hospital. We were also told what had happened at the cottage and that a team of people (including my mother's family, and two members of staff had been over to the cottage to remove any evidence. The cupboards in the kitchen were stripped from the walls and burned in the grounds of the new hospital and the kitchen was scrubbed with specialist cleaner that would remove the traces of the alcohol and the drugs that were being mixed. When the police came to investigate the fire, they were told that Good Samaritan neighbours cleaned up after the fire. Good Samaritan neighbours, who stripped a whole kitchen, destroyed all the units and the central island of a huge kitchen and scrubbed it from floor to ceiling, immediately after a fire. The police didn't bother to verify that story. It was a sleepy village in Worcestershire, I guess they couldn't imagine any different.

At the hospital I was horrified with what I saw. The smell in a burns' unit is that of burning skin. My father was bandaged head to toe and highly sedated. I was now the decision maker for the family. I carried out the decisions the way my father would have wanted them except for one. Diane and her sister Leila wanted to come to see my father, the vultures were already circling. As they were not family they weren't allowed in without my permission, I banned them both from the burn's unit. David focused on keeping the business running and I went between our home which was now in London and the hospital in Birmingham. When I spoke with Sandra, who had 20% of her body burned, she was hysterical, saying "look at what he's done to me". Sandra wouldn't live to speak to me again because she got septicaemia and died. Rachel, Sandra's ten-year-old daughters last memory of her mother was seeing her rolling around on fire in the garden. Sandra's family thought it was too distressing for Rachel to see her mother in hospital, so Rachel never saw her mother again.

My father also became septic, the race was on to get the right drugs to fight the sepsis. He was taken from his room in the burns' unit and put on a ventilator, I was told I could have the life support machine turned off. My mother wanted the machine turned off, saying he wouldn't want to live this way, and my sister agreed. My brother cried and said "no leave it on!", My decision was simple, I'm not God and I have no intention of playing God. The machine stays on until he lives or dies, that was the end of the discussion. I told my mother, if he doesn't want to live like this then he can take the decision to take his own life, I'm not taking it for him. People often ask me do I regret not turning the life support machine off.

With all the pain and hurt my father had inflicted there's been times when I wish I had turned the machine off.

My father survived. Just like his mother, he overcame near death and unimaginable odds. He was upset over Sandra dying, but not so upset that he couldn't ask my mother to re marry him. He needed a carer and, who better than my mother as who would want him now? My mother was dating Andy Slater. He was divorced and a heavy drinker and smoker. When my father proposed in hospital my mother agreed. I truly believe because she thought he was going to die or kill himself. I believe she thought she would get all his money. She sent a letter to Andy dumping him. The solicitor was called in to the hospital to draw up a will and, unbeknown to my mother, my father left her only £250,000 of any assets he had. I thought it was hilarious. My mother is so sweet and kind when she thinks you are important, or you have something she wants. She blames everyone else and nothing is ever her fault. The real Judy is obsessed with how everything looks, what people think of her and can be very vicious and nasty.

When I told my mother what was in my father's will, the look on her face was a picture. As expected, she told my father she wasn't going to marry him and went back to Andy. Andy had not long met my mother, and he thought it was ok to drive around in my father's Porsche while my father was in hospital fighting for his life. I had one of our drivers take me to my mother's house and I took the car from Andy. I parked the car at our hospital where it remained until my father could drive it again.

After his recovery from sepsis, my father was moved back to a private room. We had connections with surgeons at Selly Oak hospital and he was allowed to have one of our nurses with him around the clock. He was convinced the staff at the hospital were trying to kill him, and was a nightmare for their medical team. My father had over 50% of his body burned and skin grafts were taken from the rest of his body. My father is scarred from head to toe with burns or grafts. This image obsessed man was burned all over except for his face. Had his face been burned, I think he would have killed himself. I think most people would think that being almost burned to death and your partner dying, would help you rethink your life and change your ways. It changed nothing with my father. if anything he got worse.

Once my father was able to have his harem of women back around him, I no longer needed to be in Birmingham, so I returned to mine and David's home in London. When I turned on the TV, I saw the World Trade Center had been attacked. The markets crashed. David lost a chunk of our money that day and there was more to come. The industry also had a downturn, and the hospital was delayed even more due to my father's accident and long rehabilitation. The company was about to be lost, unless money was found, and the bank would not loan any more money.

I had the money needed to give the company some short term cashflow. I was asked to loan the company money. I said I wouldn't loan the company money but I would buy 20% for £200,000. My father was furious, and he didn't want me owning any of his company. I suggested they find someone else to give them the money. Other family members had the money to loan but refused. David and I had loaned the company money a few times when there were financial problems. I'd had enough of my family; I was in a strong position now and I played my hand. There was no way my father would accept me owning 20%, so we agreed on £150,000 for 15% of the company and an interest free loan of £50,000.

With that deal, I became an owner of a private hospital group. My parents would resent me for this as would other family members. I really didn't care what anyone thought, I had just bought my freedom from my family and freedom for myself for the first time in my life. No one would have cared if I had lost all my money, but life was about to turn out very differently.

You never know what the future will bring. Within 7 years my shares would be valued at £7.5million. The McNerlin family were on the *Sunday Times Rich List*, and

I was the highest paid employee in the history of the group. I was to build a weight loss surgery empire and put together and feature in a prime time TV series. The press called me *Donna Ross 'The Boss'*, but before I got there, I was going to go through pain the likes of which I had never known in my life. Emotional pain that took me to the edge of my sanity, to the depths of despair where the only way I thought I could make it stop was to take my own life. I was about to know what it was like to be brought to my knees.

WHAT THE READER CAN TAKE FROM THIS CHAPTER?

Often behind a seemingly confident person can be a very insecure one.

You can create something out of nothing.

Everything isn't always as it seems.

Masks are often what people wear to hide how they feel about themselves.

Anger and rage can manifest due to unresolved issues.

Life can beat you down over and over, but you can find a way out.

You never know what the future can bring, your life can change in a moment.

CHAPTER FIVE

MARRIAGE, PAIN AND LOSS

LOSS

THE FEELING OF GRIEF AFTER LOSING SOMEONE OR SOMETHING OF VALUE

David and I planned our wedding for June 1993, and it was set to be a fabulous affair. The ceremony was to be at a church in Birmingham followed by a reception at a fabulous country hotel in Worcestershire. My parents viewed it as the wedding day that they never had. My father even had a rhinoplasty to fix the big nose that he had hated since childhood. My mother planned the bridesmaids, flowers, place cards, cakes and all the stuff that goes with a big wedding. I was excited to be getting married to David who I loved beyond words, and it was wonderful to see our families so happy.

I found the biggest puff ball of a wedding dress, along with a long train, huge veil and a tiara. The whole look was very early nineties, sequins and showy, it fitted perfectly with the big, flashy wedding. I had seven bridesmaids including cousins that I didn't even know because my mother thought they would look good. Everything detail to be perfect including flower girl, height, colours, dresses, cars, and flowers. My mother even asked David to change his best man because she felt he didn't look good enough, David refused. The wedding was the day to show off the family's wealth. The wedding never felt like our wedding, it felt like my mother's.

Life looked perfect for us, and we had the world at our feet. We were both doing well at work and had a lovely home and cars. We looked like the perfect couple. Just as I had my wobble when I was shown a different life going out with my friends, David was about to have his wobble. David had decided his stag party would be a week in Gran Canaria with friends. This didn't concern me. David had always been focused on me, work, exams and money - other women never came into the picture. I was shocked when David returned from his week away and said he didn't want to get married. We were three weeks away from our wedding. He'd had fun getting drunk with his friends and had received attention from lots of women and thought he was missing out on life. I was devastated. 3 weeks from this huge wedding and he decided he didn't want to get married. I didn't even bother to try to talk him out of it. I said, "If that's what you want, you can go and tell everyone!". David told my parents and everything was cancelled. I think I cried for a week.

David and I were still living together. A week after the euphoria of the holiday had settled, David realised he had made a huge mistake. But it was too late because everything had been cancelled.

We went on the honeymoon, but it was tense. When we returned, I planned to visit see my childhood friend (Joanne) who was working in Cyprus for a year. I needed to be with Joanne and decide out what to do next. It was a good idea because we had so much fun. We went out until dawn and drove around on scooters. I was doing exactly what 20-year-olds do, I had fun away from my family, life with David and all that I had been through. David missed me so much during the two weeks I was away he said he had made a huge mistake and he wanted to book another wedding. Our wedding was rebooked for august 27th 1995. This time we were going to do it our way, and the wedding was paid for by us.

Nanny Mac was happy I didn't get married. She adored David but felt he was the wrong person for me, and she was right. Just after we booked the second wedding, Nanny Mac became ill and was having more problems with her heart. She was admitted to the Queen Elizabeth Hospital in Birmingham. Over 40 years she had had numerous heart operations, a stroke and paralysis but she needed more surgery. I thought my she was invincible - the ultimate survivor. The family were advised of the risks but she wanted to go ahead with the surgery. She would survive the surgery but she wouldn't survive very long. My father called every contact he had. He would have done anything to save his mother, but there was nothing he could do. He lost the person he loved most. She was his anchor - the one he ran too when he was in trouble. I lost my Nanny Mac. She was the women that loved me more than words can ever describe. She was my mother and grandmother.

I will never forget her last breath. The family were all with her as her life support machine was turned off. I had the seat right next to her bed with my father was the other side. I held her wrist and moved her arm to stroke my head. This was the only thing that as a child would calm me down. I fell asleep with her hand on my head. I was woken by the noise of the flatline on the machine.

My father had Nanny Mac brought home to her house as there was no way he was leaving her at an undertaker. She was buried in the suit she had bought for my wedding. I have never recovered seeing her dressed in her wedding suit lying in the coffin. My father and I suffered very badly. We were both depressed and struggling to cope with the loss of the most important person in our lives. I was to also lose another special person-this time from David's family. David received a call to say his grandfather was having emergency surgery-he didn't survive. I felt like I was losing the people I loved the most. Those people made me feel safe.

The wedding was approaching and everything was going well. On the way to the church my father said, "You don't have to do this if you don't want to. We can go somewhere and I'll have someone deal with everything". He knew I didn't want to get married just as he never wanted to get married. The good thing about my father was that I could go to him if I was in trouble, and he would know how to get me out of it. My mother would use anything I did against me.

David and I were married at Salwarpe church in Worcestershire, and we had the best day. Our families and friends were there to see us married and celebrate with us. Our reception was at the Hyatt hotel in Birmingham. We had the penthouse suite for our wedding night. It came with a grand piano and sauna and it was amazing. The next day we flew off on our honeymoon to New York, Las Vegas, Maui and Los Angeles.

We arrived in New York. It was the first time we had been to America since the holiday with my grandparents. We were staying at the Waldorf Astoria on Park Avenue. We were mesmerised by the city. We then went on to Las Vegas and had a huge suite at the Mirage Hotel overlooking The Strip. We loved Las Vegas. We were so young, just two kids in this huge suite overlooking the lights of Las Vegas, we had to pinch ourselves - we were living a dream. The next stop was the Four Seasons in Maui. Maui was beautiful with superb ocean, volcanoes, and scenery. We finally relaxed after the wedding and travelling.

The final stop was Los Angeles. We stayed at the Regent Beverly Wilshire Hotel - the hotel featured in the film Pretty Women. It was magnificent and we saw so many movie stars. Planet Hollywood was opening its first store in Hollywood and the whole of Rodeo Drive was closed off as a red carpet. We were completely star struck. What an end to the most perfect wedding and honeymoon. We shopped on Rodeo Drive, followed the stars along the Walk of Fame and relaxed by the pool with the Hollywood crowd. As we were leaving for the airport, I looked at the dress I had seen in the window of the store that covered the front of the Regent Beverly Wilshire Hotel. David said to me "Let's go and get the dress". This was my *Pretty Women* moment. We went into the store and David said to the shop assistants, "We are leaving for the airport, we have ten minutes, and my wife wants that dress". David wanted to give me everything, he really did want to give me the world.

As David and I left Los Angeles, I don't think either of us could have imagined that fifteen years later we would have a cosmetic surgery business in California. David would work in Beverly Hills with the A listers, and I'd be asked to set up a weight loss surgery business in America. David was 23, I was 22, we had no idea what life had in store for us.

I was now Mrs Ross but I refused to give up my family name, so I was Donna Michelle McNerlin-Ross. I was very proud of my family name and all the family had achieved. I didn't want to give that part of me up. My family were my identity. A McNerlin was who I was. Who was I if I wasn't a McNerlin?

David and I now had a large house in a beautiful area, top of the range sports cars, fantastic jewellery, the best holidays and designer clothes. What more could we want? But David always wanted more: More money, better cars and bigger houses. People thought it was me that wanted all these things, but it was David. He just kept wanting more and then he wanted a child. I was 23. We hadn't even been married 6 months and this wasn't what we had agreed. I didn't want children. I liked working and was focused on my career. I would go between wanting to give David what he wanted and sticking with what I wanted. In the end I relented. I found out I was pregnant in February 1996. I don't even know how I really felt. I think I was in shock. David was so excited and wanted to tell everyone. The families were so happy and it would be their first grandchild.

I was content with our house in Worcestershire. We had space and were away from my family. I did not want to move but David said he wanted a bigger family house so, in the end, I agreed we could at least look. We found a lovely house next to the church where we were married. Then we looked a further afield in Warwickshire, where we were to find our new home a mile from the centre of Stratford-upon-Avon, the birthplace of William Shakespeare. We had gone from our first house in Bishopton Road to our new home which called Bishopton House. It was a 31-room mansion.

I wasn't faring well with the pregnancy and my Crohn's disease and arthritis flared up. My consultant was concerned. My hormones were also all over the place and I was a temperamental nightmare. I hated this house and I blamed David for wanting to move and my pregnancy. I was also becoming neurotic about giving birth as I still had some medical phobias. My obstetrician was going to a conference, and I was hysterical worrying the baby may come while he was away. He suggested that I be induced. He felt that some gel inside the cervix would open everything up and I would be fine. I was booked into hospital, given the gel a few times and there was no change. My worst fear was about to come, I would be given a drip to induce labour. I was phobic about cannulas in my arm, and I knew the contractions would go from 0-10 very quickly as would the pain. I was emotionally and physically drained, but my baby finally came. Henry Thomas Ross, a healthy baby boy, the love of my life, the centre of my world and he would become my reason for living.

Our families visited and were very excited but I just wanted to get in the shower. Nothing had changed with my washing rituals because being pregnant had only intensified them. I had no idea what to do with Henry- how to wash him, feed him, change nappies, nothing. When I took Henry home, I was alone in a huge house. I only had my family to visit and Jo (the housekeeper). I had no friends in the area and my life didn't relate to any of my school friends. I was lonely, isolated and was about to suffer the most extreme type of post-natal depression. It would take me 20 years to tell anyone what was going in my head at that time.

After 3 months at home, I couldn't stand it anymore. I said to David, "I'm going back to work". I couldn't work for long as I was getting very ill again. I was having aggressive Crohn's disease flare ups. I often struggled to walk due to the arthritis and I was in immense pain. I was having asthmatic symptoms even though I wasn't asthmatic, and I would have to use a nebuliser to breathe, I kept having laryngitis and pharyngitis and was now also under the care of an ear nose and throat surgeon. No one could explain why I was constantly getting ill.

The depression I'd had when I was 18, came back with a vengeance as did my binge eating. I did not want to leave my bedroom and I slept all day. For anyone that has not had post-natal depression: You feel like you are going insane; you don't understand what is happening to you; it is horrific. I would lay in bed all day and let Jo look after Henry. I would also binge eat chocolate. At this point I didn't know I had an eating disorder and it would be years before I was diagnosed. I wasn't diagnosed with post-natal depression, just depression, because I was too ashamed to tell anyone what was going on in my mind. When David came home from work, I wasn't interested in him or Henry. What was crippling me, and why I wasn't getting better, was I had a severe form of post-natal depression and I had something called infanticidal ideas. I would wish Henry would go to bed and not wake up. I never thought about harming him, just that he wouldn't wake up. I thought I was evil, there was something wrong with me and I couldn't tell anybody for fear of them thinking I would hurt my child. I was scared and didn't know what was happening to me. It took me almost twenty years to tell anyone about those thoughts, and then a doctor finally explained to me what had happened to me.

I strongly advise that any person who reads this and feels low in their mood while pregnant or after giving birth, seek help. To any person that is having severe post-natal depression or thoughts like mine, you are not a bad person, seek help and tell your doctor you can be helped. To any person who has thoughts like I did and like me kept them within you for years, tell someone you can trust and can get help. The shame and guilt of post-natal depression dies away when we talk about how we feel or felt, think or thought. For any partner, family member or friend, there is help there and all you can do is be supportive. You can't understand what the person is going through. I couldn't see a way out, I had everything anyone could wish for and most days I wished I wouldn't wake up.

I was 24, back on anti-depressants, and my Crohn's disease was constantly relapsing, as was my arthritis and these mystery illnesses that would come and go were relentless. My life was miserable, David tried to help in his way which was take me on holiday and buy me things. He took me to Whistler skiing and I came back with laryngitis and pharyngitis. We took Henry skiing to Switzerland with my family, and we had to come home early as I was so ill. There were trips to Marbella, South of France, Mauritius, America & the Caribbean. Wherever we went, there was always something wrong with me.

I lived in a mansion, I had a good husband, a beautiful son, more money than we could spend, and I hated my life. My temper was legendary and could easily be set off for no apparent reason - I didn't know that I was full of rage. My rage was building, and it often came out at people who didn't deserve it, like David. Having Henry had been a major trigger to my childhood trauma. I had no idea that until I resolved that trauma, I would look like I had everything, but I felt like I had nothing. Nothing I could ever do or buy would fill the hole inside me, no holiday or place that I was visiting would help. What I could not escape, and what I took everywhere with me, was my head, my thoughts and my thinking.

As Henry got older and he went to nursery, I started to feel a little better. David and I had what looked like the most fantastic life. However, I didn't work and I had no friends of my own age. My mother was a constant drain on me, wanting to tag along everywhere David and I went. We had moved away from my family, which was great, but my mother moved to Warwickshire to be closer. I just couldn't stand it anymore; David was keeping me connected to my family and I wanted to get away from them. I was 27 when I said to David I wanted a divorce, he lived a life I didn't want.

Again, contrary to what most people thought, David likes to be the big fish in a small pond, and I like to be a small fish in a big pond. This was the life he wanted, not me, I didn't want a divorce from David, it was my family and this life. I was never leaving David, I was leaving them - the family.

David was absolutely devastated. I gave him one option which was to leave this house and this area. We would sell the antiques, the paintings, the cars, and go to London away from my family. Alternatively, we divorce. David reluctantly agreed.

We looked in many different areas for a new home in London, there were just so many fabulous places to live. We sold the cars; David bought a new Ferrari, I bought a Vespa and I kept my Mercedes to take Henry to school. I would wizz around London on my Vespa with the wind on my face and body. For the first time in my life, I felt alive.

David wanted a large house in London because he was used to our huge country home whereas I wanted a smaller house. Finally, we settled on a 5-story townhouse in Knightsbridge. Hyde Park was at the top of our road, *Harrods* was at the bottom. Henry was at a new school. I was away from my family and Henry and I could be together all the time. David spent Monday to Wednesday working in Birmingham and Thursday to Sunday in London. For the first time in my life, I looked up at the sky and I could breathe. I would walk down the street and I felt free. Henry had his mother back. We did everything together. He now had a devoted mother. I mixed with the other mothers, arranged playdates, got involved in the parent and teachers' association, I was becoming a mother.

I felt a freedom and happiness, I had never known, I felt I was finally free. My weight had effortlessly dropped off and my weight and eating were now stable. David started to settle into the routine of being away for 3 days a week and life seemed perfect. I was living a fantasy life. David and I started to go out more to restaurants, bars, fashion shows and live a fun life that people in their 20's do. On one of those nights, we tried cocaine with some of the cast of the TV show *EastEnders*.

After a year in Knightsbridge, David wanted me to come back to the country to live. He found magnificent homes for us in the Cotswolds including a mansion with a moat near the new hospital in Bromsgrove. I would go and look with him and then have anxiety attacks, I knew I couldn't go back to live near my family, and I loathed these big houses. David said to our friends that I would have to come back home as we couldn't keep living the way we were. I said to David "I will divorce you before I ever go back", the table just went silent. I think I knew that day, my marriage was over, I think David did too. I thought David would never leave my family and the businesses and he would always keep dragging me back.

I don't know what I really expected David to do. I'd asked for a divorce and to appease me and save our marriage, he moved to London. To save our marriage I now needed to go back to an area where David could come home every night. I just couldn't do it. It wasn't David I couldn't go back to - I adored him - it was my family. David again made a compromise and agreed to another year in London. After one year in London and being happier than I had ever been, my world was about to come crashing down.

Just before the fateful holiday to Spain (the one in which we had to charter a private jet due to the fire at my father's house) we moved into an even bigger 5 story home in Primrose Hill, which also had a separate flat.

David and I were in the worst place we had ever been, and I didn't know if we could come back from this. I said to David the best thing we could do, was he live his life and I live mine; it would be a financial disaster for us to divorce now. David found himself a flat at the Mailbox Apartments in Birmingham and would come to Primrose Hill to see Henry at weekends.

After the fire at my father's house, Sandra's daughter Rachel was left in the care of her aunts and uncles but none of them wanted to take care of Rachel permanently. They made the decision to put Rachel into care. I said to David there was no way this could happen. I always felt it was my responsibility to sort out the issues my family had caused. If not for my father mixing the Minoxidil, Rachel's mother would still be alive.

In the meltdown of my marriage, my father's horrific injuries, huge financial losses and my husband having an affair, I took a troubled 10-year-old girl I had never met into our home. David later said that taking in Rachel was the end of our marriage for him. Henry was so excited to have a 'sister', however Rachel was horrible to Henry most of the time.

After only a few months my mother decided she would marry Andy. My brother's school also closed in the middle of his GCSE'S (exams) and, on top of everything else I was going through and trying to deal with, I also invited my brother to live with me in London. He could take his GCSEs in one year at a London college and then go onto university. As usual, I took on everyone else's problems just like I'd done as a child. No one helped or intervened, I was drowning, and I was at breaking point.

Everything just built up. I was 28 years old when the roller coaster of my life caught up with me. I don't think the first suicide attempt was because I wanted to die. It was a cry for help because everything else had gone unheard. No one listened, no one helped, everyone carried on their life in Birmingham while I was left with my four-year-old son, a ten-year-old girl with behavioural issues and my brother who was 16 and partying in London. To top it all off, my husband was having an affair with a former sex worker who now worked for the company.

I took lots of pills, I couldn't see any other way. I survived the suicide attempt, but I was barely surviving. The rage started to come, I was angry with the whole world, but especially David. We were constantly arguing and the tension in the house was at boiling point. Just before David's 30th birthday, we were having an argument and all I remember was David with his hands around my neck-I thought he was going to kill me and I was losing consciousness. I reached to my side of me for something I managed to grab a small ornament and cracked it on David's forehead. It bled, and he let go.

This was my first experience of domestic violence in my own relationships. I think once violence starts, there's only going to be an escalation and there was a huge one about to come. I would advise anyone that experiences domestic violence to get help immediately.

David had booked a holiday to go back to Sandy Lane Hotel in Barbados for his 30th birthday with Henry, Rachel and me. The holiday was awful and nothing like our holiday there a few years earlier. We came home and it was a week until Christmas. We had friends over for Christmas and Boxing Day (26th December). On Boxing Day, David went to the pub with his friend. They got really drunk and when he came home and we were in our bedroom, he attacked me. My nose was badly broken, my face and neck cut and bruised, I looked horrific. David left the house, my mother was called to come and help. Her wedding to Andy was 3 days later.

The next day I went to a lawyer in London and he arranged for a restraining order against David. I was also given an order for a power of arrest. I wanted to try and salvage our marriage, but it was too late. We tried but we never came back from the violent episode. David had kept me alive through all the horrors of my life at home with my parents, we'd built this fabulous life together and now it lay shattered in pieces.

I went to my mother's wedding alone with two black eyes and bruises all over my face and neck. I couldn't be in any of the pictures, and everyone was looking and finger pointing. I went back home to London and spent the new year with Rachel and Henry at our friend's home. I had no idea what to do next. I would drink a glass or two of wine occasionally, it was small amounts, but looking back, I learned it would ease the pain I was in.

Since the suicide attempt 4 months earlier, I had been seeing a psychiatrist. He was based at a hospital in South West London, famous for its celebrity patients. I wanted to go into the hospital and knew I needed to take some pressure off myself. No one made me go. In fact, my family didn't want me to go because they didn't want me talking. For the first time in my life, I was about to start talking about what had happened to me.

Before I went into the hospital, I went on a skiing holiday with friends and my brother. The holiday was to cheer me up after the bruises and fractures from the attack had healed. I felt very lonely and fearful without David. It was the first time I'd been alone in 18 years. I slipped slightly on my skis and fell to one side on soft snow. There was hardly any impact, but I was in so much pain that I had to go to the doctors. The doctor advised me that I had badly fractured some ribs, I was told I couldn't ski. I couldn't understand how my ribs had fractured with such a soft landing - it made no sense. This was the start of my body fracturing and in the end, I would have fractures from head to toe.

I arrived at the hospital which looks like a huge white gothic castle. I was scared because I had no idea what to expect. I was taken to the nurses' station through locked doors which had keypads and codes to get in and out. I was shown to my own room with an ensuite bathroom. I was taken around the hospital and shown the facilities. I laugh because knowing what I do now, I was never ever going to get well at this hospital. The hospital had a gym which you could use as often as you wanted. The personal trainer (extra cost) was an ex-stripper, a Californian dream boy. There was a huge hot tub in the gym which was temporarily out of use because the patients were having sex in it.

The restaurant had different tables for different groups. One for staff, one for the addictions patients (with whom no other group was allowed to mix), the eating disorder group and one for the general mental health group (my group). I was given a schedule of the groups I would need to attend. I had no idea what they were, but I went along and tried them all. We had a community meeting every night to share our feelings and talk about our day. The first day I arrived I went to the meeting and was introduced and had to say something about myself. I had learned to put on the face of being happy even when I wanted to kill myself. How could I introduce myself? I didn't know who I was. How did I feel? I was speechless. I felt I couldn't relate to these people. There was a 16-year-old girl who had cut herself all over her body, a young man in his twenties who talked of putting a gun to his head and a mother who was admitted with her baby due to post-natal depression. I thought I was nothing like these people and they were all crazy. I was exactly like all these people. The one thing I promised myself was that my son would never end up in a hospital like these young men and women.

I liked some of the groups, the groups where you talked or worked and learnt something, I really disliked the art and drama groups. I realised I had major anxiety issues and I had to leave some groups or breathe into a paper bag to calm myself down. Taking off the masks that I'd developed over the years was frightening me to death. Memory, or segments of memory that I'd had for years, were recurring over and over. I would talk of the dreams I had of people being in my room at night and how when I woke, I couldn't open my eyes. I held my breath, so if there were people in the room, they wouldn't know I was awake. I didn't have many happy childhood memories. One of them was my father swinging me around in my bedroom and I was screaming with laughter and giggling. I ended up in hospital that day because my arm had come out of its socket again. I would talk of my Nanny and Grandad Mac holding each of my arms as they were walking, and my arm would come out of its socket and again I would end up in hospital. I talked of throwing soup over my breasts and cutting off my hair. I started to talk about the abuse I had suffered at the hands of one of my mother's family members and one of my father's family members. I talked about being in a bunk bed at Jean and Pete Morris's house and someone getting off the top bunk and getting in bed with me. I talked about the door opening in the same room and someone getting in bed with me. Many years later I would learn that when I felt safe, these memories would come. The clinic was the first place I felt safe in my life, that no one could get to me. I was 29 years old; and I had voluntarily put myself in a mental health facility.

My father came with David to visit me and said, "There's nothing wrong with you, if you were really crazy, you would be in All Saint's Hospital!" He referred to the psychiatric hospital his mistress (Diane) spent months in because of him. After my stay at the clinic, my parents spent years telling people I was crazy in an attempt to discredit me. I was the person who knew where all their skeletons were buried.

I was allowed to go home at weekends. One weekend, I went to see my mother and told her of the abuse by the family members. I will never forget her response: - "I knew it would all be my fault, don't tell your father" One day I understood what she meant by 'all'. She also said, "It was only kids playing, it would be like your brother touching your sister's daughter". My niece was 2 years old and my brother was 16. There was no compassion from my mother. I expected, "No, oh my god now I understand some of your behaviour and anger." There was "No, let's get you help", no, "let's call the police", no, "let's deal with that family member". I heard nothing - it was all about her.

My mother only cared about being blamed. She was the person who was meant to protect me. I was devastated. I had summoned everything to have the courage to talk and yet I had no compassion or support from her. If I received that response from my mother, what chance did I stand with any help or compassion from others? I was full of rage. It is often said that depression is anger turned inwards. On a weekend home to see David and Henry, I made a very serious suicide attempt. After the response from my mother, I wanted to die and I wasn't going to die in a hospital, I was going to die at home with my son and husband. I acted completely normally. I went to the hairdressers, returned, and I went to my bedroom and took so many pills, I don't know how I survived, I left no trace I had taken them. I went downstairs and lay on the sofa in the TV room to appear like I had fallen asleep watching TV. I later discovered that David had tried and failed to wake me. He realised something was wrong and he called the ambulance and my mother. I awoke in hospital and was very angry. I was shouting why had they brought me there? I had wanted to die, and I would keep trying - they wouldn't stop me. The doctors said I would need to return to the private psychiatric hospital or they would keep me in their NHS ward. My mother and David begged me to go back to the private hospital. I realised it was pointless asking my family for help and pointless speaking about what had happened to me. I did what I had been trained to do - act like nothing had happened. I agreed to return to the private hospital.

After 6 weeks I looked amazing, I felt so much better, and I thought I was fixed up and ready to go. I had opened a huge emotional wound. I had no idea I had opened *Pandora's Box*. The stay at the hospital was like sticking a little *Band-Aid* over a gaping wound and it wouldn't be long before it came off.

Many years later, I would request every record from this private hospital. I took the notes to Dr Pereira - the psychiatrist that would save my life. He studied my notes. He said on one of those letters alone, that my psychiatrist had written to my GP, the multi-agency safeguarding team should have been called in. There was gross negligence on the part of the hospital and my psychiatrist. My psychiatrist was later struck off by the General Medical Council for taking luxury holidays from a patient and a million pounds from her will.

Yet again, my family had got away with no questions being asked and nothing being done. How long was I going to have to scream for someone to hear me? How long would it take for someone to come and help? The hospital and the psychiatrist knew there were thousands of patients going through our hospitals and they did nothing to safeguard anyone.

I was 29 years old, a single mother with two children. I had lost Nanny Mac and David (my anchor) and I was about to start spinning out of control. I had opened Pandora's Box of which I would use anything to suppress what was inside. I had absolutely no idea what I would do next. I had given up my career and my health would cause me a problem getting a job outside the family. I would have to go back to the family.

I have heard it said that peace comes when you accept the person you were destined to be. I didn't know who I was, let alone who I was destined to be. I was about to go on a rollercoaster ride for the next 15 years that no Hollywood script writer could make up. I had no idea that I was about to rise from the ashes of my life like a phoenix from the flames. Donna McNerlin was gone. I was about to become Donna Ross.

WHAT THE READER CAN TAKE FROM THIS CHAPTER?

Seek help if your mood changes in pregnancy or once you have given birth.

Don't be afraid to say what you feel inside or talk about the thoughts you have.

Mystery illnesses will have a root cause.

At the first sign of domestic abuse seek help.

Removing the masks you hide behind can set you free.

Money and material things don't always equal happiness.

CHAPTER SIX

WEIGHT LOSS SURGERY

OBESITY

A COMPLEX DISEASE INVOLVING AN EXCESSIVE AMOUNT OF BODY FAT

While I was in the hospital, David and I had marriage counselling. While many people find it helpful, for us it was of no use because we were both finished with our marriage. I decided to stay in London to work at our clinic on Harley Street. Being in London meant that Henry could stay at his school, and although I would be working in the family business, I would be away from them. It was good to be home from the hospital and I was feeling great. I had Henry, my brother and Rachel with me. I was happy to have decided what I would be doing with my life. Yet again, life had a way of changing my best laid plans.

David and I had arranged a birthday dinner for my father in Birmingham. It was eight months since the fire and my father was recovering well. After the dinner, a group of us decided to go to a bar and continue the evening. I chatted to a guy there and we were really intrigued by each other. He was an athlete, and he had a lifestyle I longed to have. He travelled the world training and racing. He was free to do as he wished, living out of a bag. I had the stability of homes, cars and a business. We exchanged numbers and spoke on the phone. We met up and got on well. He was tall, very attractive and liked simple things in life. His purpose was to compete and be a champion.

Our relationship quickly became serious, and I started to spend more time at his home in Warwickshire. I now had some good reasons to return to the Midlands. The dynamics of my position in business had changed, Henry could be nearer David and I would be near '*The Athlete*'. I decided I was going to relocate to Warwickshire. Henry and Rachel were happy and were getting on much better. My brother had been offered a place at Birmingham University, so he was to return to the Midlands too.

We packed up the house in Chalcot Square. It was sad to be leaving but we were hopeful for a better life in Warwickshire. There was one final event we needed to attend as a family – the school summer concert. I was choked and fighting back tears because all the pain of the last eighteen months in London came up. The emotional pain was so physical – that it was taking my breath away. Two years earlier we had come to London as a family full of hope and now our family was shattered. All the teachers and parents were sad to see us go. That day my heart broke for David, Henry, and me.

We moved into a rented mansion in Leamington Spa. It was like Bishopton House. All the feelings I was trying to avoid resurfaced and I started to use food to suppress them. I was recreating the life I had lived with David at Bishopton House and, just like before, I wanted to start running away again.

Henry's new school was very academic and he didn't like it. When Henry was four, his London tutor thought that he was dyslexic. Problems with Henry's reading started to arise and he was also being naughty in class. I arranged for him to be assessed and he was confirmed as having dyslexia. I was furious with the school. I had been pointing this out to them for over a year. This would be the first of many arguments with schools over not recognising that Henry had learning and concentration difficulties. I didn't consider that the drama at home, the violence he had witnessed, his father starting another family, the separation and the moving homes were causing him distress. As I saw it, Henry had a much better life than I'd had, and I didn't consider that the damage and impact of what David and I were doing affected him. It took me ten years to understand that Henry had also suffered trauma and that was the source of his difficulties. I was unconsciously repeating the pattern and behaviour of generations of my family.

I found and bought a beautiful house that backed onto the river in Leamington Spa. My life with Henry and *'The Athlete'* was great, but I had the family to contend with who didn't like or approve of my partner. It was obvious that my issues were returning because my weight wasn't just going up a bit – it was rocketing. I lived with a team GB athlete who trained six hours a day. He ate accordingly, and I ate the same. He was amazing, he really tried to work with me on food and exercise, but nothing was working. The recurring visuals (what I would learn were flashbacks) were getting worse. After the response I received from my mother regarding my abuse, I was scared to tell anyone for fear of them rejecting me. My Crohn's disease and arthritis were also deteriorating. Fortunately, I found an amazing gastroenterologist, Dr Peter Hawker. He started me on some aggressive treatment to suppress my immune system.

I was now working at our flagship hospital. It was Dolan Park, named after my father's late girlfriend Sandra. My father had been introduced to a doctor who was working on weight loss products. One of them was a balloon that was placed into the stomach and removed after six months. It reduced the amount of food you ate and made you feel so nauseous that you didn't want to eat.

My father can be a cruel man. He endlessly commented about my weight because he believed there was nothing worse than being fat. He suggested a gastric balloon and then something called a gastric band. My mother had tried the balloon, but only tolerated it for three days due to the nausea. I was appalled by his suggestion and said I would lose weight the healthy way through diet and exercise. What a joke! For the previous eighteen years there had been nothing healthy about any of my eating habits or exercise regimes. Like so many others, I was in total denial at the extent of my problem.

I started to see patients losing weight, seemingly with little effort. I became more interested and had a consultation with one of the surgeons for a gastric band. I had a BMI of 37 and co-morbidities, so I met the criteria for surgery. *'The Athlete'* was concerned about the surgery but I felt that nothing else had worked so I decided to have a gastric band fitted. On the day of the surgery, we arrived at the hospital, but I told *'The Athlete'* to take me home. I couldn't do it. He turned the car around and we started to drive back home. However, I knew I had no choice, so he took me back again. I was scared. My phobia of cannulas and needles was terrible. I was thirty years old, but I was still that scared child. Having this weight loss surgery was life changing in so many ways, it was to become a blessing and a curse.

My father launched the weight loss surgery business and he had big plans. David asked me to look at the new business and how the sales had been structured to see what I thought we could achieve. I told David that I thought it had potential, so David asked me to work on the business and develop the weight loss surgery. I agreed on the condition that he kept my father out of the office where I worked with the staff, and I had autonomy. He agreed and said he would make sure father stayed out of the way if I brought in the numbers. I certainly did that! I went back to my core skill – sales. I moved all staff-except for my assistant-to work on the phones. They worked on converting enquiries to consultations. I worked with the surgeons, saw every patient myself and converted them to operations. I trained all the staff to work the way I had been trained, but with integrity and compassion. I took over the department at a loss making £175,000 a month. Within six weeks, we were at a profit making £325,000 a month. Month on month we were growing.

The new company was The National Centre for Obesity Surgery, and joined The National Centre for Cosmetic Surgery and our hair loss brand. The other divisions mainly used foreign surgeons whereas my division only used NHS consultant surgeons. I also worked with other hospital groups like BUPA, Nuffield and BMI group. The company was a company of two halves: One, run by my father, which people referred to as the cosmetic surgery cowboys, and my half which was run in a completely different way. We used the same software, similar sales structures, but the ethos was completely different.

I was working with two surgeons who were based in Birmingham. To expand the business, I needed to have them consult in London and Manchester. My father told me that they wouldn't go to other clinics. They wouldn't for him, but they did for me. People did things for me that they wouldn't do for others. I never asked anyone who worked with me to do anything I wouldn't do myself. I made sure people earned money according to the effort they put into the business, and I never capped anyone's earning potential. I was creating the 'dream team' - as they would come to be known.

Our business and sales models were fantastic. We just couldn't keep up with the demand, and I needed more surgeons to expand the clinics across the UK. This would prove difficult as my father had antagonised the obesity surgeons' specialist group, then called BOSS. We had effectively been blocked by them. I would have to ask the medical reps to act as intermediaries to get me appointments with the surgeons I wanted to recruit. I would have to use all my charm and convince them that, what I was doing, was different than the other parts of the company. I wanted surgeons who are what we call a 'good pair of hands'. I rated surgical skill over charm. I could teach a surgeon how to improve patient rapport and how to manage a patient, I couldn't teach them how to improve their operating skills. I increased volumes and made cuts to all fees. Many obesity surgeons would become millionaires because of weight loss surgery and were the new plastic surgeons. We were a team and we had to flow. Everyone was important, but no one more than the other. I had reduced all our costs and I increased the cost of surgery, so that the obesity department was now a streamlined business and highly profitable.

Obesity and weight loss surgery was attracting a lot of media attention. We were having articles written about us in every newspaper, then the TV companies started to approach us to make a series. We had production companies pitch every type of programme, from very serious medical documentaries to Kardashian style tabloid shows.

While my work life was amazing, other issues were developing around me and one of them was my home life. *'The Athlete'* had been great with me through the difficulties of the fallout from my separation and the weight gain. He was now holding our home life together because I was hardly ever there. While he and Henry were getting on with their lives, I was developing a new dysfunctional coping strategy. Work had become my new addiction. I would keep myself so busy that I didn't have time to think or feel anything. I would throw money at the problems arising at home to try to keep everyone quiet, but it would eventually cost me dearly.

After a day of final pitches from production companies, we agreed on an independent production company that had been commissioned by ITV. They wanted to feature me as Donna Ross, *'The Boss'*. They were to film with us for a year and follow me in my home and work life. We had to choose patients who would be characters, interesting to watch on TV and who would turn out like a swan.

The pressure of having cameras on me, focusing on my weight and image, was to trigger a whole realm of issues. I was becoming the face of the weight loss surgery industry, known as a cosmetic surgery boss and a ruthless businesswoman. I did what I'd always done and gave people what they wanted. The thinner I became, the better I looked and the more profit we made. The more I performed for the cameras, the more love and attention I received. I didn't know what I was looking for at that time, it just felt good. What I had longed for since I was a child was someone to validate me, give me approval, show me love and care for me. As a child, I got attention if I was performing, and I was about to put on the performance of my life.

I had really started to engage with patients as they lost weight and then there was my own journey. I saw people becoming, what I would describe as, sexy. They felt desired, confident and worthy, and it showed. I decided I was going to make 'fat' sexy, and that's exactly what I did.

I was having to recruit and train staff, travel all over the country and the business just kept growing. My Crohn's disease and arthritis were relapsing badly. Some days I could hardly walk. I had been given tablets to control my Crohn's disease and arthritis, but I wasn't doing as I was told. Dr Hawker told me, "No more tablets". He wanted me in hospital every month for infusions to suppress my immune system. My body was letting me know that something was seriously wrong, but I kept on ignoring my body. I started to sleep 4 to 5 hours per night and I wasn't eating well, but I was also able to eat more. I knew something was wrong. An X-ray was carried out and the radiologist confirmed my band had slipped. I wasn't taking vitamins, I didn't look after myself, and now my hair was starting to fall out. I was near the end of filming and we couldn't let anyone know my band had slipped because this would be a commercial disaster. No one cared how I was feeling, or about the pressure I was under.

It wasn't just my family who behaved this way. A famous TV obesity surgeon said to me, "Take diet pills and don't tell anyone." I felt like the abused child again. Don't talk, say nothing. All anyone cared about was me staying thin at whatever cost. There was no price you could put on a prime time series. I didn't take diet pills, I just didn't eat. I was angry all the time, and all the old feelings were coming up. Work was relentless and it was like everyone wanted a piece of me.

Another secret I was having to keep from the production company was how my nose was fractured. One of the episodes was going to show me having rhinoplasty surgery to fix my fractured nose. Lots of people in the company knew David beat me and fractured my nose, but the staff were used to being told to say nothing.

We filmed the consultation for my rhinoplasty surgery on a Saturday in Rome. People thought my life was glamorous, the reality was different. I got home from work at 11:00 pm on the Friday night and was awake at 4:00 am to catch the flight to Rome. I was filmed from the time I reached the airport and throughout the day in Rome. By the time we had dinner, it was midnight. I never slept that night. I had to be on the 6:30am flight to London because I was working in the London office all Sunday seeing patients. Two cameras followed me. Some cameramen were standing on my desk to get the right shots or angles, while I was seeing patients. This had become the reality of my life, I had no interest being on TV, it was just part of my job. It was amazing for business, so I did it.

On the last day of filming, a crane was going to be brought in to take a sweeping shot of Dolan Park. This would be used for the opening credits of the show. I asked my father to make sure we had a blue helicopter at Dolan Park for the last day of filming. The helicopter needed to take the patient up in the air, then land as though the patient had been flown in. David also wanted a shot with the helicopter in the grounds for the hospital brochure. All my father had to do for the whole year of filming was arrange that helicopter. David, my mother and father had exclusions so they could not be filmed so it fell on me as usual. The day before the filming I asked my father what time the helicopter was arriving. He said he hadn't arranged it because a helicopter wouldn't be able to land at Dolan Park. Our penalty for not completing the filming was £800,000. My father resented the attention I was receiving and importance I was gaining. He would have loved to be filmed, but had been excluded because he would have been a liability around the cameras.

If the helicopter didn't arrive, we couldn't finish filming. What followed was the biggest argument we ever had at work. The staff were used to the shouting between the family, there was always chaos, but this argument was on another level. When my father said there would be no helicopter, I just looked at him, and he knew by my face what was coming. I told all the staff that we needed to find a blue helicopter and it had to land at Dolan Park the next day. The staff were immediately on the phones. He was screaming at them not to call around for a helicopter and get on with their work but I told them to ignore him.

My father was shouting across the huge call centre, "If you pick up the phones I will fire you all!" I was shouting, "He can't do that ignore him!" I called HR to intervene. He was shouting at David's assistant Cheryl to put the phone down, I was telling Cheryl to ignore him. Cheryl was crying and the place was in chaos. My father finally stormed out after David said we had to finish filming. I found a helicopter which landed the next day. My father didn't come into the hospital for three months. He would seek his revenge – he always did.

The filming was now over. I was done. Henry had gone to live with David, I was having to hide that I had a major complication with my band, *'The Athlete'* and I were hardly speaking and I wasn't eating. I had to take a break. I was also about to play another hand for which my family would resent me. I told David I was leaving and I wasn't coming back. I flew to Marbella the next day on my own. I didn't tell anyone – I just left.

I returned home to Leamington Spa, which was now very empty. David was begging me to go back to work, but I refused. David asked our company solicitor to intervene. The solicitor called me to ask how we could resolve this situation. I said I want the same base wage as my parents and David. Despite my successes, my base wage was just a third of theirs. I had worked hard to get the company where it was and I wanted to be treated equally. On top of the base wage, I wanted a sales commission override of the group's sales. David and my mother explained to my father that the business needed me. He agreed to the sales override on the weight loss surgery and the base salary to match theirs. I had again played my hand and got what I wanted. I had to fight for everything, nothing was easy with my father.

The company was now number one in the weight loss surgery market and our contract with the suppliers of the gastric band was due for renewal. There wasn't a band company that wasn't bidding for our business. The companies and medical reps that didn't want to know our company at the beginning couldn't do enough for me now. As I brought more surgeons on board to work with us, I asked them to convert to the bands we used to simplify our processes, and they agreed. In one deal, our current supplier lost the UK gastric band market. I was gaining a very ruthless reputation.

I started to see a therapist again and she was very concerned at my rapid deterioration with not eating. We decided I would need to go back into psychiatric inpatient unit because of my eating issues. When I saw the same psychiatrist that I had seen three years earlier, he said, "I think I've misdiagnosed you, you may have an eating disorder." The doctor was the head of the eating disorders unit. He chose to put me back into the general mental health area, as I "wasn't a 15 BMI and might upset some of the thinner patients."

My eating disorder was raging out of control, and they stupidly allowed me to have a steamer in my room to cook my own food. I only ate steamed chicken and vegetables. I worked out in the gym two hours daily. I was allowed to keep three mobile phones so I could continue working. I was allowed out to meetings and I was going on shopping sprees and spending thousands of pounds. If all of this wasn't bad enough, the psychiatrist and the hospital authorised me to have surgery to change my slipped band. My BMI was 18 and the band was replaced by a surgeon I with whom I was having a casual relationship. Everyone treating me knew the state of my mental health. They all knew that I was an inpatient being treated for an eating disorder.

The most vulnerable of patients are children, the elderly and psychiatric patients. I had again been used by everyone for the sole purpose of making money. I thought everyone loved me, although I didn't know what love was. I thought if I did what they wanted, they would all love me. That's how I received love as a child, that's how I got love in my family. I just kept doing what I'd been shown. The day after the new band was put in, I was back in the gym with Mr California Dreamboy trainer and I was losing more weight.

Things turned nasty with *'The Athlete'*. He waited for his time and he took his shot. The person that I had originally met, and who didn't care about money, did now. He was to cause chaos with the airing of the TV programme. The production company hadn't got a release signed by him to appear on the show. He advised them of this on the day the first episode was due to air on ITV. He wanted money from me and the production company. It cost the production company tens of thousands of pounds, but they removed him from the show. He tried more blackmailing, but David intervened and then he was gone forever.

After six weeks in hospital, I was discharged. I came out of the hospital weighing less than when I was admitted for an eating disorder. My mother cried at how thin I had become. I was fitter and had my usual tan, although I had less money in the bank from all the shopping. *Pandora's Box* had been opened and the memories, the flashbacks, and the feelings were all coming to the surface. I had no way to process what was coming up.

'The Athlete' was gone. Henry was living with his father during the week and filming at Dolan Park had finished so I decided my life was back in London. I was doing something that I would later learn is known as *a geographical.* I kept moving around, back and forth, thinking my life would be different in a different place, with different people, away from the family or Dolan Park. The problem, as I would come to understand, was within me. My thoughts and feelings were the same and went with me wherever I was. I had no idea that until I changed my thinking, nothing would change. I kept the house on the river and used it when I worked at Dolan Park or for weekends with Henry and my friends, but my life was in London now.

Out of the blue, I got a call from Henry to say he wanted to come home. I was absolutely thrilled. I had no idea how I was going to manage as I travelled all over the country and my main base was London. I called Henry's old school and they made a place available for him without the usual entrance exam. I called Henry back and asked when he wanted to come. He replied, "Tomorrow!" He joined me the next day. When he had gone to live with David, he was a healthy weight and fit. He returned obese and unfit. Henry had seen his mother use food to cope with her emotions and he had been through so much with all the change: the separation from David, David's new family, the break up from *'The Athlete'*, his unhappiness at school and the dyslexia. My son was using food, just as I had. I was despairing, I didn't know what to do, I was 'Miss Obesity' and the face of weight loss surgery, and my son was severely obese.

January arrived and we were all very excited about the series. I had to start giving interviews for the press. I hated watching myself on TV and I hated the way I looked and sounded. I had told no one I knew socially about the show, I somehow thought I could get away with being on a prime-time series and no one would know. I had absolutely no idea what I was about to let myself in for. In the opening credits, I was introduced as Donna Ross, *'The Boss'*. I span round in my big chair in front of a huge desk, looking like something out of Dynasty. Within minutes of the show airing, my phone started ringing. All I can remember thinking was, "Oh my God, they all know I was fat!" Luckily after all that I had put my body through, if I wore a bikini you would never have known I'd had weight issues. My life was as a thin person now, I didn't want to be known as fat. I worked in the weight loss surgery industry, but I was now the finished product, and rapidly becoming one of those 'Plastic Fantastics' that I had despised.

I couldn't watch the program and I couldn't answer my phone, I just didn't know what to do. The next day at Dolan Park it was like I was a different person and people treated me differently. I would go to clinics all over the country and patients would come up to me and touch me and say, "Seeing you on TV changed my life." It was one giant lie. I was one giant lie. My whole life was a lie. I had lived this false image from Shirley Temple to Donna Ross, The Boss. I lived in constant fear of being found out and it crippled me. I hated lying to these people who believed in me and had put their trust in me.

I thought the thinner I was, the more people would love me. I kept my gastric band so tight that I couldn't swallow my own saliva. I was spending thousands of pounds on clothes. I was working all hours and I started to go to night clubs and drink champagne until the early hours. My relationship with my boyfriend was chaos. I would find out he had cheated, so I would do the same. Men viewed me as this powerful businesswoman who had this fantasy around me, and I would use that to manipulate them. My stock value had gone up. My currency was at an all-time high and I used the way I looked and my sexuality to get exactly what I wanted. Donna Ross was becoming a monster – an out-of-control monster that was full of blind rage. I was yet again covering up others lies, and I hated myself to my very core for doing it. I realised, just like when I was a child, I had something people wanted and needed, and I could get away with anything if I kept on performing and bringing in the money for the company and the industry.

The series also allowed me access to very prominent weight loss surgeons, and we appointed a group medical director for the first time who was a weight loss surgeon. I was then introduced to other clinical people who had either heard of me being this ruthless businesswoman or seen the image I had on TV or in the press. Slowly, I was managing to place the clinical people I liked and trusted in key positions.

With the media exposure of the programme and all the related press, the business exploded. The programme and the press stories were making obese people into swans. Fat was getting sexy, and we needed a new image – a sexy one. We branded everything red. It is a colour that is not used in healthcare because it reminds people of blood. we had syringe shaped pens with red ink that looked like blood, red was across the logo and to finish it off we stuck two 'pornography looking' cherries on top. We were no longer the National Centres. We were now The Hospital Group. At Dolan Park, red was everywhere. Cherries greeted you at the door and the staff all wore red suits. The Hospital Group was a sexy brand on steroids.

There could be thirty women in the open plan call centre, comparing body parts, and talking about what surgery they recently had. For many years, the surgeons had clauses in their contracts to ban any intimate relations with staff, but it never stopped them. Many of the cosmetic surgeons were having sex with different girls in different offices – each one would think they were his girlfriend. At the Christmas party, they would all get together to find out that the surgeon had been seeing lots of the girls and there were fights. Some surgeons would find themselves in the tabloid newspapers for various inappropriate relationships.

The Hospital Group was a highly sexualised environment. We had over twenty locations and people were recruited because they looked a certain way. The aim of many women was to get into bed with my father, a surgeon or other senior members of staff. David had a partner who was the mother of his two children, but he was constantly having affairs with girls, one of whom became pregnant. Diane thought she was still my father's girlfriend, along with many of the other women working at the company. One of the nurses asked my father if she could get her teeth whitened in the new dentistry department. He replied, "Get on your knees and I will whiten them for you!" Another of David's aunts came to work with me. My father sexually harassed her, and she made a formal complaint. He screamed at me to sort it out. I begged her to remove the complaint, but she was a strong woman and she refused. A settlement was reached with the solicitors. This was David's own family, so you can imagine how bad the harassment was with others.

The Hospital Group sold image and sex. It gave people what they wanted. The age of celebrity and social media was starting, and we were way ahead of the curve. The call centre at Dolan Park was like a scene from *The Wolf of Wall Street*, but the people in the call centre were attractive women. My father was Wolfie, along with David and his Merry Men, Steve and Mark. One surgeon said if you applied for a job at The Hospital Group, you would get one point for having a degree and ten if you had been a lap dancer. My father had created his own idea of heaven with all the women running around after him. No person ever received anything from my father that didn't benefit him and sadly, these women were often left bitterly disappointed.

Weight loss surgery continued to explode in the media and I became more known. We had a lot of celebrities who wanted surgery with us. I would look after the 'important' and celebrity patients. A celebrity had been outed for having a gastric band and not telling the producers of a weight loss TV show. The press accused the celebrity of cheating. The celebrity had gone to Belgium to have the band fitted and they were spotted by someone. Our PR company contacted the celebrity's management to offer for one of our surgeons to look at the band. An X-ray was performed and it was discovered that the band had been placed in the wrong position. This made it incredibly difficult to swallow, thereby leaving the person on a liquid diet or liquidising food. The surgeon advised them that the band would need to be replaced and repositioned. They had the surgery and signed a deal to become the face of the Hospital Group weight loss brand.

As with all celebrity weight loss endorsements, there is a clause for the celebrity to achieve and maintain a certain weight range. You often see celebrities with drastic weight losses, then huge weight gains as they cannot maintain their weight. For someone to endorse a product, they would have to have a weight issue, often be linked with a body image issue or an underlying emotional issue. To put the pressure of timelines to lose weight on someone with weight issues is often a recipe for disaster. This was to happen in the endorsement of The Hospital Group with this celebrity.

An article in the national press mentioned that I, Donna Ross, who had lost a huge amount of weight, had contacted this celebrity and I was her saviour. But that was not true. I was the face of 'Weight Loss Surgery' at The Hospital Group and I had to be seen to be the saviour. I had to work with the celebrity to help them lose the weight to meet PR deadlines and contractual obligations. It was a nightmare. I threw everything we had to get the weight loss needed, at the speed required, to meet the deadlines. The weight loss was coming but not fast enough. The pressure from our management was immense and enough to drive anyone with food issues to eat. Add to this the amount of trauma this person had been through in their life, I'm surprised they lost any weight at all.

My father and David wanted to know what the problem was, I'd always delivered for publicity when I needed to look a certain way. The celebrity was getting paid a phenomenal amount of money, so why weren't they delivering? We were both sandwiched between our management teams, and it was to prove a very difficult year.

I was the toast of the industry as the effect of the TV series benefited everyone working in weight loss surgery. The celebrities and patients were crediting me with their successes, I seemed untouchable. It was as if I had the Midas touch and if I touched someone's business, they would make money. The band contract was again up for renewal and, as we had major problems from erosions with the band we had changed to the year before, we were moving suppliers. Every band manufacturer around the world came to offer us a deal. I was offered trips anywhere I wanted, and I could take who I wanted with me. Dinners out, nights out, anything I wanted in order to give them the contract.

We finally made the decision to go back to the original gastric band we had used. No other company could beat their offer. That company went number one in the UK market again overnight – such was the power of The Hospital Group.

I was about to encounter another problem with my band – one that almost killed me. I had decided to stay with the staff at a hotel near Dolan Park. I got ready in the morning and then I collapsed. The medical director came out to see me and wanted me admitted to hospital to investigate. We were in Birmingham, but he was going to be operating in London. I had to travel from Birmingham to London and then I was admitted into The London Clinic. I had a CT scan to see if there was any erosion and I was told there wasn't. I was kept in for five days due to the pain. My band was fully aspirated, and I was sent home with anti-inflammatory medication and painkillers.

After six weeks of struggling to work and being in constant pain, I called the surgeon and said I wanted the band out. This time, I had to go to a hospital in Chichester. I didn't want to discuss any options about persevering with the band, I wanted it out. This was my fourth weight loss surgery operation. I woke up in the critical care unit. The band had eroded into my stomach and created a hole. The band had been removed but I was not allowed to eat. I could have only fluids. Not only had the surgeon missed the hole in my stomach when he treated me in the London hospital, he now left the port he had replaced during my third operation inside my abdomen. His aim was to let my stomach heal and put another band back in and re-join it to the port. Most erosions are caused by infection so surgeons generally accept that when an erosion occurs, the whole device must be removed. The surgeon had left an infected device in my body. When I asked him why, he said, "Because it was the most beautiful port I have ever put in." A few weeks later (at yet another hospital) the surgeon performed my fifth weight loss surgery procedure. The left port was infected. I could have developed sepsis and died. The surgeon knew there was a good chance he could lose his registration if I complained, so he did what my family did, and set about trying to discredit me.

No one knew I had these complications other than key staff at Dolan Park. What was I to do? I was the face of weight loss surgery, with my gastric band removed, all these major complications and I was gaining weight fast. A nurse who had been taking care of me suggested I might be able to have a sleeve gastrectomy. There was no way I was going back to my previous surgeon, so she suggested I go and see Professor Mike McMahon in Leeds. He was the surgeon you went to if you had a complication. I was working with him at The Hospital Group and had spoken at the Leeds General Infirmary for him at a conference about weight loss surgery. His main concern was me. He wanted me well and to have a procedure that would curb my weight gain. I had my sixth weight loss surgery procedure, a sleeve gastrectomy. My stomach was cut to be a thin tube that looked like a banana. My weight dropped again, but not as low as before.

My work life was like Groundhog Day. I wasn't creating anything anymore. I just pushed the team hard to hit the financial numbers. I always had to go over the projected numbers and increase sales targets. If the team complained, I'd say, "You know where the door is." I'd stopped caring and I'd lost my sparkle. Henry's weight was increasing and I didn't know what to do. The TV production company came back into Dolan Park to take some footage because the real show was the family and what really went on behind the scenes. My family and The Hospital Group would have made the Kardashian's look like a serious documentary. The press and TV also wanted to interview Henry and me about our struggles with obesity. I was so panicked the press would do a story. I felt like I was living a constant lie. I was thirty-four years old, and I don't think there was a day in my life that I didn't feel like I was going to 'get found out.'

My father and David decided they wanted me, the celebrity and a team of experts to do a road show across the UK. We had a theatre company come in and build a stage that we could move from venue to venue around the country. The show was produced like a theatre show. I was one of the expert panel, with a surgeon and the celebrity. The audience could ask us questions about weight, surgery, or our own personal issues. On the last night of the road show we had been informed that there was a journalist in the audience who was going to ask if I had my gastric band removed. The question came right at the end. The person chairing the show did their best to move the questions along, but the journalist in the audience was relentless. I'd had enough. The next day I flew out of the country. The PR were dealing with the fallout. I was in the tabloid press three times in five days. Our lawyers couldn't stop the stories. I had waived my right to privacy by doing publicity and advertising. My father and David did everything they could to stop the stories. They were stopped that week after our advertising agents said they would pull two million pounds worth of advertising from the newspapers concerned. It was just another cover up of the truth. Had the journalists kept going, they may have started to discover what was really going on.

I came back from my few days away to discover my father and David had fired the celebrity for breach of contract. The road shows hadn't gone as expected, the celebrity was nowhere near the size of the cardboard cut outs which we had in every clinic throughout the country. The endorsement was becoming a joke. The decision to use the breach of contract clause was nothing to do with me, nor did I have any say in it. At the same time a professor (who I worked with in London) asked to speak to me privately. He advised me that our medical director – the one that had missed my erosion and left an infected port in my body – was saying defamatory things about me. I invited the medical director for a drink and I asked him if he said these things. He never denied it and he apologised. We agreed it was time for him to step down from his position. Sadly, the things he would say about me didn't stop there.

My weight loss surgery complications weren't over, but I started to be able to eat more. I went back to see Prof McMahon in Leeds. The X-ray showed my sleeve gastrectomy had become sigmoid, meaning it curved like a snake. I would have to undergo my seventh weight loss surgery procedure to revise my sleeve gastrectomy. I was taken into the Leeds Nuffield Hospital. No name was on my door, no name on the theatre list and only certain people knew I was there. Prof McMahon looked after me so well, he did his best to help with my weight. He saw what I was going through with my family. It would be three more weight loss surgery procedures until I would need them no more. He took me all the way to the end.

I was completely fed up with the weight loss surgery industry. There was an arrogance of thinking that surgery, good dieticians and a multi-disciplinary team solved obesity. No one wanted to listen to me when I said this is a psychological issue. I didn't truly understand what it was, or how to find the solution at the time. I had access to a huge amount of data and exposure to thousands of patients. I was a patient. I was one of them, I'd had seven weight loss surgery procedures. I'd had all the complications, I struggled with food, not just daily or hourly, sometimes minute to minute. I was a food addict, a compulsive eater, a binge eater, and I'd starve myself. I have healed myself of my obesity and, one day at a time, I live free from the obsessional thinking around food that dominated my life for thirty years.

Weight loss surgery was to become more litigious than plastic surgery, and patients started to sue. Surgeons couldn't get indemnity insurance, so they couldn't operate. The industry didn't want to listen to me because they thought knew better. The age of celebrity endorsements for weight loss surgery had started. Many of the celebrities would need revision surgery or more operations. Often, they would become addicted to cosmetic surgery. When the celebrities couldn't use food, they would cross addict to other dysfunctional behaviours. Many would relapse on substances, drugs and alcohol, because if you do not treat the root cause, people will find another dysfunctional coping strategy to push those feelings down.

When qualifying patients for obesity surgery, the patients BMI and co-related illnesses are considered. Consider this: You've got it wrong – obesity is a co-related illness! It's a co-related illness to stress and trauma. It is now being suggested that obesity is a disease of the mind. I was using obesity surgery to deal with emotional issues. I was using cosmetic surgery to deal with emotional issues. I was using food to deal with emotional issues. I would use anything I could get my hands on to deal with my emotional issues.

Obesity doesn't start at a 30 BMI- it starts with your thinking. In the main, it's a result of your environment and life experiences. Food often contains chemically addictive products and there's a process when you eat. With food there can be a chemical and a process addiction. You must eat to survive and moderate the amounts of food you consume to stay healthy. We are asking people to moderate a chemical and process addiction daily, and not giving them the help, tools, or knowledge to do this. Is it any wonder why obesity is at epidemic proportions? We are looking at it the wrong way. The thinking related to obesity has to change to help people to empower themselves.

I felt my time in weight loss surgery was over and I had succeeded in what I set out to achieve. I took over the weight loss surgery division (at a loss) making £175,000 per month. When I left my role as the head of weight loss surgery division three years later, it turned over £1.6 million per month. The company never hit those numbers again, nor did any other UK company. I was the highest paid employee in the history of The Hospital Group. The company value doubled in three years. The McNerlin family were on the *Sunday Times Rich List.* We were receiving offers to sell and I was ready to cash in my £150,000 investment for £7.5 million. I was thirty-five. I had lived a life that looked like a dream although it was an absolute nightmare. I wanted to live the dream, I wanted to *really* live life the way my life looked.

WHAT THE READER CAN TAKE FROM THIS CHAPTER?

Geographical changes from place to place, home to home, or country to country may not resolve your emotional issues.

When you think you have one addiction under control several more can come up in their place.

The hurtful and harmful behaviours your parents used; you may find your unconsciously using with your children.

Your thinking will be the biggest change you can ever make in your life.

Your dysfunctional coping strategies and addictions can be passed on to your children without you realising this is happening.

You can heal yourself of your obesity, there is a solution.

CHAPTER SEVEN

CRASHING INTO ADDICTION

ADDICTION

THE FACT OR CONDITION OF BEING ADDICTED TO A PARTICULAR SUBSTANCE OR ACTIVITY

We had all agreed to sell the group and brought in accountants to prepare for the sale. I wasn't sure what I was going to do next, but I'd really had enough of everything in the UK. Our tax advisors suggested living in a tax efficient country. One suggestion being the Cayman Islands. The year before, my father had been on some crazy crusade to Cayman tracing people from (the late) Sandra's life. I had visited him there and, after all the recent drama, I could think of nothing better than living on a desert island. I suggested that we move to the Cayman Islands. He agreed and our tax advisors prepared for us to move our residency.

I was making yet another life changing decision and yet another geographical move. I mistakenly thought that living on a desert island in tax free heaven would solve all my problems. How wrong was I. It was to be the decision that would trigger all that I had been suppressing for thirty five years. I would come to use anything I could to try and put the lid back on the volcano of feelings that would start to explode. Along with that, would come any dysfunctional coping strategy I could find.

The first night we stayed in a hotel. The next morning, I woke up crying like a baby, begging (my then) boyfriend, not to leave me there. Overnight, I had turned into a petrified child curled up like a ball.

We viewed properties and I found a great apartment on the beach. My father was pushing me to get a larger apartment and live with him. We viewed apartments for rent at $35,000 per month. In the end I gave in, as it was easier to agree with him than not. I was living with my father and paying half the rent for a very expensive apartment that I hated. He had the big suite at the front that overlooked the beach, I had one of the small rooms at the back of the apartment that overlooked the road.

Once we signed for the apartment, my father flew to Los Angeles for major facial surgery to change how he looked. I flew to Italy for an obesity conference and Henry came along with me. We had the best time in Capri and it was a wonderful conference to mark what I thought would be the end of my career in the weight loss surgery industry.

My father's surgery did not go as expected and he looked like *the elephant man*. He had a nurse flown out to take care of him and Diane (the mistress) flew over as well. I agreed to fly via London to Los Angeles and be with him instead of returning to Cayman. When I arrived in Los Angeles, my father looked horrific - he was really ill. I couldn't cope with him on my own, so I asked my friend Sylwia to come to LA and then fly onto Cayman.

As my father recovered, Sylwia and I were able to have some fun, swimming, diving, going to restaurants, bars and clubs, it was great. I was looking good and in great shape but, for no reason, I would feel extremely faint, my heart would race and I would pour sweat for 30 minutes then it would stop.

Once Sylwia left it was terrible. My father was a nightmare, he couldn't go out in the sun because he was scarred from head to toe. My father would call the UK staff constantly- up to 100 times a day. I would stay out of the apartment as much as I could. I practised yoga with my teacher for 90 minutes each day. I was eating well and was in good health but I hated going home.

I started having the old recurring nightmares of people being in my room and they were getting worse. I also started having new nightmares of screaming at someone to get away from me and get out of my room. These nightmares were in the present. In these new nightmares I was an adult, not a child. I was really struggling, so I asked my friends to come over to visit. I would go out with my friends and drink cocktails because that was the only way I was able to go home and get some sleep.

Within 6 months of our move, the 2008 banking collapse happened causing devastation around the world. We had six buyers bidding for the company. Overnight we were told that the company was considered luxury consumer and was devalued by millions. The decision was made not to sell the group and make acquisitions instead.

I started to become extremely unwell again. I had swelling and pain in my legs and, at times I couldn't walk. For no apparent reason, I was suffering disease relapses.

Due to my deteriorating health, I decided to return to England for Christmas. During that time, I was at lunch with my friend who was a paramedic. I started with one of my episodes of sweating and feeling unwell. She took my pulse and it was over 225bpm - my resting heart rate was normally 65-70bpm. She called an ambulance who blue lighted me into hospital. The cardiac team in the emergency unit believed I had a virus that was affecting my heart. The doctors ran endless tests, however, no test identified any virus or other health issues. I continued to have severe tachycardia for the next twelve years and, at points, found myself in emergency room resuscitation units.

What I would come to learn is that I was having a trauma response - these episodes had been caused by flashbacks.

After Christmas & New Year, I went back to Cayman. I wanted to return to the UK and work in the company now we were making new acquisitions. My father sought his revenge and blocked me from working in the company. Due to my shareholding, if I left to work for another company, I would be competing against myself – which would negatively affect my share value.

The last few weeks with my father in Cayman, were horrific. It was just like being a child at home again. He was always chasing some woman or disappearing with women. He was also using lots of drugs to cope with the pain from his operation. Over those few weeks, I became so ill that I was told I was not fit to fly, I was trapped. The doctors in Cayman wanted to wait for drugs to come in from Miami to give me infusions like I'd had for many years back in the UK. I said I wanted to go home, I cried and begged the doctors to let me leave. Finally, an agreement was made that if I came into hospital for two days and I was fully rehydrated, the medical team would clear me to fly. That agreement was made on the understanding that if I was ill on the flight to Miami, I would stop and seek medical treatment in America. Until the last moment, my father let me down. He was due to look after Henry whilst I was in hospital but he disappeared. I had to get a friend to look after Henry, collect me from the hospital, gather up my belongings from the apartment and take me to the airport, to start the journey home.

When we arrived in England, I went straight to see Dr Hawker and I collapsed in his office. He admitted me to Warwick Hospital where I was told I wasn't quite ill enough to remove my colon by emergency surgery but too ill for routine surgery. The surgeon came and explained that I would need to have a colostomy bag. I had the company solicitors come to the hospital to update my will. Yet again, everyone was coming to visit me, because I was in a critical condition. I had been severely ill at many times in my life but this time I wanted to die. I was 36 years old and I meant to be living the dream but I was back living a nightmare. Yet again I would make a remarkable recovery, a week later I walked out of Warwick Hospital as though nothing had happened. I was weak and wobbly on my legs, but other than that, if I didn't have all the medical evidence, you would think I had made it all up.

I couldn't keep living like this, and I had to find some answers. I went to see a therapist in London who started to work on my family issues with me. The therapist could obviously see what was wrong with me but couldn't tell me. No good therapist wants to be accused of suggesting memory to their patient. I was recommended another psychiatrist, and yet again I would be wrongly diagnosed and given medication that almost cost me my life.

We restructured the company and my mother sold out completely. I didn't want to sell out because if they did well, I wouldn't benefit. I needed an income so I said I would sell 5% of my shares via loan notes and keep a 10% shareholding. This would give me a good income for six years and we planned to sell the company by then. What this deal meant was I didn't have to work, and I now owned 20% of The Hospital Group. My father's shareholding stayed the same, but David's increased and we split everything 50:50. David and I owned 40% of The Hospital Group and I had negotiated my best deal ever.

When I left Cayman I stopped contact with my father, however, I would not only speak with him again, I would return to Cayman many times. Many years later, I asked Dr Pereira why I kept going back. Dr Pereira explained about trauma bonds or Stockholm Syndrome. He explained it this way: I was like the children who are kept hostage and many years later they manage to escape but they don't get past the garden gate. Just as I had not got past the end of the road as a child when I ran away, as toxic, abusive, and hateful as my family could be, I kept going back. They were all I had. They were all I knew and, despite everything, I loved them dearly.

So yet again I had made a fantastic deal for myself. I decided that I would keep the house in Leamington and rent a house in the centre of London. My income and having not to work, meant I would have to find a whole new realm of strategies to help me cope.

I moved into the new London house in January 2010 and my birthday was a few weeks later. Sylwia, one of my closest friends, was diagnosed with breast cancer on my birthday. At the same time another close friend, Charlotte, had been suspended from her job. Charlotte was suffering from anxiety and depression and, like me, had lots of time on her hands. I was excited to be back in London, but the thoughts were still in my head, and the recurring nightmares continued.

My crash into (what someone who knows nothing about addiction would see as) a 'proper addiction' was quick and looked fabulous. Charlotte and I used to hang out together and go to the pub or have lunch somewhere. We would drink wine and have giggly girls type lunches and evenings. On one of these evenings, Charlotte met a French stockbroker and they started dating. He was a member of a famous private members club. By day the club is used for meetings and people worked from there. At night it was a completely different animal. We started meeting up at the club for a drink, on Thursdays, Fridays and Saturdays, there was a DJ and people were a little wild.

Every Sunday, I would have a dinner at my London home and invite friends over. On one of these Sundays, Charlotte asked if her boyfriend could bring a friend. When I opened the door my mouth dropped. All I could think was, 'forget bringing a bottle of wine, that's what you bring to dinner!' *The banker* had a sexy French accent and was stunning. It was love at first sight. His smile just lit up a room and he was so soft. I had never in my life experienced this before. I was thirty-seven years old, and I had finally experienced this love at first sight thing people talked about.

The banker contacted me and asked me to go for dinner with him. We started seeing each other and he was the most amazing man I'd ever met. His friends were a fun bunch of people and it took my mind off all the other things that were still bubbling under the surface. I never felt I was good enough or beautiful enough, so I started to change myself with cosmetic surgery. There was absolutely nothing wrong with the way I looked – it was the way I felt about myself. Charlotte had breast implants at the same time as a fortieth birthday gift to herself – it was to be an almost deadly gift to herself.

I was on a high, having fun, looking good, and seeing *the banker*. I had a new group of friends and was living this fabulous life in London. I was now truly living the way my life looked. *The banker* had been a playboy and was honest with me about that. I was fine with it because that was his past. By a complete fluke, I found out that someone in our London clinic had dated him. I stupidly decided I couldn't date him anymore because he had been involved with one of our staff. He had already even told me about an episode with a nurse, I just didn't know it was one of mine. *The banker* said, "Well if that's the way you feel OK, what can I do about it?" We remained close, but weren't dating. *The banker* went away travelling for three months because he was on garden leave before starting his new job. In those three months, all the pain hit me like a train. To cope, I fell into pure chemical addiction. I started living a champagne, cocaine, fabulous-looking party life. I was gaining weight rapidly, so I went back to see Prof McMahon and I asked him to help me. He said he wanted a psychological analysis for further weight loss surgery. The psychologist cleared me, and I had my eighth weight loss surgery procedure, a gastric bypass.

I decided to become a member at the private members club, and it was my new place to hang out – I practically lived there. I met a Harley St GP who introduced me to a whole crowd of fabulous looking people. They were doctors, surgeons, lawyers, financiers, property investors and celebrities. There was a core group, and then others that would come in and out. It was meeting for lunch, meeting for dinner, and parties afterwards. It all seemed so fabulous. I finally thought I had the family and friends I always wanted. I cannot tolerate alcohol well although, being me, it didn't stop me keeping up with everyone that could. I didn't understand how these people could stay so sober, drink so much and stay awake. The answer was cocaine. One of the girls said to try some and, sure enough, it sobered me right up. I could go back to play some more, and I felt great.

This was the start of two years of almost constant partying. What triggered this to happen is that my past caught up with me and all the issues from my childhood and my life just exploded. I ate, I drank, I spent, I used cocaine, I used sex. I used anything I could not to feel the pain I was in. I had the money and contacts to do as I wanted. I was out of control, and nothing could stop me. At that time, it all seemed like fun because the coping strategies were doing their job – or so I thought. The reality was I could not ever be alone. I couldn't sleep and would drive my car around London at 4:00 am because there was nothing else to do. The fabulous socialites in the party crowd were always available. I became a well-known face at the club and became really involved with the crowd there to the despair of my friends and those that cared about me.

Over time I had thawed towards my father, and I went to visit him in the Cayman Islands. On my birthday in January 2011, I slipped on a wet dance floor and fell backwards. It wasn't a bad fall, but when I put my hands down to get up, the pain was horrific. I knew I'd fractured both of my wrists. I told my father I needed to go to hospital now. When I arrived, I said, "I'm going into shock," and I was gone. I had X-rays and, sure enough, both wrists had fractured. There was no reason for the wrists to fracture, it was a slight fall, nothing major. The last fracture I had was when I went skiing with my brother while going through the breakup with David. That was ten years before, when again I fractured three ribs when my ski pole hit me slightly. Again, those fractures were not in line with the accident. I had stopped any issues with my bones coming out of their sockets as a child, but now fractures started happening, and for no real reason. I flew home the next day with two arms in plaster. I called one of the doctors I knew from the party scene, and he arranged for me to see a specialist wrist surgeon as soon as I landed. I saw the surgeon and he operated on one wrist and left the other to heal naturally.

Charlotte suggested I have a party for my birthday to cheer me up at my house. I had the food catered and staff to serve the drinks. My house was packed with the most fabulous people, people that were the top in their given fields. I went upstairs to get something and there was a queue from my ensuite bathroom all the way through my bedroom to the top of the stairs. That was the cocaine queue. I just thought, 'what is going on with my life and what is wrong with me?' But the insanity continued. Over that next year I was involved with men that were on the front cover of *Hello Magazine*, polo players, relations of senior royals, blue blood aristocracy, and some of the biggest players in the financial world. I became friends with Middle Eastern royals who wanted to give me diamonds and watches and fly me all over the world. It just wasn't me. I didn't want to be someone else that took from these rich people. I was just friends with them, and they liked me because they said I was kind.

I wanted to get out of London and so I moved back to Warwickshire, but I kept coming back to the crowd in London. They gave me a sense of belonging and an identity outside of my family. I had gone from belonging to one dysfunctional family to another. I knew I was in trouble – a lot of trouble. Things were really getting out of control. I was to be offered an escape route, that involved yet another geographical move.

After my father's facial surgery, he made a deal with the surgeon who operated on him. This was a joint venture and *The Hospital Group America* was born. My father also became involved with hair transplant surgeons and another venture was developed with a famous Beverly Hills hair transplant surgeon. A few years earlier, I had introduced my father to *The American* who was an American lawyer and businessman. I'd met *The American* when I was very ill in Miami. *The American* and I had always talked about a behavioural health unit for weight loss surgery patients. My father, David and *The American* wanted to start *The Hospital Group Weight Loss Surgery America.* I was the only person that could take on a project like that. My first centre was to be in Las Vegas, as that's where they wanted to do a joint venture with a WLS surgeon. Another doctor, who was the business partner of *The American* on this project, came over to look at our set-up in the UK. David asked me to take the doctor out in London and entertain him. The doctor was a lovely guy. He was a healthy yoga guy for part of the week and a big party boy the other part. However, he was using cocaine in London and had brought Valium and other prescription drugs with him. I was concerned. I recommended to David and my father that we did not proceed with the deal. Unfortunately, that meant I had to return to the UK.

I came home and found another house – this was to be where the final crash came. The house was two minutes' walk from the private members club, so my house became party central. I could no longer hold off the feelings that had plagued me for years. I was a mess. In social groups where people are using cocaine, however rich and fabulous it may look, it's often quite dark. The people are in their late thirties, forties, and fifties still using cocaine three times a week and drinking excessively – they aren't happy people. As I would come to learn, happy people don't need to do that.

While other people may have been happy living this life that looked fabulous, travelling around the world, I hated it. My social media looked amazing and my life looked like a dream. Yet again, I lived a life that looked like a dream but was a nightmare. In February 2012, I called up David and said, "I need help, this has all got completely out of control. I'm lost, and I don't know what to do anymore." A doctor recommended a psychiatrist named Dr Stephen Pereira. I had never heard of Dr Pereira and I didn't know that he was a world-renowned psychiatrist. I had no idea his clients were some of the biggest names in the financial world, fashion and the arts. I asked my mother and Sylwia to come with me for the consultation.

That day was to change not only my life, but my son's life and many people's lives that I would go on to help.

Dr Pereira is of Indian origin with a slight accent and a bald head. He looks like a guru type character. He told me straight he didn't need me as a client, so I either did as he said or he wouldn't look after me – I agreed. He asked me to go into a clinic for two weeks which I did. When I asked Dr Pereira when he knew I'd suffered abuse and had suppressed memory, he said the second or third time I'd met him. Dr Pereira couldn't say at that time, but he felt that if he got me to a place where I felt safe, the memory I had no idea I was suppressing, would come – just as it had started to many years ago in the first clinic I put myself in. I didn't like the clinic. I didn't like the groups and I didn't feel safe, but for some reason I felt safe with Dr Pereira. I would spend the next ten years in his office, telling him all about my life with him guiding me through the best he could without suggesting anything to me. It took me several years to find out I had fragmented memory. Much of my memory regarding the abusive life I had suffered had been suppressed. Dr Pereira could not say a word because if he did, he could be accused of suggesting things to me. So, he sat there for years watching me turn myself inside out and nearly destroy myself. He gently guided me to a path of self-discovery and healing.

Before I got to a place of healing, I would suffer more devastating traumatic events. In June of 2012 while walking to Notting Hill, I was trapped, chased and robbed at knife point. Five police cars were out looking for the robber, but they never found him or my watch. I was petrified. I called David, but his response to my robbery and loss of my watch was, "ahh well, easy come easy go." No compassion or concern for me. It would be a few years before I discovered why he held onto such resentment.

Luckily Henry had been in boarding school all these years, but he was still affected by the mother he loved and adored not being present for him. Henry had moved from his specialist dyslexia school at thirteen and gone to a new school. At one parents' evening, David was told that Henry would never be more than a D or E student. I said they can't be right; he's getting an A to E grade spread. If it was just dyslexia, he wouldn't get A grades in the subject he has. David believed the teachers, but I said they were wrong. In the summer of 2012, I took Henry away on a long holiday. We were away for five weeks, during which time Henry was looking at different colleges for his A levels. I said to him that he wasn't getting the grades to go to them. I will never forget his words, "Mother if I could concentrate, I would get those grades." The light went on – Henry had attention deficit disorder. He couldn't concentrate for very long, especially in subjects he didn't like. I did online tests with Henry and he scored high for having ADHD.

Henry is laid back, there's nothing hyperactive about him. He just couldn't focus. When I returned to England, I asked Dr Pereira for help and he referred us to a child psychologist. The assessments were made, and Henry was diagnosed with ADD. I was furious with his school. He was in their care. They had a specialist learning difficulties teacher and they had completely missed this. I took Henry home and found a place at a day school in London. I oversaw what the school were doing with Henry and he got the medication to make sure he could concentrate. I went against everyone to do this. David said the problem wasn't Henry, it was me. I argued with my family and David's family. In one year, Henry gained six GCSE's at A to C grades. This was the start of Henry excelling in education. What Henry was to go onto achieve, defied everyone's belief. I fought for my son because I believed in him, and I told him anything is possible because it really is.

In early October 2012 I started to become ill with sickness and headaches, then I fainted in a shop. I went to an urgent care centre for blood work and to be checked over. Henry wanted to come with me. The doctors checked me over and could see that there was something seriously wrong. They told me there was a neurological issue and my symptoms were acute. I asked the doctor whether I would still be alive in the morning, and he said he didn't know. Henry was outside and he heard the doctor. He was hysterical and didn't want to leave me. My poor son was again suffering more trauma of thinking his mother would die – he had to deal with this is whole life. I was taken by ambulance to another hospital where more tests were carried out. The next day the phones started ringing all at the same time. My mobile and the room phone. The nurses came running in. I was toxic. I was lucky to be alive, the medication the previous psychiatrist had given me was removed, but Dr Pereira couldn't alter my diagnosis because if he did, he would have to explain to me why.

After the near-death episode I just wanted to forget. How did I forget? Drugs and alcohol and every other coping strategy I had ever used. It was now full-blown self-destruction, but it was going to get worse.

What came along with the party lifestyle, was predatory men. A week before my fortieth birthday I was drugged and sexually assaulted in my home. Henry was home, along with a friend that was staying with me. I was woken up in bed by my son and the friend at 1:00 pm. I never slept through the night and into the afternoon. I woke partially dressed and I would never sleep in my clothes. I had this feeling I knew someone had assaulted me. By 4:00 pm I was hysterical. Sylwia came over and she said I needed to call the police. I knew the only man that was in my house the night before was a man named Oliver. I had memory of someone hovering over me to see if I was awake, I saw no face. At 7:00 pm, I called the police. They came to the house and I was taken to a special unit to be examined head to toe. All my orifices were swabbed and I had to have internal exams and pictures taken of all my body. It was horrific, I felt like the criminal.

I told the police that I couldn't tell them who had assaulted me, but Oliver was the only man in the house. I could remember being in my lounge with Oliver and his girlfriend, but I had no idea how I got from the lounge to my bedroom.

The police tracked down Oliver and he was arrested. His DNA was found in my bed, and it confirmed exactly what I had described.

I called David because I was worried about the effect on Henry. My house was now a crime scene with men in white suits all over the house. David's words, "There's always some drama in your life!" No compassion for me or the effect this had on his son. Yet again my son had suffered a major trauma. How much more could my son go through before he also cracked?

Some people believed me, some didn't. Oliver's friends didn't deny that he would do this to me. They just said that I should have dealt with it another way rather than go to the police. In the end I dropped the case because it was just another thing my family could use against me. Six years later while in Cape Town, I received a call from a man in his fifties who had been part of the group at the club. He rang me to apologise for not standing by me and believing me. He apologised for the pain that he caused and how he couldn't imagine what it would have been like going through that ,with people not believing me. He explained Oliver had gone on to sexually assault a friend of his. I thanked him for his call and kind words. What people said to me was nothing compared to what my own sister sent me. Evil texts talking about my 'so-called sexual abuse'. Not one of the women in the social group have ever apologised to me, yet they now know for sure I was telling the truth. Ironically, the compassion I received was from men.

The next few months were chaos. I tried to act like nothing had happened, but it affected my relationship with everyone. I had terrible trust issues before, but now I couldn't trust anyone not to hurt me. I started to gain weight again. I was using food to push all the terrible feelings down. I went to see Professor McMahon and explained what had happened to me. After more assessments, we had one final option with weight loss surgery – to put a gastric band around my bypass. That would be my ninth weight loss surgery procedure. I was so mentally broken, nothing could help me, no dysfunctional strategy was left to use. My mind was so overloaded with trauma, the only place to put all that emotional energy was in my physical body, my bones.

On April 13th, 2013, my body started to physically breakdown in a way the medical profession struggled to comprehend or explain. The bones in my body would fracture from head to toe.

WHAT THE READER CAN TAKE FROM THIS CHAPTER?

A trauma bond is often at the root of why we stay in dysfunctional relationships.

Believe in your children and what they are capable of. Help them believe anything is possible.

Addictions will often escalate without the appropriate intervention.

Chaotic childhoods can manifest as your version of normal life in adulthood.

What you see as other people's paradise and dream life, is often not the truth reality of the situation.

Emotional support for survivors of sexual assault is key to their recovery.

As a young child, I looked like Shirley Temple.

My fringe growing back after I'd tried to cut my hair off in the middle of the night. My shoulders were already starting to hunch over in a protective pose.

Young love. David and I on our wedding day in 1995.

Taken in the hall of Bishopton House. I grew up in poverty. Henry's childhood was completely different.

Dolan Park Hospital, the jewel in the family crown.

After my marriage break-up, I used food to cope. This was me at my heaviest.

Struggling to climb up the hills of San Francisco.

Donna Ross, 'The Boss'.

Taken at The Delano hotel in Miami. I had been chronically ill and unable to fly only a few days before. Yet again, a severe bout of Crohn's disease miraculously disappeared.

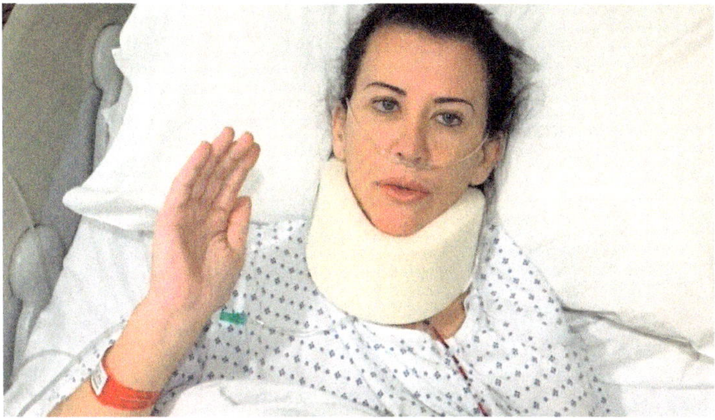

This picture was taken to send to Henry. He wanted me to show him I was alive, after yet another spinal surgery. I was mentally and physically broken.

Miss Sovra IJ Whitcroft MBChB FRCOG

Consultant Gynaecologist

Gynaecological Surgery • Hormones • Menopause • PCOS

The London Clinic
6 Devonshire Place
London W1G 6HL

BMI Mount Alvernia Hospital
Harvey Road
Guildford GU1 3LX

Nuffield Health Hospital
Stirling Road
Guildford GU2 7RF

Reference: SIJW/LME
BUPA Int BI-[redacted]
Appointment: Friday, 11 February 2022
Clinic: **Nuffield Health Guildford**

Correspondence and enquiries to
BMI Mount Alvernia Hospital
Harvey Road
Guildford
Surrey GU1 3LX
T: 01483 456836
F: 01483 576732
E: secretary@sijwpratice.co.uk

Miss D Ross
[redacted]

MEDICAL REPORT

Re: Miss Donna Ross - DOB: 26/01/1973

I saw Donna for review today. She is feeling and looking amazing since starting transvaginal infusion of ovarian [redacted] and the FSH has miraculously reduced from 58.2iu/L last august to 14.5iu/L so is well into the normal range and she is hoping for more improvement on this. The menstrual cycle has already returned which had disappeared so there does look to be some resurgence of ovarian activity.

As a result, Donna has been able to discontinue the oestrogen completely and has no low oestrogen symptoms at all and is just continuing with metformin, acarbose and semaglutide for the background insulin effect.

Donna is up to date with screening and is having regular ultrasound scans. The uterus looks normal with no evidence of fibroids or adenomyosis and there are no large ovarian cysts.

I do not need to see Donna for a year unless she has any concerns at all and she is going to continue with regular screening and blood tests and I am sure will be in touch.

With best wishes.

Yours sincerely

Miss S I J Whitcroft FRCOG MBChB
Consultant Gynaecologist

Prescribing Summary:
Metformin 500mg slow release x4 per day
Acarbose 100mg x2 per day
Semaglutide 1g per week

Endometrial Protection:
Not required

Follow-up: One year annual review unless requests earlier.

PLEASE NOTE that tailored doses of hormone replacement and insulin sensitising medication such as Metformin and Glucobay are not within the NICE Guidelines and may not, therefore, be available under the NHS. This depends upon the individual Practice prescribing policy and NHS prescriptions should not be assumed.

The letter that proves I've reversed the menopause. My FSH dropped from a post-menopausal range (>30mU/ml) before the treatment, to a functioning ovulatory range of (5.2-20.4mU/ml) after treatment. I no longer need HRT, I have a regular menstrual cycle and follicles in my ovaries.

North London Physiotherapy

[redacted]

Correspondence to:

[redacted]

4th August 2018

Re: Donna Ross (26.01.73) [redacted]

Donna was initially referred to physiotherapy by Mr Sean Curry after surgical fixation of her left distal Femoral fracture in Spring 2013. Following her rehabilitation Donna returned to Mr Curry for surgical removal of the metalwork in mid-October 2013. Prior to removal of the metalwork Donna had developed left foot pain which has been demonstrated on MRI to be a stress fracture of the left Cuboid and was immobilised in an Aircast boot for four months.

This may have affected Donna's lumbo-pelvic stability and alignment and as a result Donna experienced a flare up of longstanding low back pain. Under surgeon Mo Akmal, Donna had a two level lumbar fusion 3rd December 2013. Initially Donna made a very good recovery and was pain free, but at 6 months post-surgery she began to develop low back pain. Donna also had a fall in May 2014 and sustained a left proximal Humeral fracture. To compound this, the left foot pain continued and developed into Complex Regional Pain Syndrome. In May 2016 Donna sustained a right 4th Metatarsal fracture and a left Talus fracture, which required further physiotherapy.

In October 2016 Donna sustained Thoracic wedge fractures at T7 and T8 and on 5th November 2016 she had a Cervical fusion at C5/6 level, which required further physiotherapy rehabilitation. Through 2017 Donna was affected by Tempro-Mandibular Joint dysfunction and had further physiotherapy input from my colleague Krina Panchal. On 7th October 2017 Donna had surgery with Mr Arun Ranganathan to remove the metalwork from previous Lumbar fusion surgery following which I provided her post-operative rehabilitation. On 31st December 2017 Donna was involved in a road traffic accident where the car she was in was struck from behind. This has aggravated several of Donna's previous physical pains and required further physiotherapy.

Donna's problems have been and continue to be extremely complex. During this time Donna has also been under the care of Dr Perreira, Consultant Psychiatrist, for Major depressive disorder-moderate with anxious distress; Post- traumatic stress disorder; Attention Deficit hyperactivity disorder- inattention subtype. Recently Donna had care from Dr Ori, Consultant Neuropsychiatrist in Cape Town who has reported that Donna had been experiencing somatic symptoms of nausea and vomiting which wake her from sleep as well as psychogenic non-epileptiform seizures at night with variable frequency. Ms. Ross has also experienced episodes of faecal incontinence at night of severe watery diarrhoea followed by normal stool. These features coincided with the resurgence of suppressed childhood traumatic memories of abuse.

Now that Donna has returned home to London from South Africa, Dr Ori has recommended that Donna continues with multi-disciplinary care in a familiar and safe environment to address these symptoms. Currently the ongoing night seizures are causing physical symptoms with tension and pain over the Tempro-Mandibular joints, Trapezius muscle tension, Thoracic and Cervical region pain, for which I am continuing to provide treatment.

David Wales MSc BSc (Hons) MCSP
Clinical Specialist Physiotherapist

[redacted]

A letter from David Wales one of my physiotherapists. This shows some of the fractures I suffered when my body started to physically break down.

PROFESSOR SIMON SHORVON, MA MD FRCP
UCL INSTITUTE OF NEUROLOGY

Clinic date: 21 March 2018 Queen Square PCR
Letter typed: 22 March 2018

Dr Stephen Pereira
Consultant Psychiatrist
Stephen Pereira LLP
The Clinic
Keats House Consulting Rooms
Near Guys Hospital
24-26 St Thomas Street
London SE1 9RS

Dear Stephen

Re: Miss Donna McNertin-Ross DOB: 28/01/1973
Address: [redacted]
Tel: [redacted] **Email:** [redacted]

Many thanks for asking me to see Donna again. I saw her today and the last time she attended my clinics was in October 2014. The reason for the visit today was to discuss a new problem which seems to have developed over the last few years.

This takes the form of episodes at night which she likens to night terrors. She tends to wake up in a very fearful state. She sometimes feels there is someone in the room. She feels hot and flustered and very sweaty and is sometimes incontinence of urine and occasionally of faeces. She often has an intense feeling of acid in her stomach and feel she might vomit . She has very little memory of the events, and may wake up in the morning unaware of an attack. I was able to get a description from her partner, Paul over the phone. He describes these as follows. The attacks occur within an hour of two of going to sleep. He is awoken by what he calls a commotion. He says there are no convulsive movements nor any a positive features suggestive of epilepsy. Her jaw is often clenched and she sometimes rolls up in a foetal position. She can talk during the events, often making no sense. A predominant feature is fear, and he tries to comfort her and she recovers. The bed is cleaned up is necessary and then she goes back to sleep. On occasions these events have occurred for up to 2 hours, fluctuating during this time, but others can be much shorter and usually she estimated that they last 10 minutes or so. They occur now most weeks and usually several times a week. They are very disruptive on her sleep and she can feel exhausted by these and can be in pain for up to three days after a severe attack. These attacks have not previously occurred, and were not present when I saw her 4 years ago.

On other occasions she wakes up and feels paralysed and is unable to move. These are also very frightening. Paul describes these too, and sometimes they have lasted up to 2 hours with her unable to move during the whole period.

In the interim period, a diagnosis of PTSD has been made and she is tells me she is currently undergoing trauma therapy and dealing with, and focusing on, her suppressed memories. She has weekly psychotherapy and also physiotherapy. The therapy is going well, and her general condition is greatly improved.

Simon Shorvon • Professor of Clinical Neurology • UCL Institute of Neurology
Queen Square Private Consulting Rooms, 23 Queen Square London WC1N 3BG.

Secretary: Chelsea Gardner Email: [illegible] Tel: 0203 448 8148 Fax: 0203 448 8864
Websites: www.qspcr.com, www.shorvon.eu

PROFESSOR SIMON SHORVON, MA MD FRCP
UCL INSTITUTE OF NEUROLOGY

Since I last saw her, she told me that she had had a number of orthopaedic operations including a lumbar fusion and then an operation to reverse this, and she also has cervical spinal damage and fractures in the bones of her foot and has had a rotator cuff syndrome. The physiotherapy has greatly helped these aspects.

She has had no medication for the events, and apart from oestrogen and other hormone therapy and metformin, she is not taking any medication.

She is due to go to Arizona in early april to discuss trauma therapy and is then due for an admission to a clinic in south Africa for 3 months for therapy.

My recommendations and conclusions are as follows:

1. Donna asked me whether these could be non-epileptic attacks associated with PTSD. I think it most likely that these are related to the PTSD and have a psychological basis. I think it unlikely that they are either epileptic or parasomnias.
2. However, the diagnosis could be more definitively assessed by a recording of an attack, and I have asked Paul to try to take a video recording of an attack (for instance on a phone) and to send this to me for review.
3. In the meantime, I did wonder whether some medication to assist sleep would be worthwhile, and I have asked Donna to discuss this with yourself.

Donna mentioned that she was seeing you today and I would be happy to discuss over the phone if you wished.

With kind regards.

Yours sincerely,

Simon Shorvon

Professor Simon Shorvon
Consultant Neurologist and Professor in Clinical Neurology

cc.

Donna Ross
Via email: [redacted]

Dr Chatsuda Chleraknl
The Cavendish Health Centre
53 New Cavendish St
Marylebone
London W1G 9TQ

Simon Shorvon • Professor of Clinical Neurology • UCL Institute of Neurology
Queen Square Private Consulting Rooms, 25 Queen Square, London WC1N 3BG

Secretary: [illegible] Email: [illegible] Tel: 0203 448 8048 Fax: 0203 448 8894
Websites: [illegible], www.shorvon.eu

A letter from Professor Shorvon showing the extent of my seizures and how they crippled my life. During this time, I still managed to take no medication for anxiety, depression, and the seizures. I used my four pillars.

South Warwickshire NHS
NHS Foundation Trust

Dr P C Hawker	Consultant Gastroenterologist	Ext 4266
Dr J D Shearman	Consultant Gastroenterologist	Ext 8007
Dr B M Usselmann	Consultant Gastroenterologist	Ext 4852
Dr L Gladman	Consultant Gastroenterologist	Ext 8007
Dr A M Naji	Associate Specialist	Ext 8007
Sue Scott	Clinical Nurse Specialist	Ext 4327

Department of Gastroenterology
Warwick Hospital
Lakin Road
Warwick
CV34 5BW

Tel: 01926 495321
Fax: 01926 482601

Our Ref: PCH/JML /455266
NHS Number: [redacted]

20th October 2010

<u>To Whom It May Concern</u>

Dear Colleague

Donna Michele McNerlin-Ross - 26/01/1973
[redacted]

I am writing to introduce you to my long term patient, and I think I could probably now add the term friend, Donna McNerlin-Ross. You will make your own judgement of Donna but in essence she is a pretty active, nightflying businesswoman with a somewhat hectic lifestyle which has over the years made management of her Crohn's disease interesting to say the least.

Crohn's colitis was diagnosed around the age of 18 presenting with predominant joint involvements and modest bowel symptoms. Investigations included colonoscopy with multiple biopsies.

I first met her in 1998 when she was gave a history of intermittent bowel symptoms. She had been on long term Salazopyrin in an attempt to keep control of the disease. Following our initial consultation I reviewed the case and ensured she was given information and an education programme regarding the disease and had a full dietetic review. We attempted to control exacerbations with Prednisolone which, unfortunately, gave her significant side effects and therefore on occasions used Budesonide.

Donna's business life meant that she was not the most assiduous of attendees at outpatients and she came back to see me in 2003 when a full reassessment including colonoscopy was carried out. This showed typical appearances of Crohn's colitis affecting the entire colon. I treated her with Infliximab with, initially, spectacular results. Unfortunately at this time we were unable to use Infliximab for maintenance therapy in the UK and she was therefore started on Mercaptopurine at a dose of 1mg per kilogram. Her attendance at clinic and for monitoring was a little unstable and Mercaptopurine was therefore stopped.

She seemed to be reasonably well during 2004 but had a further relapse in 2005 which came under control.

She had quite significant problems in 2008 and was re-treated with Infliximab with good results and again we attempted to re-introduce Mercaptopurine but were not particularly successful.

Continued.....

South Warwickshire NHS

NHS Foundation Trust

Continuation of letter regarding Donna McNerlin-Ross

In 2009 she had a further cycle of treatment with Infliximab and we were exploring with our financial masters the possibility of getting her on to maintenance.

She ran into further problems in 2010 and at this stage I started her on Infliximab and put her on to a maintenance programme of infusions every 2 months. I was originally intending to transfer her to Adalimumab but as she was in the process of reorganising her business life and planning a move to the States I felt it was probably easier for her to have a two monthly infusion than for me to attempt to ensure continuity of supply of fortnightly Adalimumab injections. The Infliximab seems to have done the trick and she is looking and keeping very well indeed and I have planned for her to have an infusion shortly before she departs for America.

It seemed to me that once she is established in the States, regular maintenance with Adalimumab would be sensible but I will obviously leave this to your judgement.

We have tried Mercaptopurine on a number of occasions, the most recent she had persistent low white count and neutrophil count. On balance this drug is probably relatively unsafe and she would be a good candidate for long term treatment with biological agent.

You will also be aware she has had surgical procedures for obesity but I have no doubt that full details will be provided by her surgeon.

If any further information would be helpful, please don't hesitate to get in touch: peter.hawker@swft.nhs.uk and I will be pleased to be of assistance.

I have found looking after Donna over the last few years an interesting and at times challenging experience, but I have finally included her in a large list of patients who brighten up my clinics when they pop in and she has transferred to that list of patients with whom I feel I have become friends. I wish you the best of luck.

Yours sincerely

Dr P C Hawker MD FRCP MBChB
Consultant Physician

A letter evidencing years of illness and aggressive medical treatments for Crohn's disease and arthritis. I have cured myself of all chronic illness and live a healthy life.

Dr Rasmita Ori and I. This powerhouse of a women, as usual looking like she just walked out of Vogue.

Lesley Chorn & I. The women who gave me so much knowledge to share with others.

Getting my strength back with James Moore.

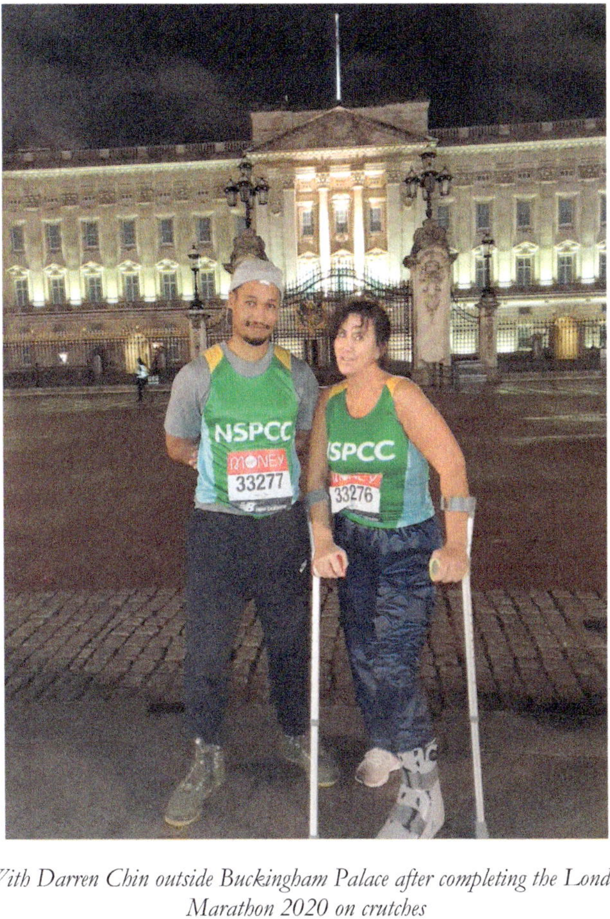

With Darren Chin outside Buckingham Palace after completing the London Marathon 2020 on crutches

Exhilarated, but drained and dehydrated, after completing the London Marathon, 2021.

Wearing my medal from the London Marathon 2021, with the team that helped me achieve it.

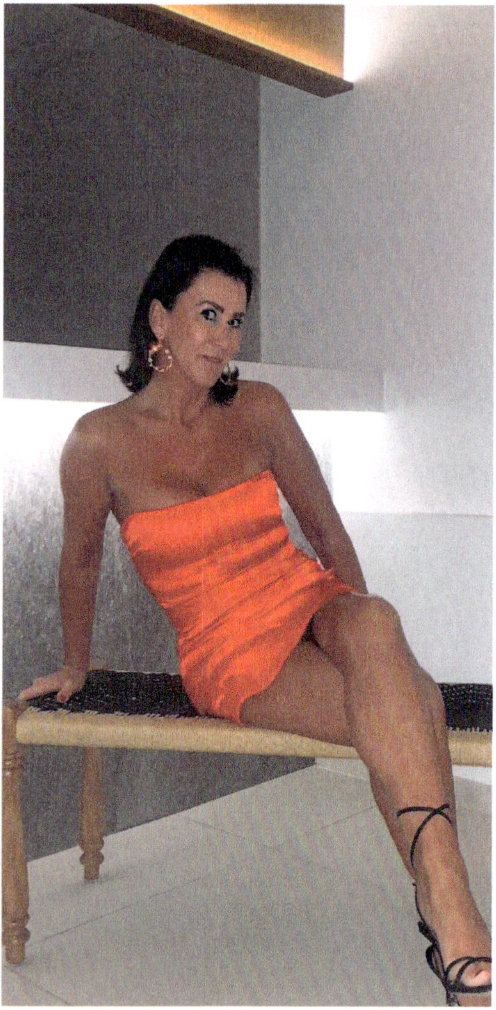

48 and feeling fabulous.

Me at 49, wearing the dress I wore when I was 33.

Taken after my confirmation by the Archbishop of Canterbury, Justin Welby, with 'The Vicar' Ravi Holy. My inner child can finally heal and be at peace.

Back in business

CHAPTER EIGHT

THE BREAKDOWN OF MY BODY

BREAKDOWN

A MECHINCAL FAILURE, A FAILURE OF A RELATIONSHIP OR INTERACTION

As a child, my arms kept coming out of their sockets. There was also the childhood neck fracture which was discovered after my father pushed me down the stairs. In addition, there were fractures that didn't relate to the impact when I was skiing during the breakup of my marriage with David, and the wrist fractures when I slipped while I was with my father in the Cayman Islands. I was about to experience relentless fractures which the medical profession struggled to explain.

I had agreed to do some work for David at our newly acquired company. My boyfriend had gone out and was going to come back and stay at my house. I had to be up at 6:00 am for work, so I asked him to be quiet when he came home. He returned in a drunken state at 3:00 am. I also received a call from the head of security at the private members club to say my boyfriend had caused a huge scene there. I was furious. I was in an emotional state and an argument ensued. He ran down the stairs and I followed him missing the bottom step. There was no impact, no big fall – nothing. My legs gave way and I collapsed onto the hall floor with searing pain up my left leg. I couldn't move. I lay on the floor for an hour waiting for an ambulance. I was screaming as the ambulance crew dragged me across the floor to get me into a position where I could be stretchered out of the house.

I was taken to the Emergency department, and an X-ray revealed that I had suffered a triple fracture to my femur and knee. I had missed one step and suffered severe fractures to the largest and strongest bone in the body. I had an operation to place a metal plate to hold my knee and leg together. Yet again, I was in a wheelchair and then on crutches. I needed help doing everything. Henry didn't want anyone to take care of me, he wanted to do everything himself.

I needed extensive physiotherapy and was told it was unlikely I would ever walk as I had before the fractures. I searched for a specialist physiotherapist, and I found a man named David Wales. David was, not only an amazing physio who specialised in lower limbs, but had also suffered a fracture which had ended his football career. Because of his own experience, he really understood the psychological impact of fractures. He would look after me for the next five years, constantly trying to work out what was happening with my body.

Around the same time a good friend called to speak with me. I was busy dealing with an issue with David and I said I'd call her the next day. The following day, before we got chance to speak, she jumped from an apartment building in the Cayman Islands. The friend was devastated over her fiancé breaking up with her and cancelling their wedding. Her poor heart couldn't deal with the pain, and this was the only way she felt she could stop the pain. I was consumed with guilt over not taking that call, and these feelings impacted me hugely.

I decided I needed to move out of central London, so I moved to the leafy suburb of Hampstead. I hated it. I felt lonely and isolated. I could hardly go anywhere because of the ongoing problems with my leg. I had developed a major scar tissue problem which meant I could barely bend my leg to walk. I walked with my leg almost straight, and I had to swing my leg out sideways to walk. David tried to manipulate my leg. He said he could work on it, but it would be very painful. I would sit on his treatment couch and scream as he bent my leg over the edge of the bed to try and release the scar tissue and get some movement back in my knee. All the physio and pain I was going through, made little difference – I needed another operation. The second operation on my leg was to 'snap' the scar tissue around the knee. As the procedure was so painful, it had to be carried out under general anaesthetic.

After the second operation, I had gained more movement in my leg but I still needed intense physiotherapy. Whilst driving to one of my physio sessions, I put my foot slightly onto the accelerator pedal and I had searing pain in my left foot. I arrived at the physio session with David, unable to walk properly. My foot was X-rayed and for no reason my foot had fractured in several places. I had to wear an air-cast protective boot while my fractures were healing. Then for no reason at all, I had the same searing pain in my right foot. I was X-rayed and there were now several fractures on my right foot. I was now wearing two air-cast boots, one on each foot. I was in a great deal of pain with the knee that had been fractured and the surgeon recommended a third operation to remove metalwork and, again, address the scar tissue. The fractures continued on my feet, and I was diagnosed with bone marrow oedema syndrome, along with chronic regional pain syndrome (CRPS).

After the sexual assault at my home, I had developed lower back pain which, at points, led me to be stuck in certain positions and unable to move. As a result, I had been seeing a chiropractor up until my femur and knee fracture. The back pain had intensified. David had worked on my spine, but I was showing no improvement. He referred me to a spinal surgeon who said he needed to fuse my lumbar spine. I now needed major spinal surgery and the trauma didn't end there. In December 2013, while having spinal surgery, my home was burgled, and all my jewellery was stolen. There was no alarm on, and I lost £250,000 worth of jewellery. The insurance company would not pay, because the alarm hadn't been set.

After the sexual assault, I had started to have, what I thought, were night terrors. I didn't want to sleep, and I developed a sleep phobia. The only way I could get to sleep was by using alcohol to knock me out. After my body becoming toxic due to medication and, what seemed like non-stop medication sensitivities, the only thing I could tolerate was paracetamol for the pain.

I would wake up with such chronic pain in my solar plexus and thoracic spine, I would scream and be unable to move. No amount of physio helped the pain. To try to resolve it, I had my spine injected by a specialist pain team but, unfortunately, the injections didn't work.

My feet fractured yet again, and none of my rapidly growing specialist medical team could explain why this was happening. There seemed to be no reason at all. The pain in my bones was horrific and the fractures were relentless.

Since the burglary, where the burglars had entered through my bedroom window, I couldn't sleep. The nightmares of people being in my bedroom were relentless. I would wake up screaming or shouting for help, soaked in sweat. I was so frightened of someone coming into my room, many nights Henry had to sleep in the room with me.

The pain was so horrific in my solar plexus, I was convinced I had another erosion from my gastric band. My (very large) medical team had exhausted all options as to the cause of this thoracic and solar plexus pain. The only possibility left was that my weight loss surgery was causing the problem. I contacted Professor McMahon, and he arranged for a laparoscopy. Everything looked fine with the band and my stomach so he referred me to a cardiothoracic specialist. He couldn't find any problems either. I made the decision to have the gastric band out, even though Prof McMahon said it was likely I would gain weight back as I could eat normally. I was in so much pain that didn't care. Every day I went to bed thinking, "Will I wake up in the morning?" When I woke up, I thought, "Is this the day I will die?"

After the gastric band was removed, as Prof McMahon predicted and all weight loss surgery data shows, I gained weight and quickly. The pain across my body did not stop, nor did the sweats at night or the nightmares. Everything was getting worse.

I decided I needed to leave the home where the burglary had happened. I put my furniture into storage and went to Thailand. Like many people who are desperate, I thought an extreme cleanse for a month at retreat may get me well. At the forefront of my mind was my weight. I didn't want to get fat. I thought starving for a month would surely solve the problem of the weight I'd gained.

I tried meditation at the retreat, but I found the explanation and what they were teaching ridiculous. I couldn't even sit still for thirty seconds, let alone ten minutes. I met a therapist at the retreat who specialised in Timeline Therapy, Hypnotherapy, and Neuro Linguistic Programming (NLP). I decided to have some sessions with the therapist. During the sessions, we got to a point around my childhood, and I can remember saying, "There's nothing there, there's nothing there." That night I woke up in the middle of the night to go to the toilet. I must have collapsed because I woke up on the bathroom floor in agony and hardly able to move. I didn't know how I had got there. I thought maybe I had slipped but it didn't make sense.

The therapist took me to the local hospital where I was X-rayed and advised there was no fracture. I knew there was. I showed the doctors the scars across my body and said to them, "I'm not leaving until you X-ray me again." After the second X-ray, a fracture of my left rotator cuff, my shoulder, was discovered. This was a bad fracture, that would need another eighteen months of rehabilitation. I was devastated. I had gone to this retreat to heal and cleanse my body, and I ended up with more fractures.

I returned to England and stayed at my mother's house. In my heart, I felt there was no hope left for me. I had gone home to my mother to die. My poor body had been ravaged by illness for the last twenty-five years, and I felt it was time to give in.

My Crohn's disease was relapsing. My arthritis was relapsing. My spine was causing me more pain, and I'd been sent to yet another pain specialist. My spine was injected again, and I was told I needed a device placed there to deal with the pain, that would cost £30,000.

At my mother's house, I couldn't stand this slow death anymore. I drank a bottle of wine and took some pills. I wanted this over with. I was woken by my mother coming into my bedroom and saying, "Oh my god, what is wrong with you?" No compassion, no "How can we help you? I know you must be scared" – nothing.

The final straw was the night my mother had to look after my nieces, because my sister had been caught cheating on her husband again. My sister Victoria and her husband had to go to sign the documents to sell their home in Turkey. The latest affair had been with the local Turkish waiter. Andy, my mother's husband, was at home. He was drunk. I sat down with him and had a drink, and then he got very nasty, verbally lashing out at me. I went into my bedroom and packed my things. As I was leaving, I said to Andy, "It's someone like you that will push me over the edge." I was inconsolable. I called my friends, and I went to the nearest one's house which was in London. That day, the friend called my mother to suggest she come and see me. My mother said she couldn't because she had a dinner that night with her friends.

Luckily, I had found Henry an apartment in London. I went there to get it ready for him to move into. The day

Henry moved in, I collapsed on the floor in front of him. I was shaking and frothing at the mouth. The next day, one of my doctors took some blood tests. I'd had a seizure, a big one. I wasn't to lock myself in anywhere where people couldn't access me easily, or be alone, until they found out what was going on. I was now having grand mal seizures. I just couldn't take any more, I was broken.

I spoke with Dr Pereira, who called Professor Simon Shorvon, one of the most eminent names in epilepsy in the world. I had various neurological tests and Professor Shorvon was very concerned. The brain scans showed nothing to be wrong. Yet again, there was no reason at all why any of this was happening to me.

I felt I was a dead man walking, but I didn't seem destined to die. The final straw came when my third pain specialist said, "Let's sit back, watch, wait and do nothing." I looked at him and thought he was crazy. I had to do something. I had to find a way.

I went back for another appointment with Professor Shorvon. He suggested I was having fugue states, which is when people wander off and they turn up days, or even weeks, later and do not know where they have been. A fugue state is the most extreme form of disassociation, where your mind completely disassociates from everything. This often happens after extreme trauma, such as natural disasters and wars. I'd decided to go to Cape Town, South Africa, for treatment for both my mind and body. Professor Shorvon's worry was that if I suffered a fugue state in South Africa, I wouldn't be safe.

Before I left for Cape Town, I went to see my mother and her husband who both apologised to me for the incident when he was drunk. I said goodbye telling them I forgave them both. I have never seen my mother since. As I sat on the runway waiting to take off on my flight, I received a call that would drive me to find a solution. The call was from my father. He'd hurt me many times, but that day he broke my heart. He said, "You may as well go, there's nothing left for you here." For all the things my father had done to me, I was his daughter and I adored him. This wouldn't be his final act of cruelty to me, but it would be his most hurtful one. I haven't seen my father since.

I had no idea how I was going to find answers to my endless problems. Nothing had worked so far. The medical people weren't able to heal me and my forays into the holistic world didn't give me any better outcomes. What I did know was that I was a survivor and if I was meant to die, it would have happened by now. I had a son and people that loved me. I had everything waiting for me and I wasn't going to be beaten.

I thought I had been fighting for my life for the last twenty-five years, I was now going to fight like I'd never fought before. I took all the rage inside me, and I let it drive me away from self-destruction to self-love. I had no idea I would discover what I did.

I arrived in Cape Town on 8th December 2014. I didn't know Cape Town at all and had booked a hotel outside the main city centre. I planned to look at facilities and find practitioners who would help me to walk again. My mind was a secondary concern at this point. I was physically weak and felt extremely exposed and vulnerable.

First, I went to the Sports Science Institute of South Africa (SSISA) to find a personal trainer or physiotherapist. I was recommended a fantastic bio-kineticist, which is like a combination of both. I booked daily sessions and planned to get strong. I walked into the SSISA dragging my left leg. I had been told I would be in constant pain for the rest of my life and never walk properly again.

I then called a clinic that I'd heard was quite tough but got results. I spoke to a lady at reception and explained I was from England and would like to view the clinic and could she recommend a psychiatrist. That call was to change my life. I was recommended a female psychiatrist named Dr Rasmita Ori. I arranged to view the clinic and was shown around by the hospital manager. I was used to my own room, grounds, and 'celebrity' facilities, where I could go in and out. This facility was different. There was a guard at the gate and barbed wire on top of the fences. You couldn't walk in and out of this facility and, to me, it felt like a prison. Once inside the facilities were good, although not as fancy as in the UK and you had to share rooms with other people.

Once I had seen the facility, I asked to meet with the psychiatrist I'd been recommended. As I waited in the hallway, I saw this stunningly beautiful woman walking towards me. The woman looked very young, doll-like beautiful, and appeared to be of Indian origin. She came up to me and introduced herself as Dr Ori. I thought, "you have got to be joking" I didn't trust women and here stood a woman who looked like she'd just walked out of *Vogue* – and I had more issues than *Vogue*. I thought it was never going to work but Dr Ori would become the first woman I would trust, and the first person I trusted enough to share my whole story.

I arrived at the clinic to start my stay with my car (which I wasn't meant to have) and two pool noodles under my arms for the swimming pool physio. I was so OCD I brought my own washing powder as no one was doing *my* washing, and three suitcases all organised perfectly. When I trotted into the clinic, the only thing I was missing was a couple of margaritas!

People do not generally put themselves into clinics. Most often they are forced to go there by loved ones or because they may lose their jobs or go to prison if they don't. I had hopped, skipped, and jumped into any place I thought would help me over the last fifteen years. I put myself behind those metal gates, barbed wire fences and guards to feel safe.

I really bonded with Dr Ori. She was very intelligent, dynamic, and answered questions I asked in a direct way, which is what I liked. Most of all, she stood her ground with me in a kind and gentle way, and that made me feel safe.

Henry called me to say that he was worried about me. He'd seen a documentary about Cape Town and the rapes and killings. I said to Henry, "Don't worry – I have never been, or felt, safer in my life."

Just as Dr Pereira had hoped, when I felt safe, the memory came. It was so confusing. At first the memory started to come as a feeling, rather than a memory. Very quickly, I was getting physically stronger. There were no new fractures, and my chronic illnesses were stabilising. I was really working well with Dr Ori, but I didn't like my therapist at the clinic. I told Dr Ori I wanted to leave. The chances of me gaining a full recovery at that stay in the clinic was about 5-6 percent. That was about the same odds as long-term success from dieting, and that had never worked out for me.

I explained to Dr Ori what I wanted to do and why. She agreed to still help me. I rented an apartment near the clinic and the SSISA. I worked on my body daily to get it strong, as that made me feel mentally stronger. I would see Dr Ori three times a week for two hours each time. We started unpacking my life and Dr Ori helped me make sense of what had happened, and what was now happening to me.

I knew I had to change my thinking, so I looked at my situation differently. I decided I would put together a programme for someone that presented with my symptoms and use it on myself. I started by looking at different treatments available for people who had issues like mine. There were lots of different treatments, but I didn't know what I should use or when and how. It was a minefield. Many clinical people were no wiser and limited to their speciality. It was the same with the alternative, holistic world – practitioners were limited to their specialities and often their own thinking.

I started with the bio-kineticist and said I needed to train harder. I didn't want to walk, I wanted to run the track at the SSISA and I wanted to lose weight. If I wanted to do that in the three months I had allotted to get well, I would need to train like an injured athlete.

I was referred to Dr Greathead, a partially sighted woman with the most amazing talent for knowing exactly where the problems are in the body. My skeleton from head to toe was a problem, but Dr Greathead looked after that. Little by little, she started to get my body back into alignment and, when the amount of training I was doing took its toll, she would manage those issues as well.

I then found a sports massage and acupuncture specialist. Lyndsey worked on my muscles and energy alignment. I was having myofascial release and I would scream with the pain. My body would push acupuncture needles out, as if it didn't want to be treated. Due to this, the treatment approach had to continually change.

I used the swimming pool daily. I had more mobility in a pool as the water supported my weight. I increased my movement, which in turn increased my confidence and hope of a full recovery. Six days a week, I was treated by at least two of the team. Some days I would be doing rehabilitation work for six hours. Every night, I soaked in Epsom salts or a mustard bath. I rested on a Sunday.

I knew the importance of nutrition and how effective it could be on healing. I met with Janine Dobson who was a nurse by background, now a highly experienced nutritionist. I had to change my thinking around food. I had to focus on the food I was putting into my body, rather than the calories. Janine requested a whole range of blood work, DNA tests, stool tests, and urine samples. She started with where I was lacking in nutrition to initially clean up my body and then used food and supplementation to re-nourish my body. It took three months to do that. There were several deficiencies that would take long term work. We also discovered my cortisol levels were off the charts due to all the stress I had been under for so long. This affected my ability to lose weight and I was also insulin resistant which, again, made it almost impossible to lose weight. I had been pushing a rock uphill in my weight loss battle and I'd worked with some of the perceived most eminent minds in obesity.

If I was to change my thinking, I had to learn to think differently. I thought back to the time in Thailand when I had the timeline therapy and the response I'd had. Something had been triggered, but at that time I didn't know what a trigger was. I enrolled on a course for Timeline Therapy, Hypnotherapy and NLP. I wanted to learn about the unconscious mind and using various ways of accessing it. I knew, at best, only 10-15 percent of our actions or thoughts are conscious, the rest are unconscious. I knew my resolution would be found in the unconscious mind. I trained intensively on those courses.

I realised that to get the results I wanted, I would need to stay in Cape Town longer. I decided to stay for six months. I started an eight-week mindfulness course where I met a doctor who suggested another place where she'd learned meditation. I thought, "I have nothing to lose", so I enrolled on a three-day breathwork and meditation course. After years of hearing about this 'meditation' and 'mindfulness', I finally got it. It wasn't about clearing my mind – it was about being able to sit with the thoughts that were in my head. The most important thing I was taught was how to use my breath to drop into a state where I could be present, and tolerate and regulate the stress and distress that I was under.

All my life, I had taken breathing for granted. I would have to learn that breath is the key to everything we do in life. I was taught the simplest, yet most fundamental, thing I had ever learned – my breath was the key to everything. If I learned different ways to use my breath, I would be able to learn to tolerate the emotions, thoughts and feelings that would come up. Instead of using one of my extensive arrays of dysfunctional coping strategies, I had a new option. I decided to continue with this group. I started with a three-day course, then a five-day course. I then went on a silent retreat for five days. At that point I couldn't be quiet for five minutes let alone be silent for five days. This is where I started to be able to be alone and sit with my emotions.

I learned to meditate in a hall with eighty people. Space was at a premium and we were packed in like sardines. I had to deal with my OCD and space issues, and I found it all really challenging. I wanted to tell people to get off my stuff and stay away from me, but I couldn't. Due to my spine issues and operations, I had to use a meditation chair to support me because we were sitting for up to twelve hours per day. Being silent for just five days gave me the space to think. I was starting to build a box of tools I could use in my fight against all that had tortured me.

I'd lived my life in noise and chaos. I was scared to be alone, to sleep, to trust anyone. I found myself in an unfamiliar country, with a psychiatrist I had gone to see on the recommendation of a receptionist. I had a team looking after my mind and body that I hadn't obsessively planned out. I was learning to relax and just go with things, to let it be and see what happens. I was learning to surrender and hand it over to something far bigger than me.

After the silent retreat, there was a Sahaj meditation course. This was a course where you received your own mantra to use to get into a deeper meditation. In one month, I had gone from an absolute non-believer to finally grasping the use of breath and meditation.

I turned my thinking back to rehab clinics for people suffering from stress, anxiety, and depression. I would say to the therapists that they weren't dealing with the real problems. I felt the clinics mainly dealt with the top line issues like misuse of alcohol or drugs, gambling or spending, sex, or love addiction. What they said to me was, "We have to go after what kills you first." I started to think around this point. I thought, 'If I didn't have it, what would kill me first?' It seemed like a simple question, but I struggled and I found myself thinking of material things.

I had to go to the basics and build upwards. I'd been going from the top down and it hadn't worked. I asked myself again, 'If I didn't have it what would kill me first?' It came to me: 1. Breath, 2. Water, 3. Food, and, if I wanted to avoid being anxious or depressed – 4. Staying in the present moment/meditation. I would come to refer to these as my four pillars, simple principles upon which I was to build my new structure.

I had also lost the ability to laugh, so I studied and learned how to laugh. I trained in Laughter Yoga. This is a practice that helps people who have lost the ability to laugh, induce 'fake' laughter through various techniques until the laughter returns. This was the ultimate, 'fake it until you make it'.

I was completely unaware that my body was telling a story to Dr Greathead. My body would mimic abuse that I was discussing with Dr Ori. Janine Dobson, the nutritionist, was looking at the blood markers of how my body was reacting to stress. The physio team were watching me go from strength to strength. The horrific pain I was suffering was no longer physical, it was emotional. The emotional pain made all my physical pain look insignificant.

I had kept in touch with friends and family while I was away, but as the treatment went on, I hardly spoke to my father, and my mother kept fishing about what was coming up. I started to talk about my life to Dr Ori. I talked about the abuse by my cousin and uncle. I talked about the relentless night terrors, where I woke up curled into a ball, my hands screwed up so tightly. I told her how I would hold my breath and keep my eyes closed in case anyone was in my room. I talked about my bed sheets and quilt being soaked with sweat when I woke up.

I cried an awful lot and felt so sad in my heart. However, I now had some skills in place which meant I could cope in a healthier way with the stress, anxiety and pain these memories brought with them. I felt sad while driving and would have tears rolling down my face and I wouldn't understand why. I described being at the cottages and looking out of the window, wishing someone would come to save me. I described how I never felt I belonged anywhere or ever fitted in. I described how I felt my whole life had been a complete lie. I asked Dr Ori why I would find tears running down my face for no reason. She explained those were the tears of the child, my inner child's heartbreak, and sadness. I didn't know it, but I was finally connecting with my inner child, 'Shirley Temple'.

After six months I had to return to the UK because I was told the company was being restructured ready for a sale. I agreed to sell my loan notes for a lot less than had been agreed five years earlier. However, I insisted that a fee was agreed to revise the botched cosmetic surgery that had been carried out at The Hospital Group. David agreed the company would pay me £40,000 so I could have my surgery revised elsewhere. I didn't want damages, just a basic fee to cover some of the revisions I needed.

A few days before I left Cape Town, I bought new trainers and stood beside the running track inside the SSISA. I wanted to run. I was strong enough now, but my brain wasn't telling my feet how to. My physio showed me how to put my heel down and then my toe and slowly, like a toddler, I learned how to run. I ran the track with tears in my eyes. I had another dream team, a team that were helping me mentally, nutritionally, and physically put myself back together.

I returned to the UK, thinking I knew so much and that I was cured. I had no idea what was waiting for me. My body broke in ways I could never have imagined. My dysfunctional coping strategies returned and I found myself in the most toxic relationship I'd ever been in. Also, my family tried to discredit me in every way they could.

WHAT THE READER CAN TAKE FROM THIS CHAPTER?

Using alcohol to sleep won't help the problem.

Sometimes doing nothing is the best thing you can do.

When you feel safe you can be open to the possibilities of life.

Emotional pain can be far more crippling than physical pain.

Connecting with your inner child allows you to truly heal.

Family are not always the people who will take care of you.

CHAPTER NINE

THE EMPIRE FALLS

FALLS

A MOVE FROM A HIGHER TO A LOWER LEVEL RAPIDLY AND WITHOUT CONTROL

I returned to the UK in June 2015. I was so excited to be home. I couldn't wait to see Henry and for him to see that he finally had his mother back. That night, I had dinner with Henry and Rachel – the girl who'd come to live with us after her mother died.

Rachel asked what had happened in Cape Town. I talked about what had come up and she kept asking who it was. I said it involved extended family members and she became hysterical. I would later understand she had been triggered by something I had said. Rachel would often stay with Diane – my father's mistress. Rachel told Diane what I had said, and the usual cycle started. Diane told her sister, Leila, and then my father. Leila then asked David what I was saying. Then both of my parents spoke to David about what I was apparently saying. Not one of them, other than David, spoke to me or asked me what I was saying or why I was saying it. David said that he'd told both my parents that he knew I had been abused, but he just didn't know by whom. My parents' response to David was, "Oh it's just Donna, you know she's crazy!"

Good parents, knowing their child had been abused, would have want to help. Yet again, just like the first time fifteen years earlier when I'd talked of abuse, they did nothing. In the last days in Cape Town, I called my mother. I mentioned the abuse, and she kept asking who it was. I wouldn't name anyone, but she kept pushing me for names. She named a list of people, asking if it was them. The last time I ever spoke to my mother was when I returned to the UK. I said I didn't want Henry near any of my family. She kept asking why. I said because I didn't have all my memory yet and I didn't know who my abusers were. She said, "I suppose that means Henry must stay away from me as well?" I said, "Yes until I know who has done this to me." She said, "I will make the decision for you – I'm not speaking to you." I calmly replied, "Only you know why you are not speaking to me," as she put the phone down.

In seven years, my mother has not contacted me. Not for Christmas, my birthday, or the numerous occasions when she knew I was critically ill.

I began looking for a new home for Henry and me in London because he now wanted to come home. Henry had taken a year out during his A levels exams. The pressure he had been under, with all I was going through, took its toll on him. He had just finished his first year of A levels and, from the sixteen-year-old that wasn't even expected to achieve anything more than D or E grades, was now predicted three A's at A level. Henry was also featured over a full page of his school's glossy magazine. He had made £120,000 that year from his fantasy trading as part of his economics A level and the school wanted to advertise that. Henry was also offered places at the top universities in London. I really thought that we had made it through incredibly difficult times. I was so proud of Henry, and so proud of myself for always pushing him to believe in himself.

I signed off on the company deal and I asked Henry where he would like to go for a holiday. We agreed on Bermuda and New York. While Henry was finishing off the college year, I went to Cyprus for two weeks to see friends. I continued the rehab on my body. I worked out in the gym and pool daily, and I saw a physiotherapist three times a week. One night, I woke and went to the bathroom. Something just came over me. I saw my small nail scissors and I wanted to chop my hair off and slash myself to pieces. I panicked. I didn't know what was happening to me. I'd cut my hair off at night in the bathroom as a small child, but that was over thirty-five years ago, and I had never cut my body. I was really frightened, but I managed to calm myself, and the rest of the time in Cyprus went well.

I returned home and Henry and I flew to Bermuda. We had a lovely time, but there was an underlying tension between us over what had happened over the past five years. Henry and I extended our stay in Bermuda by another week and then we flew to New York. I booked for us to go and watch the Yankees play. We saw *The Book of Mormon* on Broadway and a took a dinner cruise around Manhattan. On that cruise, Henry hugged me and said, "I know how much you love me Mother, giving me all these things." My thinking had changed and I realised that Henry judged how I loved him by what I gave him. Both his father and I had made up financially for what we didn't give him in emotional stability.

I met with friends in New York. *The American*, the man we were going to set up the American weight loss surgery business with, was also in town. *The American* met me and suggested we finally undertake the weight loss surgery behavioural project. He wanted to buy a large hospital in Dallas and devote a floor to WLS and the behavioural program. This was my dream. He was telling me everything I wanted to hear. We agreed he would come to London and I would set up a meeting with David because he needed a CEO for the company.

Henry and I returned to London and moved into our new home. It was stunning, but my bedroom faced a wall and it took me back to my time at the cottages. One of the cottages backed onto the farmer's field and the brick wall that retained the field went up to the bedroom windows. The name 'Terry', my father's friend, had randomly come up in Cape Town with Dr Ori and I had no idea why. I was being affected by, what I considered to be, very odd things.

I was now about to enter, what Dr Pereira would call, a perfect storm. I didn't have conscious memory of much of my trauma, and I was unknowingly being triggered almost everywhere. I lived in a place that reminded me of my childhood home, with my son who reminded me of my family, in an area I'd lived and worked for twenty-five years. Within three months of leaving Cape Town, I was reverting to old dysfunctional strategies to cope. I asked myself what had I missed? I had missed something. I was scared and lonely, and I didn't know why.

The American came to the UK at the beginning of October. He said he wasn't meant to leave the USA as he had to surrender his passport. He was involved in a bitter custody and divorce battle. He had travelled on another passport because he has dual nationality. All the red flags were there with him, but I ignored them. He met with David and I, and explained about the business plans. He kept telling me, "We've got to get David." Just as David had asked me to go to Las Vegas to check out that business with *The American*, he now asked me to go to Dallas to do the same.

I went to Dallas in November and stayed at *The American's* home. It was absolute chaos and I hated every minute of it. He had people staying at his house who were investing in his business. His father lived with him, and he argued with his mother constantly. It was like I was back in my family home. After a week, I rented an apartment and moved out. I was suffering terrible anxiety. I was biting the skin on my fingers until they bled and pulling my eyebrows out. He wasn't the sweet person that would do anything for me anymore. He was mean and rude. His behaviour was a lot like my father's. I just wanted to go home. When I returned to England, David asked what I thought. I said that everything looked like *The American* had told us. We started meetings to develop the American company with *The American*. I was looking for a place to escape.

Just before Christmas, my aunt and her daughter came to visit me in London. My aunt was helping me as I wanted to double check my memory. My aunt came with to see Dr Pereira and she gave him details of my family and my childhood. She told him that as a small child I would lie on the floor screaming. The family thought it was the 'terrible twos', but it continued. My aunt said the only way I would calm down was when Nanny Mac stroked my head. She never doubted that I'd been abused – a couple of years later I understood why. She told me that Grandad Mac had raped her as a teenager. She said her mother had sent her over to clean the house because Nanny Mac was, yet again, in hospital. My aunt was raped during that visit. She said it had changed her life. She had suffered from alcoholism and had weight loss surgery operations. Her skeleton also broke down and caused her to have numerous operations. If we stood next to each other, the scars on her body from her orthopaedic surgery matched mine, as did the weight loss surgery scars. Pictures had been posted on social media from my aunt's visit to my home, that's when the lies to try to discredit me started.

Six months after returning from Cape Town, I was completely worn down. I visited Dr Pereira on the 18th December 2015 and started to tell him more about my abuse. I thought he would call the police there and then, but he waited. I was so panicked at the thought of the police coming to speak with me. I just wasn't ready. I wasn't strong enough. I was so vulnerable that day. That was the day I met *The Accountant.* He was so different than any other man I had dated. He was short, living with obesity, and not my usual type. However, he was fun, and we got on well. We connected over life experiences, and he wanted to see me again. I wasn't really interested and said we should leave it there.

It was like glue with *The Accountant*, and I couldn't leave it there. I had no idea he had a girlfriend, nor that he was cheating on her with a few other women. We had developed a trauma bond – one of the most dangerous bonds you can have. He had severe chemical addictions and he used every coping strategy he could. He had suffered immense trauma. His mother was an abusive alcoholic and his father had died of alcoholism when he was thirteen. He reminded me of my father, and I believed if I saved him, it would be like me saving my father.

During the next six months, he physically attacked and sexually assaulted me. At points, I thought I would die. He received only police cautions because I wouldn't give the police what was needed to prosecute him for crimes against me. I had become an abused woman that was too embarrassed to tell anyone what was happening. Why was I too scared to reach out for help? Yet again, because of what my family would say and use against me.

After seeing the pictures of me with my aunt, my mother invited her brothers and their wives for Boxing Day (26th December) lunch. My mother told them to ignore everything I was saying because I was a drug addict and an alcoholic. What type of mother does that? One that protects herself first, because she had something to hide.

I just wanted to run. I needed to get out of England. Life had been great in Cape Town. I was happy, fulfilled and at peace. After everything I'd learned, how could this be happening to me? I thought if I moved to America to work on the business, my life would go back to the way it was in Cape Town. I was not only doing another geographical move, but I was also about to jump from the frying pan into the fire. I had become the battered woman you read about. This ruthless businesswoman, as I had been known, was suffering extreme domestic abuse.

I did everything I had been advised not to do. I was told not to make any life changing decisions and I was meant to return to Cape Town to focus on trauma work. Instead, I decided to move all my belongings and my life to Dallas, Texas.

Over the previous five years, the company had suffered every bit of bad luck possible. The most damaging were the legal claims from the **Poly Implant Prothèse (PIP)** breast implants that contained industrial grade silicone. Not only did every implant have to be replaced at a cost to the company, but patients sued for damages. The company was paying out over £150,000 per month in legal costs and claims, and the big lawsuits hadn't even started. Most of the cosmetic surgery companies who had used those implants went into administration and then reopened leaving patients with nothing to claim. The Hospital Group had to trade through because the biggest asset, Dolan Park Hospital, had not been separated from the business. This meant that if the company was placed into administration, we would lose the hospital. The final nail in the coffin came with a £17 million pound retrospective VAT (UK sales tax) bill. David had left the company to work on the American deal with *The American* and me. This left my father to run the company. He couldn't do it.

I wanted to wait until Henry had finished his exams before I left for America, but David said he needed me in Dallas with everyone at the beginning of April. This meant I was forced to leave my son, just before his A level exams to move to America. Yet again, Henry would be angry with me, and it would badly affect his exam grades.

Just before the move to Dallas, I started to become ill again. The mystery illnesses returned. Prior to leaving, I became so ill that my doctors thought I had tuberculosis. Yet again, nothing was found to explain my symptoms. David shouted at me saying he wanted me on the flight with him. I was so ill I wasn't sure I would make the flight. I arrived at the airport having difficulty breathing and I could hardly speak. A shock awaited me. David had brought along Steve Barnes and Mark Lester. I could not believe it. I realised I had made a huge mistake. David was with the guys, and I was left alone. I was sad and lonely-and didn't know what to do. My costs were almost £100,000 in websites, travel, removals, and a new apartment. I thought, 'Just stick with it". I was such a state, I asked *The Accountant* to come out to Dallas.

The American wasn't creating anything new. He wanted us to invest our money, use my story for PR and told me to go and look at (and copy) what other eating disorder units were doing.

One of those units was in Denver. *The Accountant* came with me. I suggested we drove up into the Rocky

Mountains, as he had never been. As soon as we got on the highway with the mountains either side of the car, I started a scream-like whimper. I was holding onto the handle above the door and making this whining sound. He had to drive at 30mph until we got to the first exit where we could get off the highway. Once we arrived, we had lunch, looked around the town and I was fine. We then had to drive back. As soon as the mountains were each side of the car, the screaming began again. It was horrific for both of us. I knew by now that something had triggered me and usually memory would follow. As we came out of the mountains, the memory came of being taken in the car, by my grandparents, to Woolacombe Bay (Devon) over Porlock Hill and across Exmoor.

We returned to Dallas and, when drunk, *the accountant* flipped over a mattress and my feet got caught in it. My left ankle fractured and so did my right foot. Yet again, I had suffered fractures that didn't relate to the impact. *The American* had not arranged our work visas or health insurance, and my health insurance covered everywhere except the USA. I said I must go back to have treatment from the team that know my body. There was no compassion from David, *The American*, or any of the others.

If the definition of insanity is 'doing the same thing over and over again expecting a different result', I was insane.

The Hospital Group was sold in July 2016 to a private equity group. It was a fire sale. I knew exactly what the new owners would do, and I refused to sign the documents. This meant David and my father invoked a shareholder drag along clause. The new owners never paid the remainder of the money. I never received one penny from the sale of The Hospital Group. After twenty-five years, I left the companies with one thing – my integrity. Luckily, it was to prove the most valuable asset I had.

Yet again, I found myself back in London looking for a new home. Only this time, my son was hardly speaking to me. The company was gone and the money I had was in David's hands. During all the chaos, a person I had helped with a home and to develop their life, stole £75,000 from me. The one good thing was *the accountant* started his recovery from alcohol. He was to help me get through the next eighteen months.

I had two choices: lie down and die, or fight. I would come to learn what a fighter I am. I decided I was going to build the obesity and behavioural programme I'd talked about. At this point, I had no idea what I would come to discover. I was going to use my twenty-five years of knowledge in healthcare, every contact I had, and use myself as the experiment. I focused on weight loss surgery first, but didn't realise it could become a programme for everyone to use.

I decided that I would start by looking at pre and post operative 'diets' for surgery. People living with obesity are often malnourished, although not in the traditional way of thinking of malnutrition. Every WLS patient had to go onto a special liquid diet two weeks pre op and several weeks post op. We had the ideal opportunity to preoperatively 'clean up the body' and post operatively 'nourish the body'. I decided I would go and learn more about juicing – something historically I'd been against. I decided I would go to a retreat that Jason Vale, *The Juice Master*, held. Jason had cured himself of illnesses with juicing, so I thought that was a good place to start. Before flying out to his retreat in Turkey, I wanted to try out a treatment called *somatic experiencing*.

After the robbery at knifepoint for my watch, Dr Pereira had sent me to have eye movement desensitisation processing – known as EMDR. It is a form of psychotherapy designed to alleviate the distress associated with traumatic memories such as PTSD. I had two sessions of EMDR and I was having flashbacks of my life in the country home with David and my childhood. I found it too traumatic, and I told Dr Pereira that I didn't want to do it anymore. I was too scared to do EMDR again, so I booked a session of somatic experiencing instead. The body holds memory and somatic experiencing helps you access and heal memory. It's an alternative therapy that works from 'the bottom up'.

I went along to Harley St, the area I'd worked in for years, to have my first somatic experiencing session with a psychologist. As he guided me through, suddenly it was like I was being pinned to the chair. I was sitting up, but it felt like I was being held down with my neck bent backwards. I couldn't move. The memory came of Grandad Mac holding me down in the caravan at Woolacombe Bay. I was a small child. My neck was held over the edge of the bed. That was how the fracture to my neck happened, the fracture that was discovered when I was seventeen. I must have been in so much pain as a little child with a fractured neck, but I was told you don't tell. I learned what no child should have to – to cope with unimaginable physical pain and say nothing. Unimaginable emotional pain and say nothing. I learned to dissociate from pain, but I would learn unprocessed pain has to be stored somewhere. Mine was being stored in my body and I had no conscious awareness of it.

I flew to the juice retreat in Turkey. I'd decided to stay for three weeks. Luckily, Jason and his wife Kate were there for ten days. I asked Jason lots about juicing, so I really understood his thinking and how I could make juicing most effective in my program. I took part in light exercise classes with low impact, because my feet were still healing from the fractures. Shortly after starting a session, a few days into the three weeks, I had a pain in my central spine. I thought I'd pulled a muscle. I continued to hike for the rest of the time for ninety minutes a day. While I was away, Henry's A level results came through. Sadly, he didn't get the required three A's and his dream of going to Cass Business School was broken. I blamed myself for moving to America just before his exams. Henry chose not to retake the exams but went to another university in London- not the one he wanted.

When I returned to London, I went to see my physio, David Wales. He was still looking after my fractured foot and ankle. I told him about the pain in my thoracic spine. David put his hands over my spine and said, "With your history, let's get an X-ray to check." He gave me a handwritten letter with a list of all my injuries, explaining that I have a very complex orthopaedic and trauma history. I immediately went for an X-ray, which showed nothing. I spoke with a friend (a trauma surgeon) and he wanted me to go immediately and see a colleague. Within thirty minutes, I was in the office of Professor Arun Ranganathan. He was amazing and wanted me to have an MRI of my whole spine.

I returned a week later for the results of the MRI. Henry wanted to come with me. I agreed. I was sure there was nothing wrong because I was walking around. We sat down and Professor Ranganathan explained that my thoracic spine was fractured. Prof explained that wasn't the main problem. He moved the images up to my cervical spine and showed me that I had almost no spinal fluid between two of my cervical discs. Prof explained I must be very careful, because any slight knock or even a slight fall and I would be paralysed from the neck down and there would be nothing he could do about it. All I thought was to get Henry out of the room quickly. I thought back to when he was sixteen and he thought I would be dead by the morning. I looked at Henry and said, "Everything will be fine." Prof explained he would need to replace the cervical disc and he would make a cut at the front of my neck. There was a risk of paralysis with the surgery, but the main problem was that Prof was booked up for a couple of weeks and then working on his charity projects in Asia. Those six weeks waiting were hell. What was worse than what I'd experienced? Being paralysed from the neck down and not being able to do anything for myself.

The vultures always come when you are weak. David had my money in his name. Our agreement was always a 50:50 split. I'd loaned him money over the last year to renovate his four homes. If he ever needed anything, I had always helped him. As I lay on my back, not knowing what the hell I was going to do, I received a call from David. He said, "I'll give you £200,000 and you must sign off on everything, or you get nothing." I was heartbroken. I screamed down the phone, "You better pray I never get up again." He was telling me to calm down because he thought I was upset about the money. I was heartbroken that he could do this to me. At the same time, I was being trolled and sent hate mail by disgruntled patients. The new owners, as expected, put The Hospital Group into administration. The patients with botched surgery or the *PIP* implants had no one from which to claim. I was fearing total paralysis and getting hate mail from people, for a deal I'd refused to sign and from which I had received no money.

It got worse. David sold the £30,000 watch that I had given him for his thirtieth birthday – that one day was meant for Henry. He also refused to honour his agreement to pay Henry's fees to study, and made Henry get student loans. David went back on every agreement he ever made with me, and he would do a whole lot worse.

Those six weeks were amongst the scariest of my life. However, the spine operation was a complete success, and I was recovering well. The mental impact was huge and the escalation in the night terrors was immense. During this time, if not for *The Accountant*, I don't know what I would have done. I would wake in the middle of the night to find that, during these night terrors, I had been completely incontinent. At its worst, this was happening up to three times a night – every night. I would wake up completely paralysed and unable to move. I was so scared and had no idea what was happening to me. I had let everything slip. I wasn't doing meditation and breath work, I wasn't eating properly, I was using alcohol to help with sleep, and I was back in the 'am I going to die today?' thinking. If I didn't get my money back from David, I could also be facing financial ruin. I was stuck, sitting with my thoughts and not using my tools.

The fracture of the spine was thought to be a very severe somatic response. It was believed that the session of somatic experiencing which brought up memory, had resulted in my body mimicking the initial trauma in a far worse way than the initial event. This was unheard of, and no therapist wanted to do trauma work with me. I couldn't go back to Cape Town because I was recovering from my spine operation. I was too high risk and traumatised for trauma therapists, so it was left to Dr Pereira to process all the trauma and aggressive somatic responses. I can remember asking him if I should have a therapist. He said, "Yes Donna, but who?" Dr Pereira wrote out a 'map' of my trauma. There were twenty-nine major items on those pieces of paper – I still have them. Dr Pereira showed me the list. He told me that most of his patients come to him with one of the things on these pages and they never got over it. He counted the trauma and said, "You've had twenty-nine in the last few years."

I started 2017 in a very dark place. The seizures were relentless. The fear of total paralysis had taken its toll. I was in total self-pity and from that place, it's difficult to see a way out.

The tachycardia was so severe that, on the 4th of February 2017, I had to call 999 and request an ambulance. My chest rocked from my heart beating so hard, and this had been going on for several hours. When the ambulance crew arrived, I was very calm and doing my breathing exercises, and they were dismissive. When they linked me up to the heart monitor, my heart rate was 230bpm. They said the machine was faulty. I said, "I assure you it's not." I was, yet again, in an ambulance, blue lights flashing and taken straight into the resuscitation bay in the emergency department. There were seven staff members in the room. They had the paddles ready in case my heart stopped. I was given a drug to reduce my heart rate, but the risk was that it could drop my rate so quickly that my heart could stop. I left one hour later with a heart rate of 100bpm, telling the staff there was nothing wrong with my heart. They could not understand that this was what a flashback could induce.

A couple of weeks later, a friend of mine reached out to me because he had relapsed on alcohol. I said I would go with him to a *12-Steps* meeting. At that meeting was an unscrupulous character, doing what is not allowed in meeting. He was looking for 'fresh meat'. This man would watch out for newcomers or people who had relapsed to 'pick up' patients for his 'clinic' in Europe. He approached my friend and I got talking with this man. He talked about his business and an expansion, and about an American investor. He carried on talking and I just knew who he was referring to. I said, "Let me guess, the American is *The American*?" Then I said, "The other one is Steve McNerlin?" He said, "Yes, how do you know?" He said there was also a finance guy. I said, "Let me guess, that would be David Ross. One is my father, one is my ex-husband and the other one is *The American* who I'm still waiting on to ship my furniture back to the UK and pay back my money."

My father had been in business with a psychologist and used our London facility for 'vitamins' to cure addictions. They had little psychological back up and it was a cash cow that prayed on very vulnerable people. I reported my own company to our regulators the *Care Quality Commission* or *CQC*. What was the outcome? I received a call from David, saying they knew it was me. The psychologist and his nurse were stealing money that the patients gave in cash. The nurse was walked off the premises by the clinical director and the business was shut down. The psychologist and nurse were never reported to their regulators, so they carried on working. They were now in business with this man I was speaking with. It seemed that my father was again working with the psychologist who stole from him. *The American* was involved and, as usual, David was the money man.

David and *The American* had gone behind my back and made a deal to buy one of the companies my father still owned. This man from the meeting was keen to name his A-list movie star clients and show me emails booking them into his facility. I asked him to say nothing about meeting me and he agreed. He saw the person who I came into the *12-Step* meeting with and realised I had important connections. This was the day which drove me, again, to find a solution to my problems. They weren't going to beat me.

I returned to see Professor Shorvon to see what could be done about my night terrors. There was something that could be done, but it involved heavy medication and it would affect my memory recovery. I explained to what happened during these night terrors, as I was still calling them. I talked about having them three times a night, every night, and on a good week, only three nights. Professor Shorvon asked if we could get *The accountant* on the phone. *The accountant* explained what was happening to me. Prof put down the phone and looked at me and asked how was I even surviving. I said," If you don't stop these terrors, I will kill myself."

I had to find answers to my problems. My Trans-Mandibular Joint /TMJ (my jaw), was so affected by what was happening at night that I could hardly open my mouth. David Wales, my physio, found me a specialist TMJ physio, Krina Panchal. Krina started working on my jaw and sent me to the eminent TMJ and maxillofacial specialist, Professor Piet Haers. The meeting with professor Haers would be the start of major breakthroughs. Prof Haers felt he would need to operate on both of my jaws. In the meantime, he would inject Botox into them to try and stop the clenching. Prof had also noticed that many of his patients had underlying hormonal issues. He asked me to see a gynaecologist and hormone specialist, Miss Sovra Whitcroft. I was to learn about the impact of hormones and how the jaw is one of the simplest and biggest markers for people to identify, stress, anxiety, anger, and rage. Krina worked on my jaw, David Wales on my body, Prof Haers on my TMJ, and Miss Whitcroft on my hormones. I started to show improvement, although many days Krina would say, "I worked on your jaw two days ago and it's like I did nothing."

I went back to the drawing board. I decided to work on step four of my four pillars. I booked my course to train as a mindfulness-based stress reduction teacher (MBSR). I needed to stay present and stop the chronic fear state in which I lived, over what could or would happen to me. I researched what could be happening to me at night and I came across non-epileptic PTSD induced seizures. I continued working with Dr Pereira on my trauma and I asked him if he thought I was having these types of seizures. He said yes. At this point, what would kill me first was the effect these seizures were having on my life. The problem is there's almost nothing you can do about things happening when you are asleep. It was a race against the clock to find a solution to the problem with these seizures.

I left it a few weeks and called David and told him I knew what he and *The American* had been doing with my father. I received a call from *The American* apologising and trying to explain. I had to go to Dallas in April to pack up my apartment and ship my stuff back to the UK. He asked if he could see me in Dallas and I agreed.

I completed my MBSR training in April and then I was due to fly to Dallas. A few days before I was due to fly, I came down with such a terrible response to, what the doctors' thought was, severe food poisoning. I spent three days in hospital being rehydrated.

At the airport, I was so crippled with anxiety that I didn't think I could board the plane. I was in a terrible state. I arrived at my apartment to find my furniture damaged, as the staff had been using the apartment. I met with *The American* for lunch, and he was horrible, blaming me and being a bully. I was in tears. *The American* would go from being super nice to shouting and bullying if he wasn't getting what he wanted. He didn't pay for my furniture to be shipped back, he said it could be stored at the building where the company laboratories were.

I was relieved to fly home. I finished my training for my master practitioner qualifications in Life Coaching, Timeline Therapy, Hypnotherapy and NLP. My tutor,

Wayne Farrell again talked about Dr Bruce Lipton. During the course of my research, I saw Dr Lipton was in London in August 2017. I had to go and meet him.

David had spoken to me about working on some of the behavioural projects with *The American.* I said I would consider it if *The American* met with Dr Pereira, so he understood how bad my PTSD was. *The American* agreed. Dr Pereira gave very limited information in that meeting, and I think I also wanted him to see *The American* for himself. *The American* was cordial. Dr Pereira told him that when there was a group of men, I could feel ganged up on and scared. *The American* meeting Dr Pereira was lip service. *The American*'s true colours were about to be shown.

The American and I met with David. *The American* wanted me to settle my financial affairs with David. The offer had tripled from David's original offer, and I still refused. We were at my private members club and *The American* started shouting at me in front of the security cameras and other people. *The American* knew I had two claims: 1. via the money he had still not returned which I could claim as an investment, and 2. via David. I sat there and looked at David ignoring *The American.* I kept saying over and over, "Are you going to let him do this to me, just like you let my father?" *The American* stormed off. He knew I wouldn't do what he wanted. David looked at me with tears in his eyes and said to me, "You broke my heart." There it was the reason for all the horrible comments – sixteen years after we broke up, his heart was still broken. David had pain and resentment against me, and *The American* was using that.

Afterwards, David looked at me and said, "Are you dying? Your face looks like a skeleton." The issues with my jaw had affected my face. I said, "No, but I if I stay around all of you, I will." As I left, I met Steve Barnes who *The American* had fired from the USA company six months earlier. David had placed Steve in the UK company. Steve arrived with a well-known psychiatrist who had been the assistant medical director at the facility I stayed at, where my psychiatrist had been struck off for taking gifts and a million pounds from a patient. This psychiatrist also had a very chequered past and found himself in front of the General Medical Council (GMC) because of inappropriate behaviour with his patients. *The American* wanted this psychiatrist to write a book about how he had turned his life around and then be the face of a new behavioural healthcare brand. *The American* was paying him to be on retainer. Nothing ever came of the European behavioural health business. *The American* was having other issues back home.

I called *The Accountant* in tears. I asked him to come and pick me up. I said, "I have just lost everything!" If I stayed around these people, I knew I was dead. There would still be several years going backwards and forwards, trying to get what belonged to me. That was the first day in my life, I decided my life was worth more than this.

May 2017 was such an important month in my life. I found messages on *The Accountant's* phone to other women. I knew I needed to look at my personal relationships, so I started working a *12-Step* program for relationships, sex, and love. I was to meet my mentor, the second woman I would come to trust in my life. I started to not only work on my trauma with Dr Pereira, but work on understanding my relationships.

August 2017 was another interesting month. I found out that *The American* and David had bought my father's UK company and agreed on monthly payments. They had defaulted after a few months. Mark Lester was fired by *The American* after he said he caught Mark stealing. Mark came back and started working for my father. Mark told my father about all the financial impropriation that he said David had been doing for years at the companies. Mark completely sold David out. *The American* agreed a non-disclosure agreement with Mark. Mark signed it and no further action was taken. The reason for that agreement with *The American* would transpire in the research for this book, but I had a very good idea why then.

Dr Lipton was speaking at a conference in August. I had originally planned only to listen to him, speak to him and leave. I stayed and listened to all the speakers for the three days. This is where I started to finally understand what I had been doing and why I wasn't getting the long-term successes, even though I had many tools to use. A geographical move wouldn't work because my environment was in my head. I had to change my thinking and I'd already got my foundation in line with what was being said at the conference – that was my four pillars. I now knew I could also change the expression of my DNA. I listened to Dr Joe Dispenza and his talks, and data around meditation and healing the body by changing our thoughts. At this point, I didn't even imagine that all my chronic illness would, or could, be completely resolved. I had been chronically sick most of my life and I could not imagine any other way of life. What I heard was amazing, but I felt there was something missing. I still wasn't sure what. All I knew was I now had hope. I knew I would find a way to the answers I needed. I would just keep going back and forth to the drawing board and trying things out on myself.

In September 2017, I started training to teach mindfulness-based eating (MB-EAT). I also wanted to bring that into my program which was starting to become far more relevant to more things than WLS and obesity.

I needed to have another surgery on my spine to remove the metalwork from my lumber spine that was carried out in 2013. That was planned for October 2017. Dr Pereira warned me that in the twilight phase coming out of the anaesthetic, I could have flashbacks. I had informed Professor Ranganathan, but he didn't seem worried. My big fear was that would happen, and I would totally embarrass myself with people I knew from my industry. The worst happened. In the recovery room I started screaming, "Get her away from me, get her away from me!" Professor Ranganathan came running into the recovery room. He pulled the nurse out of the room. She had blonde hair poking out from her theatre cap and I thought she was my mother. The poor nurse just didn't know what had happened. My memory was about to 'pop'. Dr Pereira had been watching for all the signs and he knew I was close. He had told me that you can never be sure exactly how the mind will release memory or when. It would be like throwing a jigsaw puzzle up in the air and it landing on the floor, and I would have to piece it together. I said, "Can't you just tell me what you are seeing?" All he ever said to me was, "It will all make sense in the end." This drove me nuts.

The plan was to finally return to Cape Town in January 2018 to start my trauma work. The spinal surgery went well, and I was getting myself prepared to go. I'd now started to go to groups for everything: Family of origin groups; workaholic groups; underearner groups;

survivors of incest groups; couple groups; debtor groups; spender groups and food groups. I wanted to understand what lay beneath them all. The common theme was trauma. What was common was just as Dr Lipton had talked about – your DNA being a blueprint. What I was seeing was a common theme of a traumatic blueprints.

I had to make another trip to Dallas. This time it was different. Miss Whitcroft was stabilising my hormones. Prof Haers had managed to avoid surgery using other methods. The physios were getting me more mobile and stronger. I was understanding myself more and my family of origin. The work I was doing and what I was learning was really working. I arrived in Dallas and *The American* was completely different. This time he was kind, apologetic and humble. He knew I wasn't going to be broken, so I guess he was scared I would talk. I let him think I might. I gave him a touch of his own medicine. I was finally taking back my power.

Henry was also in a good place, doing well at university and being predicted a first-class honours degree. Henry was working on his emotional intelligence with Dr Pereira and the trauma he had suffered because of his childhood environment. I can remember saying to Henry when his father and *The American* were driving me crazy, "Your father and *The American* will have me jumping off that bridge if they carry on." Henry just burst out laughing. He said, "Mother, the only thing you aren't good at is committing suicide". He carried on laughing. He said, "I know I shouldn't say it, but it's true!" We laughed so hard together, I knew then Henry would be ok.

I had a simple Christmas, and *The Accountant* and I had a lovely New Year. We went to *Winter Wonderland* and then to a restaurant in Soho. *The accountant* had done some therapy and he did have a very kind streak. We decided after midnight we would take some food to homeless people. On the way there, a taxi crashed into the back of our car. I was three months post spine surgery. My trip to Cape Town would be delayed by a few months so I could have more physio.

My night seizures were getting very frequent again. However, I needed no medication for anything. I just used my four pillars and my large box of tools I was expanding with my knowledge. I was getting myself ready for the place I'd been avoiding going all my life. I was going after my memory. I was going to live, breathe and eat trauma. Trauma was at the root of it all, so that's where I was going to go.

What I had no idea of, was the extent of the pain I would feel. If you took all my fractures, my operations and illnesses and put them into one, they were nothing compared to the pain I was going to feel. When the memory came, and it did, I would get down on my knees, sob, and beg God to make it stop.

WHAT THE READER CAN TAKE FROM THIS CHAPTER?

If you are reverting to old dysfunctional coping strategies. Try to ground yourself and connect with your environment to see what your triggers could be.

If your children come to you and talk of any form of abuse. Listen, love, and support them, ask them how they feel they would like to receive help.

If you are suffering any form of abuse in a relationship, there are charities and authorities that will help and support you.

Take your time to undergo trauma treatment. Make sure you are ready to cope with whatever may come up.

Your body can often hold memory and the stress and trauma associated with these.

Your life is worth more than a business, work or money.

CHAPTER TEN

RELIVING HELL

HELL

A PLACE OR STATE OF MISERY OR WICKEDNESS

On the 24th April 2018, I was finally returning to Cape Town. I thought with all I had learned, and the work I had done on myself, I was ready and able to cope with intensive trauma treatment. I really had no idea and no-one one could have prepared me for what was coming. Dr Pereira and Dr Ori hadn't told me that they expected the memories to be extremely traumatic. Not only in view of what I'd already told them, but the extent of my somatic illnesses and fractures. Dr Pereira wanted me to stay in a clinic, not because I needed to be in a clinic, but because when traumatic memory is recovered, some people can have psychosis. At this point, he didn't want me to take any risks.

Returning to Cape Town after almost three years was like going home. I thought I'd start by taking a silent retreat for five days before I started treatment. I wanted to calm and quieten my mind. My mind was too busy, and the unconscious fear of what was coming was bubbling. After the retreat, I saw Janine Dobson (the clinical nutritionist) who helped me on my last stay. Janine arranged for lots of tests to be carried out, so we had extensive knowledge of what was going on within my body. The next person I saw was Dr Greathead. I was absolutely thrilled to see Lynda again because she had worked wonders with my body last time. Finally, I met up with Dr Ori. I was very different than the last time she saw me. Dr Ori was no different. She was happy, and vibrant as ever and now she was also a mother herself.

Dr Ori had found me a trauma specialist named Lesley Chorn. Lesley was in her fifties and very caring and motherly. I wanted to get going on the trauma work – the hardcore stuff like EMDR. I thought I was ready, but Lesley was having none of it. She had been prepared for the type of person I was and the level of trauma I had suffered. I thought I knew breathwork and meditation, but Lesley was going to teach me breathwork on another level. She was going to use breathwork to bring up the trauma memory. She taught me how to ground myself, how to bring myself back to the present moment if I was disassociating when the memory came.

On one of our first days, we were in a room where there was gas cylinders and clear medical gas masks. I said to Lesley, "I can smell gas." She said, "There's no smell of gas." I insisted I could smell it and became so distressed we had to move rooms. The next day I went into the same room for a nurse to take my observations because I needed to be constantly monitored due to my history of tachycardia. Once again, I said I could smell gas and said I must get out of the room. Just as I used to run from the dentist chair, I 'ran'. I was in flight mode. I told the staff I was going for something to eat. I got into my car and had to get away from the clinic and that room. I was panicking and I could feel myself disassociating, but I couldn't ground myself. Lesley had taught me to look at the trees or the sky, but it was dark and I didn't know how to ground in the dark. The next day I laughed with

Lesley. I said, "Next time you teach someone to ground, make sure you teach them how to do this when it's dark!" It was little things like this that I learned myself to share with others.

Lesley then started with the breathing techniques. She assured me they would bring up the trauma. I thought she was mad. She taught me holotropic breathwork and, just as she said, I would end up crying. I didn't know why I was crying, but Lesley said it was good as I was releasing the trauma. I was yawning and burping constantly. Lesley said this was also releasing the trauma. Then Lesley taught me TRE, which is trauma release exercises. Lesley explained that, when you see a lion go to battle with another lion, after the fight, they shake themselves. The animals are releasing, shaking off their fear and trauma. I learned how to induce tremoring to release my trauma. She also explained somatic experiencing, and the similar theory behind that in releasing trauma from the body. Lesley helped me understand EMDR because this was the treatment where I'd been really distressed in the past.

Dr Ori was helping me process and make sense of everything that was coming up. I needed to understand *intellectually* what was happening to me *emotionally*. I was understanding how my personality was developed, and why I chose women like my mother and men like my father. She helped me to understand why I had chosen the friends I had, why I chose certain types of people to work with me, and the role models I chose. Dr Ori helped me understand why I thought the way I did, and where it came from.

Janine was stripping me back from the insides from a hormonal and nutritional perspective. She watched how the various markers were altering as my trauma was released. She was bringing up, and helping me release, the trauma. Dr Greathead was re-positioning my body as my body re-enacted the positions of abuse, fear or protection. Dr Ori was processing the trauma.

Lesley then started to go into the deep trauma work. I thought my memory would recover chronologically, but that wasn't the case. I thought I would recover my childhood memory first and the last would be the trauma memory as an adult. It was completely the other way round. I was hoping the childhood memory would come first, so I didn't have to speak about the shame I felt over the things that had happened to me as an adult.

We started with EMDR. The memory came of one of the nights with *The Accountant* when he had physically attacked and sexually assaulted me. I was so full of shame and just wanted to lie to Lesley about the visuals I was seeing in my mind. I said to myself, "If you lie about this now, you will be lying forever." I told Lesley what he'd done to me. When Lesley saw the rage come, she would have me whack a pipe over a mattress, have me scream and shout. Lesley had to get the rage out of me – the apocalyptic rage that had been trapped inside me for years. The rage that could be triggered and come out at the most inappropriate times, and at totally innocent people.

Lesley also noticed that I was blocking, and becoming aware of, how the various methods were getting to my memory. Lesley would switch from one treatment modality to another, from EMDR, to somatic experiencing, then to holotropic breathing. Some days when we hit on the big traumas and I would have lots of memory recovery, I would be sweating, shaking, and have horrific diarrhoea. It was like my body was releasing trauma from every pore and every orifice, by any means it could. Some days we just had to stop treatment, some days we could push harder. I knew when Lesley called time and said that I'd had enough, that was it. She wouldn't budge, no matter how much I wanted to push on.

My frustration was that the memory wasn't coming quick enough. I wanted to know what had been done to me and I wanted it in detail. I didn't want someone else knowing what they had done to me, and I didn't.

I also wanted to complete the programme at the clinic, as well as all the other work. I wanted to learn about co-dependency, personality disorders, trauma, addictions, grief, loss, anxiety, depression and all the other things they taught on the programme. I already knew a great deal of information about these subjects, but as I evolved, I would look at the same thinking and treatments in a different way. The programme at the clinic was repeated every three weeks, so I was repeating some of the programme and understanding more and more about myself including why I was the way I was, how it was affecting me in my life and what I could do about it.

Dr Ori had put provisions in place, and she assured me if I did hit psychosis, she would have me out of it in twenty-four hours. I was undergoing six to eight hours a day of intensive trauma treatment, and two hours a day at weekends. I was so frustrated that the memory wasn't coming. I thought I would never get my memory back.

I was to discover there was a way to get my memory back. Dr Pereira had used a 'patient' as an example. He had told me about a patient who felt she had been abused. This patient wanted to go into the Amazon and take ayahuasca. At the time, I told Dr Pereira this patient was crazy and asked who would do that. Much like I had told him he was ridiculous when he suggested mindfulness, I was about to have to eat my words again.

Lesley kept seeing me so upset, thinking I would never get my memory back, she said I may want to look at the multidisciplinary association for psychedelic studies. When I did, it made sense what Dr Pereira had said to me. I thought people who took psychedelics were hippy, weird tree-hugger types. Little did I know that I would come to believe these medicines were critical ingredients to heal trauma.

I realised I would need to return for more treatment. Lesley wanted to bring in a clinical psychologist, Jefferey Rink, who specialised in hypnotherapy and regression, and I thought that was a good idea. I was set on finding a doctor with experience in psychedelic plant medicine who used them clinically.

I had been using myself as the experiment for all types of therapy and treatments for years. Now I was going to experience the effects of hypnotherapy and regression, and psychedelic medicine.

I returned to the UK in June 2018. My relationship with *The Accountant* was over, although it would take another six months before all ties were severed.

I spent six months immersed in the memory that had come up and was continually coming up. I thought to myself, 'I'm sure this can't be true.' The truth was, I didn't want any of it to be true. I set out to prove my memory wrong. If I could prove my memory wrong, then I was crazy like my family said – that was a much better option. I obtained all my medical records from my

GP going back to my birth. I then obtained my medical records from the two stays at the clinic almost twenty years earlier. The records confirmed exactly what I'd been saying for years.

The aunt who had been helping me came with me to all the places that I had memory of abuse. I went to Montague Road in Smethwick, where so many of my immediate and extended family had lived. I went to Brand Hall where my grandparents' flat was, and the 'orphanage', as I called it, had been on Perry Hill. I went to the road where Uncle Fred the paedophile lived. I went to Haden Hill Road where my parents renovated the house next to this man 'Terry' whose name kept coming up in my memory. I decided I would knock on the door of the house, next door to where I thought Terry had lived. I spoke to the young man in the house, and he said a man named Terry lived next door. As I walked back to the car, a man was in the garage working. My aunt said, "Oh my god, that's Terry!" As I turned to look, the garage door and his workshop were the same, everything was just as I remembered. We then went to the cottages where my aunt had spent lots of time. I told her what had happened to me there and she said, "I believe you".

I found my childhood babysitter, Janet McKenzie, and met her for lunch. We laughed about what a lovely little brat I was as a child. Janet talked about my mother and

Diane, and my father having the two women around. I met up with my best childhood friend Joanne Parsons and we laughed about old times. We were with other friends, and she said I was no different than back in the day when I was a poor kid in Birmingham. Joanne was surprised I ever had children. She said, "Why would you want to? Your mother treated you like a babysitter." David once said to me, when I cut ties with my family, "I can understand your mother, she treated you like Cinderella, but your father, you used to light up when he came home."

Everything was confirming my memory not disproving it. I had been running memory and fact checking past Gary, my father's cousin. He was shocked that I knew about Fred the paedophile, and said that was the biggest Cowdell family secret. I fact checked with my aunt who knew both sides of my family well. As I set about proving my memory false, the more I proved it correct. The more I looked inside the family tree, the more I saw the generations of abuse, mental illness, and trauma.

Over those six months I went anywhere I could to listen to people with abuse, trauma, OCD and any form of addictive behaviours. I wanted to understand the thinking, what had got us all to this place. I also started deep inner child work. I went to a *Heal for Life* survivors' retreat and really started engaging with my inner child. I met a man there who I really connected with. He said he was a comedian. He was incredibly funny, but he would also tell me he was a vicar. I meet many interesting people on my travels, but Ravi Holy the vicar, was one of the most interesting and helpful on my inner child journey. I explained to Ravi that my seven-year-old child was still waiting on the steps of the church for God to save her. Ravi worked through a lot of traumas with me, and he would find the most amazing way to help me finally heal my inner child.

Christmas 2018 was the best. I went to the theatre and for dinner with Henry on Christmas Eve and he even came to midnight mass. He cooked Christmas lunch and I took him to a pantomime on Boxing Day. As I engaged with my inner child, I was really encouraging him to engage with his inner child.

I had been writing my book, *Behind the Knife*. We put the cover up on social media late January 2019. I got a call from David saying my father was, "blowing up his phone" asking him what I was saying. David said he was threatening to sue me and take out an injunction – for what I didn't know because I hadn't even said anything yet. David was saying, "It's a great story for the press, your father threatening to sue you when you haven't even said anything yet." I wasn't interested in doing anything other than releasing my book.

What it triggered was a horrific fear response. On the Saturday evening, I started having lots of pain and by 4:00 am, I was having to lie in a hot bath to try to ease the pain. I sat on my bed and Henry was rubbing my back. I called Mr Sirat Khan (a trauma and orthopaedic surgeon) who knew my case well. He sent me to hospital. When I arrived, I asked the medical team to call Professor Ranganathan and tell him that I was there asking for every painkiller they can give me. Prof knew I refused painkillers, so he knew how much pain I must be in to ask. That week, all my friends rallied round to support me. *The banker* came to visit me as we were now like family. Henry, as ever, looked after his mother. The arms of the medical profession also wrapped around me. Mr Sirat Khan, Professor Arun Ranganathan, Dr Sean White and Mr Alistair Windsor all looked after me that week and Dr Pereira oversaw everything. Dr Akbar de Medici came to see me and suggested I see a physiotherapist named James Moore. I was taken from my hospital bed, with the cannulas still in my hand, to see James. I had no idea who James was or his very prestigious background. I couldn't move my arms more than a few inches from my side and I just needed help. That was a meeting that would lead me to show people that anything truly is possible.

The book had to be pulled because I had to return to Cape Town immediately for more trauma treatment. James started working with me to get some movement before I left. What James achieved in a few weeks was miraculous.

As I boarded the flight, I felt like I was fighting for my life. I could not keep living like this. I started straight away with the usual team. Janine took the bloods, Dr Greathead started work on my body, Lesley started the trauma work and Rasmita oversaw everyone. I met Jeffery Rink and I wasn't sure what to make of him at first. I have never seen anyone make so many notes. Just like Lesley, he wasn't starting any hypnotherapy until he had a full background that he had taken himself. Outside of this group, I had found a doctor who specialised in psychedelic medicine and specialised in trauma. I was hitting my memory from every single angle. I now had the dream team looking after me.

Jeff was filming all his sessions. I filmed all the psychedelic sessions just in case my family decided to call me a drug addict again. Lesley and I filmed some of the sessions too. The memory started to come – it was extremely painful. The worst ones were with the hypnotherapy and the psychedelic doctor. With those treatments, I was reliving my life and traumas and this time I was feeling the emotional pain.

I had to drink a potion the psychedelic doctor gave me. It was absolutely disgusting. I laid on a bed, I had a thick eye mask on, and I had my own pillow and blanket with me. I had monitors on me constantly checking my observations. The music the doctor chose was playing loudly. The doctor explained that I might see colours or shapes to start with and then I should breathe and relax and let my mind go where it wanted to. It was horrific. I saw no colours, just skeletons in top hats pulling me down. I saw the old BBC holding screen with the girl in the middle and the girl was me. I kept going down and down with prison like bars around me. I thought I was going to hell. Every single time we used a psychedelic, I had to go through this. While I was in Cape Town, psychedelics were used twice a week using very large doses. What I would go through over the next ten months using psychedelics was hell. I was reliving hell.

What I accessed was grief - years of grief and loss, and the emotional pain that came with it. My journeys, as they are called, would last five hours and I would cry for five hours, just sobbing. I saw oceans of tears and as I looked at them, I thought they would never go, and I would never heal. I saw all those that had hurt, harmed, and abused me. I also saw all those I had harmed, and the harm I had caused others. I was crying the tears of the little girl sitting in the church who could never let anyone see her cry. I was crying the tears of the adult me, the loss of a life, a marriage, loves lost and never gained. I was feeling a lifetime of grief in a matter of hours, and it seemed like it would never end.

My grief and loss seemed infinite, and I often just wanted to make it stop. Within the journey, I would be in my bedroom as a child, then in the hospital as an adult. This moved at such speed that I thought I had gone psychotic. I hadn't. The doctor explained I was going from trauma to a safe place, then back into the trauma, then a safe space. I would see the reservoir of tears and it was getting less and less. It was working, and I was releasing the grief.

With Jeff Rink I was going into the trauma as the person that was suffering the trauma. I would speak like a child or have the mannerisms or accent I had in that part of my life. It was so odd because it was like I could hear myself speaking, but it was another person. I explained this to Jeff, and he would reassure me everything was just as it should be. I really liked Jeff. His precision about everything and being word specific made me feel safe. Jeff was the person who explained to me that with my cosmetic surgery, I had been trying to find a physical resolution to an emotional problem. I kept doing and undoing my cosmetic surgery as he described it. I had also talked about some surgery I'd had, and I said it was like genetic mutilation. Jeff picked straight up on it and repeated what I'd said back to me. I said, "No, I meant genital mutilation." What Jeff was highlighting was that I was trying to cut my DNA out of me.

Lesley was processing the trauma memory that was coming up and it was coming fast. Lesley and I would have quite a laugh when I told her some of the thing's I'd got up to in my life. She would say, "Donna you are something else," and start laughing. I would say, "I know," and we would giggle. Lesley would go on about astrology, I would say, "Whatever Mystic Meg," however I noticed a lot of what she was pointing out to me was correct. I got interested in the astrology and I booked to see Lesley's astrologist – Bernadette Medder. Oh my, the day I met that woman, what Bernadette taught me is timing. There are good times to do things, not so good times, and sometimes terrible times to do things. Yet again, I had to eat my words regarding me saying people were ridiculous in their thinking.

Lesley referred me to acupuncturists and Dr Thomson, another body doctor. Lesley also referred me to Richard Higgins. She tried to explain to me what Richard did, but you can't really explain it. The work I do with Richard is healing generational trauma and energy work. Through numerology, I was also able to understand my personality better. The speed at which Lesley and her team were processing my trauma was phenomenal. The work across the board with this amazing dream team was something else. I was healing my past, the present, and futureproofing myself with everything I was doing.

During my stay in Cape Town, I received a call from David to say *The American* had gone off the radar and effectively double-crossed him. David had been fired from his USA role as CEO. I had told David over a year ago to get out of the American company and focus on the UK one. He wouldn't listen and I was about to find out why. Again, I would have to stop the trauma treatment and return to Cape Town another time.

I returned to the UK to one hell of a storm. The day I landed, my father had gone into the office of the company *The American* and the Americans still owed him the money for, and attacked David. My father smashed a mirror, threw furniture and took chunks out of the wall. The staff could hear all the shouting, but my father didn't care. When he saw rage, the army could be there, and he would carry on. Steve Barnes was getting in the middle to try to stop my father from hitting David. It was the insanity that I had left. My father wanted his company or his money.

I met with Steve Barnes and David the next day. What I saw shocked me. David looked horrific. He had gained a lot of weight. I could see his drinking was out of control again and he looked worried sick. He said he'd known for a long time there were issues with *The American* and the American business, but not only had he invested all our cash, he signed for loans in America and secured UK assets for a company he didn't own. *The American* had used every single one of us, and when you were of no use, you were discarded.

Steve Barnes started crying, saying, "You don't know how scary he is, Donna." He meant my father. "We are really scared." I looked at Steve and said, "Can you repeat what you have just said to me?" He said it again, still crying. I started laughing. I said, "Are you really saying this to me? I had to fight, not just my father, but all of you on my own, while I was facing death and critically ill!" I told them they needed to go to the police. They said they were frightened of what he would do to them. I laughed and said I would contact the police and make the complaint after Henry finished his exams. I told David he needed to do what I had told him a year ago with the UK company. I said I would help them if I could, my co-dependency was still very much an issue at this point.

I also received a hysterical call from my aunt, saying my father had visited her and she was scared. After the attack on David at the office, my father had turned up unannounced at her home. He had brought her some tablets for her heart and started talking about me. He suggested 'they' had got me in a room in South Africa and convinced me I had been abused. My father then got his smartphone and showed her people with false memory syndrome (as abusers like to call it) who were being sued. He then said he would invite my aunt to his sixty-fifth birthday party, which he'd had the weekend before, obviously to make her feel included. My aunt said she couldn't help me anymore because her daughters were petrified. The drama that I'd expected had started.

Over the summer, relations with David were quite good and we discussed doing some business together. Henry got his first-class honours degree and was going to do his masters at Cass Business School. During this good period, we met at a business lunch with two of the medical people I knew well. There was a plastic surgeon at the lunch. David talked about a breast implant problem that was discovered by the plastic surgeon several years ago at Dolan Park, our old hospital. I had no idea. David said the breast implant company sent people over from America to deal with the issue. I knew nothing about this, but David said our company solicitors were involved and they had the information. I had no idea at the time how many millions of women this affected.

As expected, the happy times didn't last for long and once I'd personally secured a loan for David and Steve Barnes, I was not needed. To my shock and horror, after everything he'd said and done, Mark Lester was back working with David.

I was ready to go back to Cape Town but, before I did, I wanted to re-trace my life again. This time I went to all my childhood homes, our offices at Crown House and Church Square and then Dolan Park. I went back to the cottages and a man was outside one of them. We got chatting and he said he'd been trying to find history about the cottages. He took me inside and showed me around, and I recorded what he said, which was again in line with my memory. I then decided to drive back down to Woolacombe Bay. This time I drove to the seafront along my usual route, but as I drove out, I went a different way. As I was driving up the country lane, I saw a caravan park. I pulled into the caravan park and as I was driving down to the office, there it was – what I'd seen repeatedly in my memory. I got out the car and there was the view down to the sea with the two points of land coming together to make the bay. The bars that I'd kept seeing in the flashbacks that looked like prison bars, weren't. I now understood they were the parts of the caravan windows.

There was no more proof needed. I just had to go and face whatever would come, my mind would give me whatever it thought I was ready for.

I arrived in Cape Town and my focus was just get the memory and be done with this. I was about to make two huge mistakes. The first was that using psychedelics is very quick to recover memory, but you cannot process trauma at the speed we were going to be recovering memory. I decided that if I was going to work with the psychedelic doctor, I should see Dr Ori to document and help me understand what was coming up. I would have some sessions with Jeff, but I thought I didn't need all the intense processing work with Lesley.

We started on the psychedelic treatment. This was when I needed the processing more than ever. What would come was deep rooted suppressed memory and I had memory flooding, years of memory coming at once. I was going to hell and at points, I didn't know if I would come back. This time, to avoid having to go to the toilet, I wore an adult nappy. I wanted to stay in the process. I went through my usual horror of being dragged down by skeletons and seeing me as Shirley Temple on the BBC screen. I had become more used to how to use the psychedelics and if I asked my mind the questions or information I wanted, it may take me there. I asked to go to the most suppressed therefore traumatic memory. I was shown the usual life purpose, how to view things, to see life and destiny more clearly and have a better understanding of myself.

Memory came of the night I was drugged and sexually assaulted in my home. I saw my lifeless body draped across Oliver's arms as he carried me up the stairs from my lounge. I could not move my body. I was paralysed by whatever I'd been given. I relived everything that happened to me that night. I knew everything that was happening to me, but I was unable to move. The memory was just heart-breaking, so painful. The memory also came of the cottages, the link between Terry (the builder who lived in Haden Hill), his wife and the abuse. The cottages were my most fearful and suppressed memory, of which the memories are still limited. I was just a very scared ten-year-old child. What also came was what happened to me in the Cayman Islands, why my life fell apart the year I spent there, and why I became so incredibly sick. The most painful memories were still to come. Over several weeks, I relived my childhood and everything in it. To this day there are three people who I love dearly, and I wouldn't be alive without their love and support: My son Henry, my father and my Nanny Mac. My life as I knew it, and everything it was built on, was about to be burned to the ground. Where do I even find the words to say this – the memory came of why Nanny Mac stroking my head calmed me down. From a small child, in the most horrific ways. Much of it, Nanny Mac was not aware of, some of it she was. Memory came, and when it came I saw the visual of Nanny Mac stroking my head to keep me calm while Grandad Mac abused me.

The memory then flashed of all the times I'd felt safe with Nanny Mac stroking my head when I was a baby, when I'd run to her house to get away from my parents' chaos and she would stroke my head while we watched TV on the sofa. I understood why I developed the mystery virus, Crohn's disease, and arthritis after having to spend time sleeping in a room with them on the holiday with David. Worst of all was the memory of the moment she took her last breath. I held her hand and moved it so she could stroke my head. The one thing in the world that could make me feel safe was shattered, at that moment, my life was shattered. I was screaming, "Make it stop! Make it stop!" I was on my knees begging God to make it stop. I was shouting at the doctor to make it go faster, give me more, make it go faster. The speed at which this memory was coming was phenomenal. My eyes were flickering, and it was like looking at the data that's downloaded in the movie *The Matrix*. My unconscious mind was downloading years of memory into my conscious mind, at lightning speed. There was just too much to process. The memory was now in the warehouse of my conscious mind, and I could be triggered easily.

My memory wasn't finished with burning my life to the ground. During a hypnotherapy session with Jeff, I regressed to the little Shirley Temple child. I understood why I had the memory of the orphanage. Jeff films all his sessions, so the mind takes you wherever it wants to go. My mind took me back to sitting in my Nanny and Grandad Macs' car. The car was facing downwards on Perry Hill, in Brand Hall. I was sitting in the back seat of the car, with my face up against the window looking at the orphanage. Nanny Mac was telling me, "If you tell anybody, you will be taken away like Uncle Freddie's children and you will never see your family again." Under hypnotherapy, and in a child's voice and crying, I'm saying, "I don't want to be taken away from my family, I don't want to be taken away from my family."

To save my own life, I had to walk away from all my family and everything that went with that. My worst fear was being taken away from or losing my family, as dysfunctional as my family are, they are my family and I do miss them. Why have I talked? Because secrets keep you sick and I don't want to be ill anymore.

Another memory that also resurfaced was of Nanny Mac shouting at Grandad at the house in Galton Road, "If you touch her (that being me) again I will leave you!". My father had started to make money and my crippled Nanny Mac was no longer reliant on Grandad. I want to be clear, my father had no idea that my grandfather was abusing me, because I truly believe he would have stopped it.

My life was now in ashes and there were only two choices – stay in the ashes or rise like a phoenix from those ashes. I was going to rise, and I was going to rebuild a healthcare empire. I did not know exactly how I was going to do it, but I would.

The first job was to rebuild me.

WHAT THE READER CAN TAKE FROM THIS CHAPTER?

Prepare yourself with grounding work before undergoing therapy. This will help you to deal with painful emotions, or memories that may come up.

It can be helpful to sit with, and take your time to process and accept flashbacks and memory that comes into your consciousness.

Fear can produce extreme somatic responses within the body.

Grief and loss, when processed, can give you a feeling of peace and serenity.

Psychedelic medicine is very powerful and should not be undertaken lightly.

False memory syndrome is often used by those who wish to discredit the abused. It has been proven to be scientifically inaccurate, damaging to survivors and unhelpful to the public.

CHAPTER ELEVEN

THE MENTAL, PHYSICAL AND COSMETIC REBUILD

REBUILD

BUILDING SOMETHING AGAIN AFTER IT HAS BEEN DAMAGED OR DESTROYED

My life lay in ruins and the pain I was feeling was pain that I had never felt before. If I talked about what was at the root of my pain, I would desecrate the memory of my Nanny Mac who was my world. I went back to Birmingham and talked through what I should do with my father's cousin Gary. Like many others, Gary loved Nanny Mac. I asked him if he believed me and he said, "I do-you have never changed your story throughout the time you have been talking to me about this". He said how difficult it was for him because of how much he loved my nan. I asked him what he thought I should do and he said, "You have to do what's right for you". Whatever my decision, there would be consequences, there was no easy choice.

I thought about how I'd managed to overcome all that I had. That was rooted in what Nanny Mac and my father had taught me. They taught me how to survive. Since her childhood, Nanny Mac had survived unimaginable odds. She had been told many times she would not live. My father had also survived unimaginable odds throughout his life. What I had survived, most of the medical profession could not comprehend, never mind explain. The key word was they were survivors and I'd been taught how to survive, not live. In many ways I'd had this amazing life, but I'd never lived a day in my life. I was always in some form of trauma response. While my mother was a hard worker, my father was the brains of the family and had a brilliant mind. He built an empire from absolutely nothing, my parents had nothing. My father would tell me, "You are like me, not like them"., He meant the squeaky women around him. He'd raised me to survive. He taught me (not my siblings) all that he knew because he knew I was the strong one. I remember he once said, "You are like me, but you don't have to be like me". He didn't know another way of life. I'd managed to find a way to live rather than survive. To rebuild my life, I would need a combination of the strength of Nanny Mac, and what my father had taught me, together with all I had learned along with my new way of thinking.

Deciding to live your life differently is as easy as that. The work required to re programme your mind takes an immense amount of time and effort. You are reversing generations of programming and very often you are triggered to revert to your default mode. To rebuild and live a different life, I would have to do that from the inside out. No more could I 'paint the outside of house' when inside nothing had changed. I could look at my life in ashes as a gift to rebuild from scratch or I could play the victim. I'd played the victim, the poor me card- I'd learnt that from my mother. I'd decided I was going to build a *new house.* I would build from the ground up. I would de construct and re construct myself, mentally, physically, and cosmetically.

I had taken my mind apart with the psychedelic medicine and seen the inside of my mind over and over. The psychedelic medicine had 'rubbed out' or softened some of the old neural pathways making it much easier to re programme my mind. I had gained the knowledge I needed to rebuild what I wanted, whether that was through my learnings or by experience. I knew I had to stay present, so I had to practice breathwork daily. I had to strengthen the mind muscle and that meant a short core practice meditating in the morning. That was the gym for my mind and I would get stronger every day. I see so many people who sit around like a Buddha talking about meditation and spouting so much rubbish. My view was that if you can only sit there for half an hour a day and the rest you can't bring your mind back to the present moment, what's the point? Modern life isn't lived sitting like a Buddha. You can teach your mind to live in the noise and the chaos. My mind was genius at living in noise or chaos and it had two fantastic coping strategies that had been with me throughout my life. Those coping strategies were disassociation which, I describe to people who don't know what that is, as automatic pilot. For example, when you drive your car and you get to the shops, but you are thinking how did I get here? The other coping strategy was the dysfunctional strategies that at first seemed great, then I ended up in absolute ruin.

The first thing I had to develop was bringing my mind back to the present moment. In the now, nothing could hurt me, in that very moment I was safe. If I felt safe, I didn't need to disassociate to escape my pain or use my dysfunctional strategies to numb so I would feel nothing. I had to learn to live with the noise and chaos of the world we live in. I'd used everything I could to avoid that for almost fifty years. Once I started to stay present and practice living-not just surviving, it slowly got easier. I would often think of the past. I would say to myself "You are an absolute idiot, how could you lose everything? Look what you had. You had everything anyone could have wished for. You have thrown your life away, it's too late for you now, the time is gone". When I was present, I could say to myself, "You threw nothing away, you chose to walk away from that life. You were unhappy, suicidal, and you had no idea how to live. The people in your life were toxic, you were toxic to yourself and others, that's not who you are now".

If I wasn't present, I would think about the future and I would be crippled by fear. I would say to myself, "They are right, the family told you that you only got where you were because of them". I'd repeat to myself what they told me; "You are nothing without us. You will never make it on your own without us". When I was present and in the moment, I could say to myself, "The figures don't lie, you built a huge business". I would tell myself how I help people every day with my knowledge. What I had to face was fear, and fear is at the root of many of the things we do as humans. I had to learn to sit with, and face a lifetime of fear. My fear would often come out as rage and that was often more fear for what may happen to others more than myself. Or my fear could turn me into an extremely frightened four-year-old child, who wanted to curl up in a ball.

The driver behind much of my fear was the my crippling co-dependency. I knew I had to face my co-dependency head on because it was a fundamental part of my operating system. For those that don't know what co-dependency is, a brief explanation could be characterised by preoccupation and extreme dependence (emotional, social, and sometimes physical) on another person. I was preoccupied with what those close to me were doing, so I didn't need to look at myself. If I could control someone else's world, I didn't feel so powerless in mine. I had co-dependant relationships with my son, friends, and David. The co-dependant relationship with David would cost me dearly. I lived a co-dependant life and most of the people around me were co-dependant. What this meant was as I changed and recovered from co-dependency, I would have to let go of those around me. Not only would I walk away from my family, but most of my friends.

I would often be triggered into a fear response because of the download of years of memory into my conscious mind. There was no way it could be processed at the speed the memory had been recovered. That meant, in the main I was a calm changed person but, if I was triggered, I would revert to the old coping strategies and operating system.

Re-programming my mind was the most difficult process of all. It took daily practise and I would often return to old strategies and then I felt like giving up. Sometimes, when I felt like that, I stopped my daily practises and I was OK with that. The main thing I was changing was the negative self-talk and now noticed when I was speaking to myself in a horrible way. When you grow up in a harsh and punitive environment or family, negative talk is normal. I didn't grow up in a nurturing, encouraging environment- I grew up in a toxic one. While I was very encouraging with my son, and told him to believe anything was possible and not to listen to anyone that wanted to 'kill his dreams', my talk to my son was very negative. I was parenting as I had been parented, so as I changed the way I talked to myself I changed the way I talked to him. However, even with my son I could be triggered back into my old operating system. I still can.

I had to keep practising and practising and noticing when and why I reverted to my old thinking and operating systems. I used pillar 1 and 4 of my four Pillars: breathwork and staying present. These were the two key things that I used to rebuild my mind. They were free and cost nothing. You can do all the therapy and self-development in the world, but I found the two key things to base change on were free. Using your breath and bringing your mind back to the present moment and noticing what's going on in your mind. When you can do that, it will really help you be more conscious and therefore aware of why you are doing what you are doing. Sometimes, when I observe my own thoughts, I can understand why I used anything not to be in my own head. I can tolerate most of my thoughts now and I assure anyone, if you practice and persevere, you can learn to tolerate your distressful thinking as well.

Dr Pereira was helping me process and understand my thinking. What I was noticing was as the trauma was being processed and my mind decluttered, as he called it, my brain was becoming sharp and super focused. I was coming up with new business ideas and going back and forth to the drawing board. I had one of the most brilliant and eminent minds in psychiatry helping me and I would ask him if what I was thinking was possible. He thought about it and said, "Yes". I wanted to take all my knowledge and build something that would give everyone what I'd been receiving. I was starting to believe in myself from a recovered place, because while I often looked 'healed' my driver was still often fear. I know what fear can do to the body and it can make you very sick. Slowly, I was replacing fear with self-belief and trusting in the universe. I believed I had some sort of destiny. I really had no explanation for how I was alive nor did the brilliant minds I had around me. I had to put these amazing gifts I was receiving to good use. Instead of feeling sad and sorry for myself that my life had been burned to the ground, I was starting to feel extremely blessed, lucky and, most of all- grateful. There is a saying in recovery that really resonates with me, "We will be grateful for what has been given to us, what has been taken away and what has been left behind". How I was now living my life was from a place of gratitude. I was rebuilding my mind as a grateful person, I was even becoming grateful for the not so good things that were still happening to me because, in the long run, even those things seemed to have a purpose. Now my mind was getting stronger and clearer, I could really focus on rebuilding my body.

My body has been broken from head to toe. I had a cervical spinal disc replacement, I fractured my left rotator cuff (shoulder), both wrists, nine ribs, and cervical spine. I had my lumbar spine fused, I suffered a triple fracture to my left femur and my left knee. I fractured my left ankle and I've had over six fractures on both of my feet. I was diagnosed with Crohn's disease and arthritis when I was seventeen and I have been riddled with many other chronic illnesses that would come and go throughout my life. I needed to get my body strong again.

Even when my body was completely broken, I would walk around in gym clothes and trainers. People would often ask "Have you just been to the gym?" I would say, "Yes". I'd sadly learned in my family you never let people see that you are weak, that's when they attack. I'd wear my gym kit and I could hardly even move. I'd post pictures looking healthy and well and I had a whole team of medical people working on my body.

I'd had amazing care from my physio (David Wales) who helped me to achieve miracles with my physical recovery. When I met James Moore during my hospital stay in January 2019, I was to achieve another level with my physical body. James not only looked after me himself, but he also brought in his whole team to take care of me. James' team work with Olympians and ultra-sports people and athletes. Among many other credentials, James was head of performance services at the British Olympic Association, and he was Deputy Chef de Mission for the Rio 2016 Olympic games. I now had the *Formula One* team of people looking after me and getting me back to strength and health. I remember telling James when I could hardly move my arms that I wanted to complete a marathon. James always taught me to believe I could do anything I wanted. He understood the psychological impact of injury on my body and how that could impact performance.

James brought in Professor John Dickinson to work on my sleep and breathing. He brought in Darren Chin, a 100m relay European gold medallist, as another physio and coach. Mike Naylor is head of nutrition for the English Institute of Sport and provides expert nutrition to 20 of team GB's Olympic sports. He was brought in to look at my nutrition. Jim Pate came in as the physiologist and oversaw all the testing. Professor Greg Whyte devised my strength and training plans. If I had any physical issues, I would see Professor Mike Loosemore at the Institute of Exercise, Sport, and Health. When I had any injuries, James arranged for me to see the leading medical names in that speciality. My body was now being treated like a *Formula One* race car; I was being treated like an Olympian whose body was being rehabilitated. James took me on as a project and he would help me achieve my dreams. He understood my mind, physical and mental trauma, the mind body connection and most of all, he understood me. James, like me, believed anything was possible and he could translate the physical body like no medical person I have ever met.

James helped me build my physical self-back in ways I could never have imagined or even dreamt. He was preparing me for a marathon within fourteen months of meeting him. I no longer felt physically weak and vulnerable. I started to feel that I was physically invincible. With this phenomenal physical dream team, I rebuilt my physical body in ways no one could have imagined.

I was still left with the issue of the damage I'd done to myself aesthetically. If not through my OCD and anxiety, through trying to find a physical resolution to my emotional issues. Until Jeffery Rink (clinical psychologist) in Cape Town brought this to my attention, I had no conscious idea that's what I was doing. I also had the issue of the botched surgery I'd had at The Hospital Group. While I was linked to the business and family, it was difficult for me to see anyone in the industry in the UK. The medical world is extremely small. When you and your family own one of the largest cosmetic and weight loss surgery brands in Europe, people talk. After what happened to me being sold out by people close to me for my weight loss surgery complications, I was scared to seek advice or help for the required cosmetic surgery revisions.

My aim was to put my body back to the way it would have been had I not been trying to change who I was. Like many people who have cosmetic surgery, I was using the knife to look how I thought my industry and society wanted me to look. I had no idea who I was, so I asked surgeons to take me back to my more natural looking self. I asked them to reverse the damage I'd done to myself. Luckily, I met surgeons who wanted to help me.

In March 2010 while seeing *The Banker*, I'd had a lot of cosmetic surgery in one procedure, everything I'd had done needed to be revised. I'd had the skin from my upper eyelids removed and I had scars in two completely different places which needed to be revised. I'd wanted a slight revision to the cartilage on my nose. Too much cartilage had been removed and my nose needed a cartilage graft. I'd had a breast uplift and my breasts were uneven and needed revision. I'd had bits of liposculpture in different areas and that was uneven. I had wanted my labia to be slightly reduced and the surgery had left the sides uneven. I'd pulled the ends of my eyebrows out due to the anxiety and stress and some of my hair had fallen out with the stress and anxiety. My teeth and jaw had been damaged by the seizures and I'd had an implant where I'd had a molar removed as a child. I was in the middle of my dental treatment when the company was sold. The new owners didn't pay the dental laboratory, so my dental work didn't get finished. The amount of sun damage I'd done to my face with my obsessive tanning was immense. I had scars across my body from all the orthopaedic surgery. Lots of those scars were causing me pain so they needed to be revised. I had a body of two halves that didn't match. I was like a patchwork quilt of scars. Most of all, I wanted to be the person I was- Donna-not some form of caricature.

I started with my nose first. When I had been in Thailand, I had had a seizure and fallen, breaking my nose. Ever since I'd struggled with breathing through one side of my nose. I was referred to Mr Charles East who is one of the most famous rhinoplasty surgeons in the world. Mr East grafted cartilage from my ear and he spent five hours rebuilding my nose. I had another issue with my eyes. I had something called bilateral ptosis, which is where the upper eyelid droops and can affect vision. I was referred to Mr Naresh Joshi-again one of the most eminent oculoplastic surgeons in the world. Mr Joshi corrected my ptosis and had to cut my upper eyelids to do this. At the same time, he was able to even up the scars. I then saw a hair transplant surgeon who carried out a hair transplant to my bald patches and eyebrows.

I was still extremely concerned about having the badly botched work revised in the UK. I asked doctors in Cape Town for recommendation. I first went to see a dentist called Dr Mark Bowes. He wanted to take things really slowly with me and alter my 'bite' so I wasn't in so much pain. After getting my bite more comfortable, he needed to replace all the veneers in my upper mouth. Dr Bowes referred me to see his colleague Dr Howard Gluckman because my dental implant also needed to be replaced. When I met Dr Gluckman, he discussed the amount of gum recession I had due to years of obsessively brushing my teeth. He said he could graft my gums and reverse the damage I'd done to myself. Dr Bowes also referred me to a female plastic surgeon named Dr Nerina

Wilkinson. I felt comfortable with her, but I was still extremely 'cagey' with her about my background and how I'd ended up with so much botched surgery. She planned to first revise my painful orthopaedic scars, then revise all the botched work. She also reversed the damage I'd done to my face with the sun with a powerful laser. She rebuilt my body cosmetically and put me, as best she could, back to the Donna I would have been before I'd done so much damage to myself.

Away from the prying eyes, I had mentally, physically, and cosmetically rebuilt myself in Cape Town. In the UK with James Moore and his 'dream team,' we were taking my physical body to another level. Dr Stephen Pereira was working through my trauma with me and getting me mentally strong and ready to return to my life. I had all these amazing medical people who knew my story and we were helping me rebuild myself. From the ashes I was starting to rise, I still didn't know who I was, but the mental and physical was a good place to start. Finally, I was becoming me, not Donna Ross, just Donna.

WHAT THE READER CAN TAKE FROM THIS CHAPTER?

When telling your truth about the abuse you have suffered, it is best to do what is right for you.

As well as inheriting generations of dysfunctional behaviour, you can also inherit amazing skills to achieve and survive.

Meditation is far more than sitting like Buddha for 20 minutes a day. It's about training yourself to be present for your life.

Positive self-talk can slowly reverse the impact of the negative talk that you may have suffered during your life.

Co-dependency can be one of the most debilitating and self-defeating strategies.

You can be broken physically and mentally and you can overcome it all.

CHAPTER TWELVE

THE PANDEMIC – ADDICTION, ANXIETY, DEPRESSION, OBESITY AND PAIN

PANDEMIC

A DISEASE PREVELANT OVER A WHOLE COUNTRY OR THE WORLD

I returned to the UK on the 2nd January 2020. I had no idea this would be one of the most transformative years of my life. I had decided I wanted no more intense trauma treatment. After the episode with the psychedelics where my memory came flooding back, I couldn't go through that again. That episode had not only pushed me to the edge of my sanity, but I'd also felt like this must be what psychosis feels like. I said to myself, "Enough, you have been through enough!".

As my self-talk became gentler and softer, I didn't feel the need to be so aggressive with myself. I no longer needed to know every detail about what happened to me. I was starting to trust myself and the memories that were now part of my consciousness.

I didn't realise that I had made two major mistakes. The first mistake was not processing the memory and related emotions as they were recovered with Lesley Chorn. The second one was not I had not made provisions for processing the traumatic memory when I arrived back in the UK. In my mind, I had a warehouse full of a lifetime of trauma but in my consciousness. It was raw memory and attached to it was an emotional charge that could set off a nuclear bomb. I was a ticking time bomb and my house that I'd rebuilt was about to be hit by a tsunami of emotion-the likes of which I had never seen.

I realised fear was at the root of my operating system. Fear of loss. When you lose anything, even something very small, there is a grief process. By that, I mean the emotions attached to that loss. A loss could be a marriage, a home, a friend, a loved one, a job, or money. The world was about to be hit by a fear that we had never seen in our lifetimes. We were about to be hit in the face by the fear of losing our lives, the lives of those we love and our world as we knew it. No one could have predicted, and therefore prepared, for what was coming.

The day I returned from Cape Town, I felt odd being back in London. I couldn't wait to get home, but now I was in London I felt like a fish out of water. I can remember standing waiting for a train and thinking just jump. I was scared to death but didn't know where was this coming from and why? How could I tell anyone, after all the work I'd done, that my mind was telling me to jump on the tracks. Every smell, noise, sound, person, and piece of music felt like it was triggering something within me. I was jumpy like a cat on a hot tin roof. I thought it will pass and assumed it was just an adjustment to being home after hardcore treatment with psychedelics. I was feeling shame and guilt. After all everyone had done for me, how could I be feeling like this?

I was due to have a bilateral ptosis repair with Mr Naresh Joshi. When I saw him for my preoperative appointment, he picked up what he thought may be a neurological issue. He wanted me to see a neurologist right away and he called his colleague Dr Angus Kennedy. I panicked- I couldn't go through anymore ill health. I was worried the psychedelics had caused some form of neurological damage. I just kept thinking what I have done, I was trying to hold it together, but failing miserably. I thought after this round of trauma treatment I would come back and go straight to work. Dr Kennedy felt there was no neurological issue, and I was just processing trauma.

The following weekend both David and I received anonymous threatening phone calls. These came out of the blue and we were confused and scared. That was the final straw. I felt very unsafe and I moved into a hotel. Only one friend knew the location. Had I put the measures in place or stayed in Cape Town to process the memory that had come up, I would have been fine. I was having a PTSD response and I was in flight mode. I ran to the Midlands, and I went to stay with a friend in West Bromwich. I just wanted to go home and feel safe. This was the closest I could get. I was a frightened child because all those memories had been triggered.

I was training for the 2020 London Marathon which took place in April. No matter the weather, I had to train, and I would go every day to train in Sandwell Valley Country Park. It was February and the weather was horrific. Storm Dennis was hitting the UK. I still went out in waterproof clothing and a poncho to get my miles in. During the storm, in the middle of Sandwell Valley Country Park, and exposed himself to me. He then followed me. As I came around the lake, I saw someone in waterproof clothing and, as I got closer, couldn't believe my eyes. I had to look again. The man was calling to me with his hand. Once I realised what was happening, I started to pick up speed. The man was following me still performing the act. I called 999 and the police told me to stay on the phone and they were sending officers out to me. The person on the phone wanted to know his location. I couldn't run fast because I had to keep looking behind to see where the man was. The man carried on walking quickly but calmly. I was screaming. The police sirens were all around us but I was in the middle of the park and the police couldn't get to me. I was hysterical after all the years of sexual abuse, I thought this man would rape and kill me and throw me in the bushes. Trying to get away from this man were some of the scariest minutes of my life.

I felt like I was a stalked animal and the fear was unimaginable. The worst thing was the calmness of this man. He was still following me, and you could hear sirens all around us. Finally, when I was almost at the car park, the man calmly turned and walked away but the damage had been done. I was hysterical and in a full-blown PTSD episode. I went back to my friend's house and sobbed. I was forty-seven years old and feared there was no time or place in this world where I would feel safe. I had learned everything I could and done everything possible to heal myself. I gave so much of my time to others to help them and these things were still happening to me. I asked the universe to give me a break, just give me a break. There's only so much the strongest of people can take before it all becomes too much. This was the point where I thought I just want someone to help me, look after me and protect me. Yet again I went back to London to my home- I needed to be home.

The news constantly reported a virus affecting China, Europe, and other parts of the world. Lots of people were dying but it still seemed so far away from us. Within a month of returning to London we were in lockdown due to the outbreak of the COVID-19 virus.

I was in my small apartment in the centre of London. I lived alone and I would have to sit with all the unprocessed emotions and memory that had been brought up. After years of immune suppressant treatment and other medical treatment, my white cell blood count was under three- the average is seven. My medical team had spent years trying to increase my white cell count, to no avail. I was warned something as simple as a virus could kill me.

I started to feel ill. I was boiling hot, sweating profusely, very weak and was sleeping seventeen hours a day. I could hardly lift my body from my bed, then I started to cough and cough. I called the NHS helpline and, because I hadn't been to an infected country or near a person who'd been confirmed as being infected with Covid-19, I was told to go to my local hospital with suspected pneumonia. I asked a nurse friend to take me. I was examined and told it wasn't pneumonia, it was a virus.

I returned home and got progressively worse. I saw what was happening on TV and feared dying alone in a hospital. I then developed breathing difficulties. I was weak, coughing, tired, and drained. I thought I've survived all that I have, to be killed by a virus. I used my four pillars and focused on using different breathing techniques to regulate my breath and keep me calm. I drank as much water as I could. As weak as I was, I got myself to the kitchen to make a juice to get good nutrition in my body as I couldn't eat solid food. I meditated because fear would kill me if I didn't stay present. I was fit and healthy as I'd been marathon training. I used all that I had learnt to keep myself present, hydrated, and nourished. With my white cell count so low, I'm not sure how I survived, but I did. The virus took a huge toll on me. Two weeks later I barely had the strength to walk five minutes to the shops. My muscles still ached, and I was weak. Living alone like so many, fuelled loneliness and I had to sit with all the emotions and flashbacks. I was starting to recover after the initial shock returning to the UK. What I'd started to notice was pain was increasing across my body.

Several weeks later, the same symptoms came again. I was full of fear because this time I knew exactly what it was. There was talk on TV about various drugs that were working at reducing the effects of Covid-19. I knew a man that I was sure would have them, or know how to get them. I'd met *the Builder* the previous November. I thought he seemed very pleasant and a gentleman. *The Builder* had asked me to go out a couple of times, and we'd discussed starting an obesity business together. *The Accountant,* in many ways, had been the young version of my father before he became successful. I believe *The Builder* was the man that was big enough for me to play out the business and adult relationship I had with my father. Like many people did during the pandemic, I was about to get involved with a man because I was scared and lonely.

I called *The Builder* and asked if he had the medication that was in the news. He said he would arrange whatever I needed. If there was a man that was big enough, strong enough and rich enough to keep me safe from everyone, it was him. I was worn out and wanted someone to protect me- he could and would. I saw a very soft side of *the Builder.* He was kind and gentle. He would come and fit up furniture for me and make me cheesecake. Through him, I could see the soft side of my father. Like my father, he employed the women he dated or had dated. That's a sure way to make sure no one can abandon you. I now understood why my father employed these women.

The perfect storm was about to hit. My father emailed me. We'd had no communication in five years and he was checking I was ok because of Covid-19. All those memories that I hadn't processed from the psychedelic trauma treatment got triggered in ways I couldn't imagine. When you are in a traumatised state, you often don't know that you are. I was in the eye of the storm and spinning. *The Builder* became *my father*. He had to be the best at everything and win just like my father. He had to be right like my father, he was wealthy like my father, a builder like my father and in the medical business like my father. When crossed, he could be vicious like my father. This lovely man, that had so far done nothing to me, was completely unconsciously becoming enemy number one. The universe had sent me two gifts to help me process my relationship with both my mother and my father to find a resolution in a safe way.

I got in touch with *Jackie*, a woman that used to work for me in sales at The Hospital Group (Jackie wasn't her real name, it was a nickname given to her by staff at the company in reference to Sylvester Stallone's mother and the amount of cosmetic surgery this woman had had in the past. I told her that *The Builder* and I were going back into the WLS business and would she be interested in joining. She agreed and *the Builder* and I went to meet her at her home. I should have seen it that day - *Jackie* liked rich older men. She had spent the night with *The American*, the American 'business partner', when we were in the Cayman Islands. One of her favourite lines that would have us all laughing was, "a Porsche can cover a bald patch".

As with so many people during the pandemic, sitting with all these emotions, a lot of rage was coming up. This was unconsciously directed towards *the Builder.* It was the rage that I had towards my father. I had fallen into a fear state. What compounded that was that *Jackie* would call me and want to chat for hours about him and me. People come into your life for seasons and reasons. I believe he was the man I felt safe enough to play out what I wanted to say to my father and come to a safe resolution. I'm so grateful to *the Builder* for that.

After the breakup with *the Builder*, friends took me out for dinner and this was where I met *The Italian.* We had dinner then they wanted to take me to a bar in Mayfair. I agreed and as we walked in, I noticed a stunning looking man in front of us. The waitress sat us next to his table. We sat on high stools and mine was right next to his. My chair wobbled and he said, "don't worry, I will catch you". My friend kept telling me he keeps staring at you. I said, "don't be ridiculous". He then started to chat to me, asked where I was from and where I lived. He said he was from Italy and lived in Mayfair. We only chatted for ten minutes. As he got up to leave, he said. "Would you mind if I leave you my card", I said no and took his card. He said he was opening a restaurant in the city and really wanted to take me there for dinner. I messaged *The Italian* a few days later and he asked me to go out with him. I said I would in a few weeks.

I went on a few dates with him. He was lovely. He was honest that he'd been a playboy, but he treated me very differently. I had so much respect for him. He had come from Italy in November 2019. His background was in clubs and restaurants and Covid 19 had hit his industry hard. Four months after moving to England, and he couldn't work so he set up a new business. Then he took a risk and brought a restaurant in the middle of the pandemic. His life mimicked mine. We had very similar personalities and we were both really driven fearless people.

I was still training for the London marathon 2020-now a virtual race where your running number was tracked by satellite. Four weeks before the marathon, friends had taken me to dinner. I placed my foot to the ground, felt pain and I collapsed to the floor. I knew I'd fractured my foot and I could tell by the pain that it was serious.

There was no point going to emergency department because my orthopaedic history and somatic responses were too complex. I called James Moore and he arranged for me to see Professor Nima Heidari the next morning. A scan confirmed a fracture.

The fracture was a Lisfranc fracture-a very severe fracture of my left foot. I was devastated that I couldn't take part in the marathon. Prof Heidari suggested I take part on a knee scooter where I pushed with one leg but I tried it and it was impossible. Then I tried a wheelchair, but my upper body wasn't strong enough, I didn't know what I was going to do. My foot was being scanned weekly and James Moore was doing what he could with my foot. I couldn't do any training and I was told I had to bed rest because, if this fracture displaced and there was a high chance it could, my foot would need surgery.

Jackie called me every day, often several times a day talking about *the Builder*. Ten days before the marathon, *Jackie* said something to me and I thought if she wasn't already seeing *the Builder*, she soon would be. That weekend she disappeared. She called me on the Sunday afternoon and said, "You'll never guess who I saw yesterday?", I said I had no idea although I knew exactly who it was. She continued in this manner finally asking me to guess. She said, "*the Builder*" to which I replied "How long having you been screwing him?". There was silence then she said, "I haven't". She continued to deny it until I said, "You know what I've been through, are you really going to do this to me?". The denials stopped and the aggressive projection started. That was a monumental day for me in my recovery. I didn't allow myself to be gaslit. I trusted myself, my gut instinct, and my reality. I stood my ground. I realised that I didn't want to be a hard nose salesperson and I didn't want those people working with me anymore. *Jackie* was like my mother. She wanted my life and what I had. It was a relief to be able to see and let go of those women. It was like I could finally understand and let go of my mother.

A week before the London marathon 2020, I said I'm going to complete the marathon on crutches. I had learned to put my hurt to good use, it just drove me harder. I saw James Moore on the Tuesday and Thursday before the marathon and I told him what I wanted to do. He said, "Donna, there's a huge risk of displacement of the foot". I asked what percentage, but he didn't know because there's was no data because no one he knew has ever completed a marathon four week's post Lisfranc fracture. He estimated 85% chance of displacement. He said I have to hop a marathon since I had been on bed rest for a month. I decided to see Prof Heidari on the Friday to see the scan results decide. Prof said, "The foot is healing well. keep all the weight off your left foot and give it a go". The instruction was the slightest pain and I stopped, and I listened, my life and my body were now priceless to me.

I also saw Dr Pereira before the marathon He said, "When he saw the email to say you had had another fracture, I thought poor Donna, but she's near the end now".

I was in a fear state around *The Builder* but it was nothing to do with him. All the memory that had been brought up and not processed in Cape Town, had been put through my body again. If the emotions and energy from trauma aren't processed, they must go somewhere. I was going to have to make one last trip to Cape Town. Before that, I was going to do my best to complete a marathon on crutches.

Darren Chin agreed to do this marathon with me. Henry also asked if he could meet me and walk with me. I said, "I may not even make a quarter of a mile, let me see how it goes and I will call you at thirteen miles if we make it halfway". I chose a route that meant something to me- Regent's Park, then through Marylebone into Hyde Park, through the streets of London and finish at Buckingham Palace.

We started the marathon and I was scared. James had told me that if my foot displaced, it would need surgery and my feet would be different widths. He said I would have to forget wearing any of my shoes again. We started off slowly but, as the time went on and my foot was ok, I started to speed up. It was like going down memory lane. I went past Henry's little flat overlooking Regent's Park. We then went past Primrose Hill where David and I had our last house together. We continued down Harley St, then past the private members club where I'd found so much trouble. As we lapped Hyde Park I started to laugh. As we were walking past mine and David's first London home in Knightsbridge, my mind was clear like a fishbowl. I was pacing myself with my breath. My breath-my life force was driving my body and at the same time clearing my mind.

Henry met Darren and me at Hyde Park Corner. We were at twenty-one miles and Henry was going to walk the last five miles with us. Henry was so proud of me. As we walked along Piccadilly, I saw the *Hard Rock Café* where I used to take Henry as a child. We passed *The Ritz* where I had taken Henry after he had gained his degree. Piccadilly Circus reminded us of *The Trocadero* where I would take Henry as a child. I pointed out all the landmarks to Henry and reminded him of our life. As I walked, I thought how far I'd come. I was a poor kid from Birmingham and I'd found myself living a life I could never imagined. Every step I took was driven by those that said I couldn't do things, those that hurt and abused me. I would show everyone that I could and would do what I set out to do. I'd show that I was unstoppable, that I would not be silenced, and that I would tell my truth. I walked through Covent Garden and showed Henry where my father had taken me to

Freed's to my tap dancing shoes. and *Tuttons* where we always went to eat when I came to London with my mother. We remembered *The Lion King* where Henry (aged 3) had shouted at the top of his voice, "it's not Simba Mummy, it's a man!". As we walked towards Buckingham Palace, we walked through Trafalgar Square. My parent's honeymoon was a day trip to London, and they had pictures taken next to Nelson's Column.

As we arrived at Buckingham Palace everyone else had finished but it didn't matter. I done what I had set out to achieve and shown what was possible. I'd shown how strong I was. I'd proven to myself that I was unbreakable, the only person that could break me now was me. I'd done enough damage to myself. Henry was so proud of me. I don't think he could believe I'd done it. When I walked into the Centre for Health and Human Performance two days later, they all stood up and clapped. These were the team that looked after Olympians, and they were standing and clapping for me. James had said, "If you complete it, I'll be impressed", and James was not someone easily impressed. James explained that what I had achieved was like doing a marathon and a half on one leg. What my poor mind and body had been through over the years was immense. In real terms, a marathon was nothing compared to what I'd been through. In under two years, James and his team took me from a hospital bed to a marathon and it wouldn't be my last marathon.

I spent the most amazing month with *The Italian.* He was so soft and gentle and told me, "You met a playboy and now you just have me". I don't think he thought he was enough. Looking at him and all his insecurities, was like looking at myself. Through *The Builder* and *The accountant,* I'd been able to see my father. Through *The Italian*, I was seeing myself. It was like looking in a mirror. He would constantly ask me, "Why are you with me?". I would say, " I don't know - I just am". He would ask all my friends as well. I saw his heart and his determination. I was so proud of him but not for the way he looked or because he was the 'Italian lover'.

A few days before I left for Cape Town, we were in a taxi on the way home and he turned to me. I knew what was coming. He said, "I have feelings for you. I need you to be honest and tell me how you feel. I'm not asking you do you feel the same, I'm asking you could you feel the same. If you can't. you need to tell me. This will make me soft, and I can't be soft". I didn't know what to say so I said nothing. I felt the same but the problem was that I'd been hurt so much. I didn't believe anyone could want me. The night before I left, we had dinner at home. We had sushi and nice wine, Michael Buble was playing and *the Italian* pulled me up to slowly dance. He could sing like Buble. I started to giggle and he asked me why

I was laughing. If there was a fairy tale, this would be the ending and Donna gets her prince. My whole life I'd wanted my Prince Charming and here he was.

I went to Cape Town in November 2020, Covid-19 affected people very differently in Africa- they starved. I met people who said they would rather die than go through another lockdown. I finished the required treatments and I was speaking to *The Italian* most days. I kept extending my trip. I was scared to go home because I'd have to see him. Covid forced me back to England. A new variant had originated in South Africa. One of my friends had died and two others were hospitalised. I had now seen the stark reality of Covid-19 and it was frightening. I was also unwell while I was there but fortunately, I wasn't sick as I'd been the first two times, so I thought it wasn't Covid. The hospitals were now full in South Africa and the borders were closing. I had to get back to England, I flew out on the 31st of December 2020. What a year it had been. I had survived so much, and I had come so far, I felt I was finally finding my peace.

I arrived back in London on New Year's Day 2021, I said I couldn't see *the Italian*. It was one of the worst calls ever and he was so hurt. I had fallen in love with *the Italian*, but I had been hurt so much in my life and I just didn't want to get hurt again. I let someone very special go. You learn what someone wants you for when you part. He wanted me for absolutely nothing. That was a painful lesson to learn. I hoped I wouldn't make the mistake of letting someone I loved go again.

The first round of UK lockdowns were bad, and that data was showing all forms of addictive substances or behaviours skyrocketing. From day 1, I was telling people what was coming. It was like looking at my life and everything I had been through. While clinical data can't be gained quickly, data from alcohol sales, domestic violence helplines, online gambling, and porn subscriptions had all increased. It was all starting to show. The second lockdown was going to be over the winter and many people faired a lot worse than the first time. People had now been living in a state of fear and trauma for a sustained period. The dysfunctional coping strategies were starting to show in the data. People were not equipped to 'sit with' the emotions they had spent lifetimes trying to suppress. Rage was surfacing that had been suppressed for years. The Black Lives Matters movement started. In the UK, women were protesting following the killing of Sarah Everard by a police officer on Clapham Common. Women were sick of not feeling safe to walk the streets. People were starting to let rage out globally.

After having lost a year of their lives being stuck at home, some young children and adolescents experienced abuse at home within dysfunctional families. I looked at the damage that had been done to my son by having to live this way. I looked at his lost year from school and looked at the impact it had had on his life. I spoke to all the specialists I knew in areas of medicine & wellness. I used my case and my son's case as an example of how they would be affected. What I had been saying since the early days of the first lock down, was showing. The data wasn't showing the extent of problems yet, but what we were seeing was bad enough. Trauma is trauma, and as Dr Pereira said, one of the things on my list of twenty-nine is what most of his patients come to see him with. He also said they often never get over it. If my experience, and what I was seeing, was correct, there was a tsunami of mental illness, physical illness, and a break down in society, the likes of which we had never seen before.

It was like I had a crystal ball, and I could see what was coming. There weren't going to be enough life vests, rafts, or masks for people. We didn't have enough psychiatrists, psychologists, therapists, counsellors, and coaches to deal with what was coming.

The tidal wave of mental illness is on its way, and we are starting to see the wave building. We don't have enough medical or wellness people that understand the somatic responses in the body to fear and trauma.

The slowest form of medicine is psychological and behavioural health. I'd been asking Dr Pereira if what I'd been working on was correct. I knew there was a solution, but how did you get people to listen when you told them there was a tsunami coming if they couldn't see it? As Dr Pereira said when I asked him how other specialists could misdiagnose me so badly "How could they have not seen that my body was sick because of emotional pain and trauma?". He replied, "People only see what they want to see. It's too late when the tsunami is upon us"

We need to sound the alarm now. Get our life jackets on, learn the skills to deal with the issues that may arise. Learn the skills to read our bodies, learn very simple skills and strategies to help us cope.

The tsunami is coming, we need to prepare.

WHAT THE READER CAN TAKE FROM THIS CHAPTER?

Fear and loneliness can often be reasons why we get into inappropriate or dysfunctional relationships.

We can often repeat cycles of trauma and dysfunctional relationships until we find healthy and safe resolutions, and then we are able to let them go.

You never know who can come into your life. Love can be found in the most unexpected places, with the most unexpected people, at the most unexpected times.

People who gaslight you often do this to cover up their own lies and wrongdoings.

Your breath is the most powerful force your body has. It can drive your body, clear your mind, and calm your emotions.

If you find someone you love, don't let past hurts make you fear giving and receiving love again.

CHAPTER THIRTEEN

THE TSUNAMI IS COMING

TSUNAMI

AN ARRIVAL OR AN OCCURANCE OF SOMETHING IN OVERWHELMING QUANTATIES OR AMOUNTS

As I look around the world today, the family environment of my upbringing, closely mirrors many facets of the culture, the way of thinking and the way we live our lives. My family based their very lives on how everything looked to the outside world. If *Instagram* was around in the seventies, eighties, and nineties my family would have been major influencers. The image was shiny and they expected me to be perfect and live up to that unattainable image. It is shocking to think that image covered trauma and the life I lived, was completely different to those glossy images.

The last two years have merely amplified, magnified, and expedited dysfunctional behaviours and coping strategies that had already been rapidly increasing. The way we think, our society, the constant bombardment of images and unrealistic expectations of perfection are bringing out the most dangerous and narcissistic elements of our personalities. The instant gratification, the get rich quick, the lose weight now, the belief that beauty and perfection buys us happiness culture has been around for many years. Often, if people don't achieve these things, which are rarely attainable, they revert to ways to numb their perceived failure.

When you look at the real world versus the *Instagram* world, if it's all so perfect. You must ask yourselves why millions of people around the world -both adults and children- are depressed and anxious. Modern society's way of living has altered our natural processes and we are suffering the consequences.

The medical profession looks at me like I'm some kind of miracle but I'm not at all. The only thing that makes my story different, is the amount that's happened to me. Whether that be the traumatic events, the chronic illnesses, or the physical breakdown of my body. If you broke down my story or medical case into individual 'bits', most people would relate to an element of it. When you read my story and how I break it down, you may then be able to understand the reason why some of the things you relate to are happening to you. If you break my story down into one hundred different parts, I'm so mainstream, common, and relatable that it's unreal.

I would like to explain the definition of trauma again. Trauma can be defined as a psychological emotional response to an event that is deeply distressing or disturbing. When loosely applied, this trauma definition can refer to something upsetting such as being involved in an accident, having an illness or injury, losing a loved one or going through a divorce. Extreme trauma can be sexual abuse or torture. Everyone processes a traumatic event differently because we all face them through the lens of prior experience in our lives. The marker for how we process trauma is often our family of origin and the environment of our upbringing.

If we look at the theory of epigenetics and understand that 95-97% of the expression of our DNA is changeable, we then understand that only 3-5% of illness is fixed. Therefore, I was able to heal myself of all my chronic illness and it wasn't a miracle because there is a scientific explanation. What is of interest is how I healed myself of all chronic illness.

I would like to mention the definition of fear again. Fear is defined as a distressing emotion aroused by such things as impending danger, evil or pain. Whether the threat is real or imagined, it is the feeling or condition of being afraid. The key for me here is real or imagined. Most of our fears are based on things that have never happened to us nor ever will. When I say to people the worst thing that can happen to you has already happened, this is because the very thing you fear hasn't happened to you yet. An example in my case of perceived fear and a severe reaction, is my fractures. When we examined every single fracture I suffered, I was in a state of fear. Even if the emotion looked like rage, fear was underneath it. When David said my father was threatening to take out an injunction against me for what (he thought) I would say in my book, I had such a fear response, that I was hospitalised because the pain response was so severe and my capacity to move was severely limited. I couldn't even wash myself or go to the toilet without help.

The fear I was suffering was based on my childhood traumas. I feared what might happen to me, even though the reality was that, in the main, I was in no real danger. The fear response we have (whether the fear is perceived or real) is the often the same. In our world, there's a fear of not being good enough, a fear of fear of not fitting in, a fear of not being beautiful enough, or rich enough, the fear is of not being enough of something. Therefore, the fear is I'm not enough. In my case, I could never be enough because my reality wasn't real. My life, and the image that my family portrayed, was a lie. Just as I did, I see people living two lives- what I call the *Instagram* life and their real lives. People are living in a split or distorted reality to cope with the fear of "I'm not enough".

For over two years, most of the world has lived in a fear state. Much of that time the population of the world has been highly traumatised by the ongoing events and traumatised by living in that prolonged fear state. The impact of living in a prolonged state of fear will adversely impact your mental health. We are aware of the impact on mental health and globally, there is an understanding of what can be done to improve your mental health. We understand the need for pharmaceutical interventions, along with the long-term benefits of wellness modalities such as mindfulness and yoga. If we then combine wellness modalities with the short to medium term use of pharmaceuticals, along with diet and exercise, you will have a substantial magnification in your results.

I think we are all grasping the damage that the pandemic has had on mental health. I don't believe we are anywhere near close to understanding the tsunami that will come over time. Mental health issues can sometimes take years to present themselves. This is often due to varying levels of resilience from person to person based on their life experiences. When I say the tsunami is coming, I'm talking about the physical health implications. How do these fear and trauma states manifest in the body?

If 95-97% of all illness can be mapped in the mind, and globally we have lived in a sustained state of fear and trauma for over two years, the problems with mental health are going to be minor compared to the physical manifestations which will magnify and multiply. They will do this because as you get ill, you get fearful. As the fear increases, so does the physical response. The fear keeps on fuelling the physical illnesses. When the medical profession with their current way of thinking does not readily accept or understand somatic responses based on fear and trauma, that leaves people with no explanation for their illness. This then fuels the fear which fuels the illnesses.

I became sicker because I was worried that no one could explain the reasons behind my illnesses. Once I understood that my illness was a manifestation of a response in my mind, the emotional charge and energy was taken out of my fear. Instead of the perpetuation of the cycle of physical illness increasing, my symptoms decreased. This was with no medication or medical interventions, merely by understanding what was or could be happening to me. What was reduced was fear, and fear was the driver in my mind that was driving my physical illnesses.

The reason I wanted to devote a chapter of my book to this, is because the knowledge of this alone can be more impactful than some other interventions. I'm still fearful and often that fear can be chronic, and I can have the same response as I used to. The difference is that I now understand and can read what's happening externally and how that can manifest in my body. I can tell the difference between a somatic response, even if it looks like a chronic illness, and let's say a seasonal cold that anyone can pick up.

The basis of our healthcare system is reactive. It's not a healthcare system, it's a sick care system. I now understand the driver behind most of my illnesses and from where they manifest. When I'm going to be under periods of pressure or stress, I'm aware that may manifest in my physical body. This takes away or limits the fear I feel and shortens the somatic response should it occur.

We are aware globally that mental health issues such as anxiety, depression and stress are the main causes of time off work- followed by musculoskeletal issues such as back pain and neck pain. What I don't see asked on surveys, is how much of the mental health issues come from the worry of physical health issues and their implications? The root of the problem will not be resolved until the cycle of the mental fuelling the physical, and the continual magnification of both, is addressed. I can say from personal experience and what I've seen with people I've helped, is that once you understand this process and you learn the simple skills to help, the energy and charge is taken out of the fear.

So far, I have discussed the root cause of somatic responses. What also comes because of fear and trauma are the masking strategies, the dysfunctional coping strategies. The behaviours we use to numb out not to feel. I talked through the escalation of these strategies, from the hit of oxytocin the day I was born, to the hit of food, to the hit of sex, to the hit of love, to the hit of alcohol, to the hit of cocaine, to the hit of exercise, to the hit of spending, to the hit of working and so on. The 'hits' available in the world today are immense.

Our society is focussed on instant gratification and instant numbing of emotional pain, but again, the emotional pain goes somewhere. Just because you're numb and you don't feel it, you suppress that pain but it's still building. Where is it building up? In the mind. Where does the mind manifest? In the body. Whatever behaviour we use to cope with stress, trauma and fear, the results find their way into the mind and then the mind becomes overloaded and it manifests its way into the body. The mind's way of speaking is through the body. A psychologist would call reading the body somatic experiencing or reading the body somatically. Medical doctors may describe reading the physical illness in the body that seems to be rooted in the mind as body literacy. The root cause is the same, the translation is the same, the name of that translation is different.

We can see there's a huge potential problem, so what's the solution or solutions? Two things I feel are key. First, there needs to be an understanding of the acceptance of the extent of the problem. Along with that, the other understanding is there's not enough medical or wellness people globally to deal with the problem. Second, is education and knowledge. You would be wise to learn to read your own body. Learn to read your body, no one should be able to read your body like you can. After all, it's your body, empower yourself to gain the knowledge to break the cycle.

The pandemic and the lockdowns didn't just affect parents. It affected grandparents and children. In some families it affected four generations. There are children who saw domestic violence that they would never have seen if not for the pandemic and the lockdown. Those families that never would have been in the category for domestic violence, now are. The children have had domestic violence become part of their reality- their version of normality. That affects what they now think is acceptable behaviour. They are far more likely to engage in violence within their relationships. Then their children will see domestic violence and it becomes their version of normal and it happens in front of their children.

I have used domestic violence as an example, but this applies to any of the realm of behaviours. It can be alcohol, drugs, online shopping, gambling, pornography, workaholism. Strategies that children observe their parents using to cope with stress or anxiety. Strategies whereby they see their parents finding some relief. The strategies can be healthy ones- about 20% of people improved their quality of life because of the pandemic and lockdown. They would have passed on healthy strategies to their children, given examples of positive change rather than negative and damaging examples.

We also don't account for the fear children had watching their parents not being able to see or care for their parents or loved ones. The fear of abandonment or loss a child may feel not being able to see, or say goodbye to, a loved one. Merely hearing of an experience of a friend or one of their family members can induce that fear. The rates of self-harm among children and adolescents are at levels that never seen before. The mental health of a generation is described as being the tip of an iceberg. This not only affects this generation of children and young adults, it can affect their behaviour patterns which can affect their children which can affect their grandchildren and generations to come.

In the introduction I described a stress response as manifesting in ways we wouldn't normally associate with trauma. I described two of those responses as anger and rage. People are fearful and they are angry, often that anger comes out in rage. We currently have the war in Ukraine. We have the *Black Lives Matter* movement and we have the rage of women at Roe vs Wade being overturned. In the UK, we have numerous organisations striking- more than I have ever seen in my lifetime. People are angry, their movement was restricted and rights removed during the pandemic.

Now the global cost of living is rocketing and people are worried about how they are going to afford to live. They are again in another state of trauma. A global recession is looming and after two years of living in a state of fear, the likelihood is yet another prolonged period of fear. It is fear on top of fear on top of fear. People will use whatever they can to cope, and we are seeing every form of addiction sky rocketing.

How best can we help teach people about trauma, how it manifests, what they can do about it, where it's likely to affect them and their children and loved ones? What can happen if we don't make efforts to heal with this generation? How, as parents, it can affect not only our children but grandchildren? We need to sound the alarm now. We need to educate people about fear and trauma and its effects.

The positive is that we can heal from trauma. There is a solution, a way to heal the somatic manifestations and the compulsive and addictive behaviours that we develop as a result. We are on the verge of the legalisation of psychedelic medicine for patient assisted therapy. We have a better understanding today of the effects of trauma and how we can heal from it, more than we ever have. The key is education and empowering ourselves with the knowledge to fight the tsunami that is coming.

My story or my medical case achieves a few things- it gives people hope and shows the capacity to overcome anything. It shows the power of the mind and the strength of the body. Most of all, it shows the capacity to heal. I believe the body and mind want to heal more than they ever want to be sick. I encourage people to empower themselves, realise that have a choice. You don't need to be perfect. It's OK to keep on trying. Better you try a little every day than not at all. It's OK some days to be fed up with the constant effort it takes to reverse the harms and damage others did to you.

The most empowering day for me, was when I realised that I had a choice that meant nobody was doing anything to me anymore. I had a choice to do nothing, or I had a choice to do something. For myself, my son, those I love and future generations of my family, I chose to heal from the pain and trauma others inflicted on me. That pain and trauma I then went on to perpetuate and inflict upon myself. I decided it was time to recreate myself and bring all the knowledge I had gained into a healthcare ecosystem where you can *futureproof* against the tsunami that is coming.

I was on my journey to find a way to stay alive and I wanted to share the knowledge that I had gained with people who would not ordinarily have shared my opportunities.

I would sit with Dr Pereira and say, "It's OK for me sitting here with you, but what about the people that don't have a Dr P and they don't understand what's happening to them? I have access to the most eminent names in healthcare, I need to share this knowledge that I'm gaining".

My medical bills were over £2M and I had been sick all of my life in one way or another. This could have been avoided. My pathway could have been mapped from conception had my family of origin been considered. The alarm bells would have been set off at the first sign of trouble because it would have been expected.

I realised that I had suffered needlessly my whole life and had many unnecessary operations. Even the cosmetic surgery was pointless because I had tried to use a physical/surgical solution to solve my emotional problem.

When I set out on my journey seven years ago, I didn't even know I was suffering from trauma, and you would have had to torture me to get me to admit that I was fearful.

I don't think anyone could have predicted the pandemic bringing the fear, trauma, chaos, discontent, and pain to the world.

I decided I would set up a foundation to gather information from the most eminent names in healthcare to people who needed it most. Medical people were happy to speak to me on camera and I knew we needed to use technology to reach people. Health is global, and the pandemic disrupted the healthcare industry. People are now happy to be a part of, and belong to, virtual healthcare. We can now take great information into people's homes.

There is so much misinformation and people are suffering. There are simple solutions to, what seems like, insurmountable problems. Simply acknowledging that obesity doesn't start at a BMI of 25 or 30, it starts with how you think around food when you are a healthy weight. I explain to people how diets work, so why is the industry built on you failing? The same applies for treatment centres- the success rates for full recovery in one stay are pretty much the same as going on a diet. The process of why this is happening is quite simple to understand when you break it down for people.

What I started was to refine and simplify complex processes into a streamlined effective programme that was easy to follow. I saw the future of healthcare as a predictive system, not the current reactive system. We live in a *sickcare* system. We don't work with *health*, we work with *sickness*. Our system works on the 3-5% of fixed DNA, not the 95-97% of the expression of our DNA that we can change. I don't know another industry that would work on the 3-5% that is fixed rather than 95-97% that can be changed.

I had been using myself as an experiment with everything I had been trying out. I would work with the medical and wellness professionals and go back and forth to the drawing board. The main thing was educating people- you only know what you know. People cannot be prepared for something if they know nothing about it. I had been in the healthcare business for over twenty years, and I did not know any of this information.

The future of healthcare is predictive and regenerative medicine. We must give people the information and knowledge in advance to stay healthy. If I'd had this information, the course of my life, my son's, and those around me, would have been completely different. A predictive health system is a behavioural system. It is possible to map a care pathway from birth that sets alarm bells off for people who are predisposed to emotional issues manifesting in the body.

I was having DNA testing and blood work. This told the professionals (that knew how to read it) what was happening. They could then predict where I would find issues and map my pathway. Not only was I healing from my chronic illnesses, but I was also now predicting and *futureproofing* myself.

While I was dying, I thought if I survived, I would develop a healthcare brand that had a different way of thinking. I became the experiment, DR Health and Medical are the innovators. and Predictor Health is the future.

I had rebuilt myself on every level and I was taking all that I had learned to people, but I still had one last fear to face before I was finally healed.

WHAT THE READER CAN TAKE FROM THIS CHAPTER?

I'm not a miracle. There is a scientific explanation for how I have healed myself of all chronic illness.

The biggest fear can be the fear of not being enough for anything.

Everyone processes trauma differently, and that process is not comparable as it's based upon our life experiences.

Trauma in the mind can manifest in the body. Illness can cause more fear when there is no medical explanation, which fuels and magnifies the cycle.

The basis of the current healthcare system is reactive. It's a sick care system, not a healthcare system.

The pandemic and its effects will affect many generations to come.

CHAPTER FOURTEEN

LOVE, HOPE, PEACE OF MIND

LOVE

EROS: EROTIC, PASSIONATE LOVE
PHILIA: LOVE OF FRIENDS AND EQUALS
STORGE: LOVE OF PARENTS FOR CHILDREN
AGAPE: LOVE OF MANKIND

If I truly wanted to be authentic and talk from a place of wholeness, I would need to face my fear of love. The people who said they loved me and would take care of me had hurt me. When someone said they loved me, my inner child thought the next thing they would do was hurt me. My other chronic fear was of abandonment. Even worse than my chronic fear of abandonment, was being abandoned with a child. My father abandoned my mother and I paid the price. David wanted a child and abandoned me. These were my deepest fears and, even after all the work I had done on myself, they were still there. I knew I had to change the way I lived to be in a healthy loving relationship. I asked the universe for a man for whom I was willing to change the way I lived my life. I only had to be willing, I believed everything else would work out as it should.

The universe was about to deliver what I asked. Friends had invited me for dinner then onto the private members club. As I walked into the room, I saw a handsome man with a beautiful smile. He kept looking over at me and we got chatting. He said he was a musician and seemed like a lovely guy. Within an hour, he asked me if I'd like to go to his house in Ibiza. I paid no attention to that- a musician asking you to his house in Ibiza was something of a cliché. We carried on chatting and exchanged numbers. I received a message the next day but thought no more of it.

A few days later, while having physio with Darren Chin, I received a message from *The Musician.* The message said, "Hello darling, I'm in Ibiza would you like to join me for a long weekend". I nearly fell off of the couch. I thought about it, and decided I would go. I had never done anything like that in my life, I have never travelled to another country for a man. My friends thought I was nuts. They couldn't understand it because I didn't even know the guy.

I completed my half marathon and went straight to the airport. He was waiting for me when I arrived in Ibiza. At that point I wondered what I was doing there-I had no idea he never did things like this either. I was so worried I would have a seizure because I'd only slept for two hours on the first night. He cooked me brunch every morning and then we went to the beach and relaxed. He was quiet, calm, and easy going and I liked being around him. He told me that he spent half of the year in Dubai, and he would have to go back to Dubai in a month. He asked if I would I go and see him in Dubai and I agreed.

When we returned to London, he stayed with me a few nights a week and we got to know each other more. He decided he was going to stay an extra month in London. I told him about my trauma and how I had used the psychedelic medicine to heal. He mentioned he had some trauma and - have no idea why- but I suggested using the psychedelic to help him heal. I said I would do this with him.

I called an amazing therapist with extensive experience with psychedelics and asked if she would oversee the process. I was used to large doses, but she suggested we use small amounts. For some reason, I wasn't scared at all going on this journey with him. The therapist suggested I set an intention, and she asked me if there's anything I would like to achieve and I said, "I want to open my heart". *The Musician* was, not only, classically trained but was a DJ that played in big clubs and he also produced music. In fact, he produced music for us to use. I was to learn the significance of music with psychedelics. We lay down and put our eye masks on, so we could observe our minds. The therapist spoke with us before we drank the medicine, and she would speak with us after. I was about to have the most beautiful experience of my life.

My previous experience with psychedelics had been traumatic, but this time I wasn't scared. I rested my head on his chest and he held me in his arms. I have never ever let anyone go near my trauma with me, yet here I was laying in the arms of a man I'd only known for six weeks.

He'd produced beautiful music and it was all about love. There we were-a pair of love addicts going on this journey together. As the medicine started to take effect, I saw colours. I thought maybe I would finally see what other people saw. I could hear the musician saying, "Wow!" I asked what he was doing and he replied, "I'm painting like Picasso". I was giggling at him having such a beautiful time.

I'd warned him that my trauma was severe and I didn't know what to expect. Then the memory of my traumas came and I told him, "I'm seeing my usual flashbacks". He pulled me so close to him and he held me tight, I don't think I'd ever felt so safe in my life. He wasn't just holding me- he was on the journey with me. He was alongside me when I was reliving these traumas. The tears rolled down my face and he pulled me even closer. Then he went quiet, and I knew he had hit his sadness. As I lay in the arms of this kind and gentle man, my heart opened.

The visual was like the *Raiders of the Lost Ark* scene where they open The Ark and there's the bright light and it's beautiful. I could feel my heart opening and it was like a bright wide beam of sunshine coming out of my chest. First, I felt love for the musician, then I felt this overwhelming deep love and I felt love for mankind. I knew at that moment, no matter what happened, I would love *The Musician* forever. Also, like the scene from the movie, I just unleashed my deepest pain. My heart hadn't been broken- my heart had been shattered repeatedly since I was a small child. I had no idea I'd just unleashed the last and most painful memories.

I was the living example of the mind and body connection. I would come to understand it is the heart, mind, body connection. I could not heal fully until my broken heart healed. I would have to feel this pain to complete my cycle of healing. I had no idea I had stored pain in my heart, and I could not comprehend the next level of pain I would feel.

The Musician stayed for an extra month and then he returned to Dubai. I had to focus on another marathon. I'd completed the marathon the year earlier but it had been on crutches. I wanted to speed walk a marathon to show people you really can overcome anything. James Moore and his team had worked with me to get me ready. We had a strategy that I would walk a constant 7.3km per hour and I would walk the marathon in under six hours.

Unfortunately, disaster struck the night before the marathon when I got food poisoning. I was so ill, and severely dehydrated. There was no way I could re hydrate my body quick enough for the run. On the day, Henry came to see me off. He kept telling me not to do run because he said I was too ill. The same as the year before, I said, "I'm going to give it a go!" Two miles into the race, my hands started to swell due to the dehydration. There was nothing that could be done so I either stopped or I kept going. I maintained the strategy of 7.3km an hour up until sixteen miles and then I hit *the wall.* I was severely dehydrated with ten miles still to run. The task was just like my life. I had to choose to give up or keep going. That's my mind strength, I will never give up, that's why I'm alive. In fact, I finished the marathon but it was a silly thing to do when I was so dehydrated. The pictures that were taken that day show my puffy and swollen face.

Two days later, I flew to Dubai to see *The Musician.* I was so happy seeing him again but I had no idea what was coming. As soon as I got to his apartment, I felt strange, something had changed in me. The first night I got flashbacks. I panicked but I didn't want to say anything, thinking it might be a one off. It wasn't and they were relentless- I was having flashbacks in the day as well. I knew I had to return to the UK because of the likelihood that the seizures would start. I didn't want to say anything to him. I didn't know what had been unleashed or why this had started- I'd been fine in the UK, I wondered what was wrong with me again and thought I couldn't keep living a life like this. I was also starting to feel angry, which meant I was scared. He is the gentlest, most sensitive and soft person I have ever met. Seven days into the three weeks I had planned to stay, I told him I had to go home. He gently asked me "But why?" I didn't know how to start to explain my life. I'd told him quite a few things, but there was just so much to tell. Dr Pereira, always says to me, "Give people your book, let them read it and then they can ask you questions. It's just too much for people to comprehend, it's easier if people read and digest the information first".

I was scared. I was in someone else's home, in another country. I felt trapped and wanted to run. I didn't realise I was triggering his abandonment fears. Over the next few days, I said I had to leave two more times and then the situation blew up. What I was seeing wasn't a forty-two-year-old man- it was a traumatised child. For the first time in my life, I thought, "I'm not doing this", and I walked away. I did something else I've never done in my life While I moved out of his apartment- I didn't leave Dubai. He couldn't understand why I wasn't going home. He said "Why are you staying? I would be going home to my family". How did I even explain the family I'd walked away from and why?

I'd become very good at running but, for the first time in my life, I stayed. I believe abandonment is the core wound of so many people and they don't understand what it is. I had triggered his abandonment. I stayed for him because I didn't want him to ever think I'd left him. Luckily *The Banker* was in Dubai and he's seen me in a full-blown PTSD meltdown. *The Banker* knew what my family are like, and we have always been there for each other. We met up and I felt calmer. He advised, "You need to go home". I flew back to London two days later.

I had to try to figure out what had triggered this full-blown PTSD episode. I was either not wanting to be alone and going out, or I shutting myself off from everyone. I feared going to sleep again because of the flashbacks, but it didn't appear I was having seizures. We thought I'd had another somatic fracture- this time of the ribs in the area where I'd fractured them twenty years ago while skiing after my breakup with David. The pain was just as severe as the initial pain. I saw James Moore and he wanted Prof Loosemoore to check my ribs, but he found nothing. Two days later the pain disappeared. My body was now only mimicking traumatic episodes which this is quite normal and as expected. I was re-experiencing the pain from the somatic injury as I processed the emotion around the memory of that time. This was an amazing sign because things were getting better and my body wasn't fracturing anymore.

In Autumn 2019 I was at a business lunch with David. At one point someone raised the issue with regards to a problem with a certain type of breast implant. This problem had been discovered at Dolan Park Hospital several years before. The discovery was made by the surgeon who was at that business lunch. Two of my closest friends had that brand of implant removed. Charlotte (who had her breast implants for her 40th birthday) had the silicone dug out of her breasts. Toni removed them after a (negative) cancer scare. Within one week, her chronic back pain was halved. The alarm was raised as soon as the discovery was made but those implants continued to be sold to patients for many years after. David said our company solicitors had the information regarding the alarm being raised with the manufacturer. He also said the manufacturers had flown in from different locations around the world to discuss the issue.

I had to have my breast implants changed and the surgeon who made the discovery offered to carry out the surgery. He used the breast implants he developed as a result of the discovery he had made. I had known the surgeon almost twenty years, and really felt like my life-in many ways-was coming full circle.

On the day of surgery I cried. The surgeon was a friend of David. I said to him, "You know I've done everything I can to reach out to David and ask him to come and do things differently". He said "I know Donna. I can vouch you have gone back to everyone that has made mistakes and bad choices and offered them the opportunity to do things differently". I said, "I've known David since I was eleven years old and I told David I don't want my rise to be your downfall". I was sobbing. He gave me a huge hug, he knew what it had cost me to walk away. What I didn't know was the extent of what David had done yet. I also didn't know the extent of the problem with the 'certain' type of breast implants, but I was about to find out.

I told *The Musician* I would be back as soon as I'd addressed some issues in the UK. I was no good to myself or anyone until I finished what I'd started. I had to finish my book, but the fear of what would happen to me when I released my book made my ill. I also needed to be cleared to go back to work, and I was having the flashbacks again. It seemed like every time I was almost at the finish line, something happened to me. There was just a huge amount of fear, fear of success and failure. The more successful I'd been, the unhappier I had been- I feared success. The fear of failure was because my family told me I wouldn't make it without them, and I didn't want the "I told you so".

A few weeks after my surgery I went to dinner with the surgeon who had carried out my procedure. I asked him to explain what had happened with the discovery of the problem with these implants. I also asked him to what had happened with regards to informing the affected patients. He explained what had happened and he also said, "It's not just that 'certain' type of breast implant, it's any breast implant with that coating and shell, so any implant that copied certain brands". I asked the question I had been avoiding-how many women be affected? He said ten million globally! My jaw just dropped- Ten million women! I could never have imagined this number could be affected.

The next thing I thought was "Why me?" So many people knew of the issues and did nothing. I was fifty yards from the finish line after everything I'd been through and overcome. Now not only was I blowing the lid on my family and my life, but it also seemed I would be blowing the lid on one of the biggest healthcare scandals of our time. I know what it's like not to be able to sleep and I wanted to sleep at night. If I did nothing with this information, then I was as guilty as everyone else. The question was how I would handle this information not to cause mass hysteria. First, I wanted to double check the information I had been given.

I'd stayed in contact with *The Musician* and we messaged quite often. We never spoke on the phone, we would leave voice notes for each other, text, or email. Everything was taking so much longer than I had planned because of how I was feeling. I was two-three months away from returning to Dubai. He made a huge impact on my life and our meeting was about to have a major impact on healthcare. He was 42 and I was 48. He had never had children and would want children at some point. That was something that wouldn't be possible for me because I was in the peri menopause. I had two fears- One was, after doing all this work on myself, I would fall in love with a man that wanted children. The second was having a child with that person and being abandoned by them. He was the first man for whom I was willing to change the way I lived my life. I only had to be willing, because if I was willing for one person, that meant I could be willing for someone else.

In the past I had looked at fertility treatments, but I was not willing to change my life for anyone, so there was no point. With him, I was willing to change my life which meant I would be willing to change it for others. I started to look at fertility treatments again and I picked up something that I thought the doctors were missing. I had an amazing Gynaecologist and hormone specialist, Miss Sovra Whitcroft. I had been following protocols Sovra used and had been tweaking them. My hormones were stabilised as was my weight and they had been stable for five years. I had been so ill, and the medical profession didn't know what was wrong with me so I had been tested for everything they could think of. I was like one big human experiment with more data than we knew how to use. I had a theory which I ran past Miss Whitcroft,. She thought it was a bit gimmicky, but she went with me on it. I also had been having bone density scans for eight years, because of the fractures.

I gathered all the historical data that was relevant to what I was hoping to achieve and prove. There are a few areas of medicine that I know very well: WLS and obesity; Cosmetic treatments; Pain; Orthopaedics, and behavioural health. I believed that the procedure I was going to have could reverse the menopause. I felt the frequency being used was wrong. Similar procedures are used in aesthetic treatments and in musculoskeletal/orthopaedics. The frequency is much shorter in those treatments. I was also using the protocols from Miss Whitcroft combined with other things I'd developed. I gathered all my data from the bone density scans and tests. I have a skill for putting a combination of things together, and try out what I'm doing on myself then go back and forth to the drawing board until I get the optimum combination and results. Had I not had all this historic data, it wouldn't have been as easy to prove. I then asked physicists who had specialist knowledge in this area. They looked at the global data and agreed that the frequency was wrong. Even better, with the protocols I wanted to use, we would have clinical data to prove the procedure worked in 120 days. This is unheard of in the medical field.

I was still unsure what had caused all the flashbacks, but as I used my processes, everything was getting much better. I still wanted to understand what had happened, so I did some research. I came across the heart, mind & body connection. New data was showing that the heart signals the brain, and the brain signals the body. The cycle is heart, mind, body connection. If you ask most people where they feel emotional pain, they will likely say their heart. When we used the psychedelic and my heart opened and I felt overwhelming feelings of love for *The Musician* and the world, however I had released the most severe emotional wounds. Unconsciously, I related all this emotional pain to him. He opened my heart, so he had 'caused' the pain, when of course he hadn't. The wounded part of me didn't see it that way, which is why I was feeling angry with him. Add that to the fact that his way of processing was not speaking while he processes, my abused inner child felt like she had no voice. This is a good example of what happens so often in life. The anger that I felt towards others who had severely harmed me, totally unconsciously, I was projecting at the musician. The most kind, loving and beautiful soul I'd ever met in my life, was triggering anger that belonged to others.

I had to do the emotional work and connect with the pain in my heart. I had to feel that pain of my core wound and that would start with the abandonment by my mother. I had to finally sit with the pain of the way my mother treated me. All I ever wanted was a mother's love and I looked for that in friendships with women like my mother. If they couldn't be me, they wanted to destroy me. I had to accept, at 49, that my inner child still wanted her mother to call on her birthday and Christmas. My inner child wanted her mother to call when she was sick, call to say she loved me, but it was never going to happen. I have the memory of why my mother can't speak to me- I don't need to write it in a book.

I had to feel the pain of what Nanny Mac allowed but, whatever the reason, those events tormented me my whole life. The women that I loved more than anything in the world, allowed the worst harms to happen to me. I choose to take the best of her. She taught me how to survive and beat the odds. Nanny Mac loved me more than words can say and I knew that.

I had to feel the pain of the loss of my father. We fought a lot because he raised me to fight and survive. When I come up with my ideas, I want to tell him, but he's not there. We email occasionally and we have spoken on the phone. I love him dearly and I will miss him every day of my life. The reason I'm able to do what I do, is because of my father. He taught me how to do what I do- I just chose to do it a different way.

I had to take my rose-tinted glasses off with David. I had to stop seeing the boy I fell in love with, and see him for what he had become. I found out David had used our own son to hide his assets from HMRC (UK tax office) and administrators trying to recover money for the patients seeking damages from when he was CEO at The Hospital Group. He had also used Henry to hide assets from me when I was looking for his assets in our financial hearing. He had used our son (who was innocent of everything) while he was having trauma treatment with Dr Pereira. David had manipulated and coerced his own son to assist him. I will always love the boy I knew.

Most of all, when my heart opened and the demons came out, I had to look at myself and the hurt I've caused. I can only live my life differently one day at a time and deal with whatever comes when it does. You don't detonate a bomb like I have and expect the fall out to not hit you.

I struggled to understand why my heart opened in the way it did. Then I realised it was the music and I felt safe in the arms of *The Musician*. Music accesses a different part of the brain which is why patients with Alzheimer's disease or dementia can still remember music or songs. When I was in Dubai, I was talking through some ideas with him. We came up with a way to individualise the music for each person using psychedelic medication. The psychedelic opens the mind, and the music takes the person from a feeling of safety into trauma and back to safety and so on. I'm very blessed to have amazing minds around me in behavioural health who I run my ideas by. In the field of psychedelic medicine, I'm lucky to have access to both brilliant clinical and shamanic minds.

I continued my fact checking regarding what I had been told about the 'certain' implants. The number of ten million women globally considering all brands with that coating and shell is correct. I spoke with the Clinical Director at Dolan Park Hospital at the time of the discovery and they confirmed what had happened, and what I had been told was correct. I contacted the company's solicitors requesting the information regarding the communication between The Hospital Group and the manufacturers. After several requests, as ever they ignored me. I asked David if he would give me the information but he just said, "I don't want to get sued by anyone, so no!". Ten million women worldwide have breast implants in their bodies which carry an increased risk of developing Breast Implant-Associated Anaplastic Large Cell Lymphoma (BIA-ALCL) This is not breast cancer-it is a type of non-Hodgkins lymphoma (cancer of the immune system).

At 33, I was a very powerful women in a world dominated by men. Today I'm proud to call myself an empowered woman. I feel sad that people with female organs are biologically biased. Women want to start families later in life, but our biology limits that. If I had male organs, I could continue having children until the day I die. As an empowered woman, I would like the same opportunities as a man, so I found a solution. The treatment to reverse the menopause worked. Not only did I come off all HRT, I have follicles in my ovaries so if I want to have children naturally- I can. My bone density is up 12% in my spine, and I feel better than I ever have in my life. Hormones is how we age and I'm getting younger. I found a way to buy back the time that my abusers stole from me.

Often in life we look back and think why on earth did we do that or did we really love that person. I went back to

Dubai four months after which I had to leave *the musician* to return to England and finish what I started. As Bernadette (my dear friend and astrologer) says to me, "Donna, what is true and what is real?". I needed to know if what I had felt for *The Musician* was true and real. I needed to know if I had felt real love and the only way I would know was if I saw him. So I went to watch him play a set. When I looked at him, I knew what I felt was true and real. I realised the time I spent with him was short, but the impact he's had on my life will last forever.

I ask myself why I had to go through all that I did. I believe the knowledge I have gained must be shared with others. As a *whistle-blower*, I know that I will pay a price, but how can I not share knowledge when people may die if I don't?

As I sat with Dr Pereira, I reminded him of what he would say to me when I only had fragments of my memory. To my immense frustration, he would say, "It will all make sense in the end". I explained to him how I felt my life had been one long 'yellow brick road' and I was just like *Dorothy* in *The Wizard of Oz*. As a child, I would imagine clicking the heels of my red sparkly shoes, to escape my life. When I found myself in his office years later, I was again like Dorothy asking, "Oh will you help me, can you help me?". I went on my journey with some of the most eminent medical minds in the world. They guided me along the yellow brick road of my life, all the way to The Emerald City. Like The Lion - I found my courage, like The Scarecrow - I found my brain and most of all, like The Tin Man - I found my heart. The Tin Man asked The Good Witch of the North, "But why didn't you tell her before?". The Good Witch replied, "Because she wouldn't have believed me". That's why Dr Pereira couldn't tell me. When I reached The Emerald City, he was there waiting for me. Like The Good Witch would say to Dorothy, he said to me, "You don't need to be helped any longer". What I've found is a home with those that love and support me, a home within me and now I know, I had the power all along.

I received a call from Ravi Holy, the vicar that I met on my Inner Child Healing week. I said "Hello Vicar!" laughing. I'd been discussing with Ravi being confirmed. I still saw my seven-year-old self, standing on the steps of the church waiting for God to save her. God was about to come calling in a way I couldn't have even dreamed of. Ravi said he had been able to arrange to get me confirmed, by The Archbishop of Canterbury. He gave me the date of Saturday the 16th April 2022, which was Easter Saturday evening. It was also Passover and Ramadan. They coincide only every 33 years.

Before the ceremony, The Archbishop of Canterbury asked why I wanted to be confirmed. I started to cry and he asked me why I was crying, I said, "My seven year old self is still waiting on the steps of the church for God to save her". He said, "I can understand you think God abandoned you". Crying, I replied, "No I know God saved me. I'm alive and it feels like a miracle".

Standing alone with the Archbishop, he blessed me and we prayed together. What bigger sign could God send? The universe had conspired to save me and keep me safe. That was the day my inner child found her peace.

WHAT THE READER CAN TAKE FROM THIS CHAPTER?

Love is the answer.

EPILOGUE

I'm often asked what happened to the people and organisations I mention in this book.

I haven't seen or spoken to my mother in over seven years, she lives in Spain with her husband. I've never had a Christmas card, a call on my birthday, a call to check I was ok during the pandemic, nothing. I would imagine shame and guilt keep her away.

My father lives in the Cayman Islands. He travels around the world sourcing, pills, potions and products. He still comes up with great business ideas. After forty years, Diane the former mistress remains in his life - She's still waiting for her mortgage to be paid.

David continues in healthcare businesses, with Steve Barnes and Mark Lester. He's no longer the 'front man', he likes to keep assets out of his name. David has four properties, including a country estate. He drives a Range Rover and an Aston Martin among other sports cars. All of David's children are in private education. His partner Bridget Daley has a very lucrative Airbnb business renting out the properties he owns, the ones I loaned him the money to renovate. Sadly, I no longer have contact with David. No patient or administrators have received a penny from David.

Steve Barnes also lives in a country house and drives a new Porsche. His wife Lisa Barnes has a non-surgical cosmetic business, patients receive treatment at their country house. No patient nor administrator have received a penny from Steve.

While undertaking research for this book we investigated Mark Lester. Mark has numerous companies registered at Companies House. Mark was CEO of healthcare companies that have been put into administration, owing substantial sums to suppliers. I have emails and payments from these companies clearly showing the payments were made for money that David owed personally.

The American 'business partner', was indicted by a grand jury. The defendants in the indictment are charged with engaging in organised crime (a first degree felony) and securing the execution of a document by deception (a second degree felony). If convicted, he could face life imprisonment. *The American* was also denied admission to the state bar of California for failing the state bar moral character minimum requirements, for his criminal activity. David, Steve Barnes and Mark Lester were involved in a healthcare business with *The American* during the time the alleged felonies took place.

The law firm that represented my family and our businesses, have documents relating to the recalled implants. I have made numerous requests for this information, I was ignored. The law firm are also defendants in a case brought by administrators accusing them of assisting the directors of The Hospital Group to intentionally move assets, they deny this accusation. In 2021 and for several years beforehand, this law firm represented David against me in a financial hearing. I was trying to recover marital assets and money that belonged to me. After twenty years of representing David and me, both personally and in our businesses, this law firm maintained there was no conflict of interest.

The lawsuits regarding the P.I.P implants and the companies and individuals involved rages on. Barclays Bank are accused of assisting the directors of The Hospital Group to intentionally move assets. Barclays in no way assisted the directors, in fact it was quite the opposite. Barclays would not allow the group to be restructured by way of administration. This was the reason why I refused to sign the documents to sell The Hospital Group. It was clear what any new owner would do. Barclays Bank should not be included in any legal action by administrators.

The Banker is happily married with a family. Our friendship is caring and loving, based on trust and loyalty. We have become family and he will be in my life forever.

The Italian is as gorgeous and charming as ever. He contacted me on Christmas day to let me know that he had sold his restaurant and made a 40% profit. He was my little girl fantasy-The knight in shining armour.

The Musician is busy producing music and DJ'ing around the world. He was so different than any other man I've had in my life, he's so soft and gentle. He will always have a special place in my heart, after all, he was the one that opened it.

I'm constantly asked if I'm scared speaking about these very powerful and wealthy individuals

and companies. I have lived my whole life in fear of what would happen to me if I talked, I will

no longer live in fear or be silenced. I have been called crazy, insane, had numerous character assassinations, received many threatening phone calls. I have been threatened with legal action and been worried for the safety of myself and my son.

I have found my voice, I learned what integrity is and I will tell the truth-my side of the story. The various details I give in this book have been in the public domain for many years. I refer to some of them in the media and news article section. I write about what was happening behind information that is already in the public domain. It was simply knowing where to look and how to piece it together. The sad truth is after thirty years, a few of the players may have changed, but the game remains the same.

When my body was breaking down and I was slowly dying, Dr Pereira suggested that my health might improve if I was to walk away from the family and businesses. I told him that I would not leave without my money. In the end I asked the universe for one thing- that my son and myself could be out of the cycle of trauma and abuse. I traded everything I had for my life, my son's, any more children I may have and future generations of my family. There is no price that can be put on that the lives of those I love.

The world is becoming a very different place. Abusers and those that abuse power are being brought to justice. The *Epstein*, *Weinstein* and *Maxwell* cases among many more are showing the abuse of money and power to buy silence and cover up illegal activities is no longer being tolerated. Not only are the people with the money and power being held to account, but also those who assisted them, worked for them, and financially gained from their activities. Without many people covering up for and helping my family, they would not have evaded justice for all they did. All of those that assisted the criminal behaviour did so for power and money.

In telling my truth, I have found my peace. Whatever I have done in the past, I can't change, however I take full responsibility for my actions.

One day at a time I do my best to live my life differently. I am truly sorry for anyone who has been hurt by my actions or my omissions.

NOTES FROM THE AUTHOR

A percentage of the royalties from this book will be given to The Donna Ross Foundation. This will be utilised to take specialist health and medical knowledge to people affected by trauma, addictions, mental and physical health issues, obesity, womens' health and breast implant associated-ALCL. For further information please visit

www.thedonnarossfoundation.org

I have worked in the health and medical industry for thirty years although I am not a clinician. The experiences in this book are my own, and my discoveries using my extensive knowledge along with the help and guidance of health and medical professionals.

Whilst my aim has been to make my story relatable for anyone to understand, I have a duty of care and a responsibility to those that read this book. I have taken the decision not to discuss any pharmaceutical medications I have used. I do not discuss which psychostimulant/psychoactive medicines were used. These medicines are extremely powerful and require a robust grounding programme and clinical care pathway for anyone wishing to experience their healing powers.

I have mentioned several trauma treatment modalities. However, my suggestion is that no trauma treatment should be commenced without first undertaking an extensive grounding programme.

In the spirit of the cherished tradition of anonymity, I have not named any specific 12 step recovery programmes. The helpful organisation section will give some suggestions to anyone suffering from the issues I've discussed in this book.

It is appropriate to keep details of my sexual abuse and assaults private. There are many reasons for this decision. Details of assaults can be very triggering for survivors of abuse or those suffering from PTSD. I also do not believe specific details of events add any value to my story. My aim is not to sensationalise important issues that need to be taken very seriously.

ACKNOWLEDGEMENTS

There have been many people who have helped me to create this book. Many shall remain nameless, others have heard of my story and encouraged me to share my knowledge.

Dr Pereira
I don't think I would be alive- let alone telling my story- without your help. You encouraged me to share, what you called, the journal of my life. You have helped me think in a different way and guided me gently through this process. I have been extremely lucky to have access to your brilliant mind when going back and forth to the drawing board. You helped me to understand the processes required to extrapolate the details from my past. I found a place of resolution, wholeness and belief that I could write this book. You told me that "it would all make sense in the end" and it did.

Toni Russo
Your command of the English language and clinical ethics has been an asset in writing the book. Your love and support helped me through so many of the dark times. I don't know what I would have done without you.

Rasmita
You gave me so much support. When re living my past while writing, you were on hand to talk me through the

somatic symptoms. You were the first person I told my story to. This book would not exist without your help and support.

Murray Harkin
It's been a very long process and I know many times you thought I would never finish the book. Thank you for your directness in what was needed to induce a change in peoples thinking. When I worry about the pressure of the media and what horrid things could be said about me, I look at what you endured and managed to come through. I know with you by my side I'll be ok.

Idriss
Your friendship, kindness and support has been immense. You always asked me if I really wanted to do this and supported me in the choices I made. You make me feel safe.

Ryan
When I was up against the clock and thought I would never get the book completed in time, you stepped in and took the technical stuff off my hands. I will be forever grateful.

Rob
You were the final piece in the jigsaw puzzle, meeting you pulled everything together. Finally, I could write about love from a place of pure love. I think you are amazing.

Henry
You are the love of my life. You gave me a reason to live when I otherwise had none. You make me laugh and you accept me as I am. To you, I'm just your mother. You never doubt I'll achieve what I set out to do. You are fiercely private, so thank you for allowing me to share some of your private life with others. Your story of triumph over adversity will help and inspire many young adults and children.

Bernadette Medder
My business and timing Guru. Your guidance helps me know that the difficult days are not infinite. The timing of the release of a book is key, thank you for your continued help with dates, timing and strategy. I have immense gratitude that you came into my life.

Lesley Chorn
Thank you for being the sounding board for my ideas and what I believe will come due to the pandemic. You help me get a clearer picture of what to write and how to write it. Thank you for giving me so much knowledge which I share with others in this book.

James Moore
Thank you for helping me make sense of some of my ideas. You have helped me combine my understanding of the mind, body and hormones. So much of the knowledge I share in this book is due to you and your

exceptional team. You're a genius, I've never met anyone that sees the physical body and how to maximise its potential the way you do.

Sovra Whitcroft
Your processes helped me manage my hormones, menopause, obesity and cure my insulin resistance. You have given me so much knowledge which I'll continue to share.

Gary Glasgow
You are one of a kind. Your support when I wrestled with how to deal with talking about generations of family trauma and abuse was immense. You told me to do what I had to, to tell my truth. The gratitude I have for the endless nights you spent talking to me when everyone thought I hadn't got much time left to live, pulled me through. You never once doubted me, you believed every word I said. I'm proud to call you family, you are an amazing father, husband to Lisa and friend. Nanny Mac would be so grateful for how you've helped me. I truly believe she would want me to tell my truth. I love you dearly.

Wayne Farrell
Thank you for sparking my interest and setting me off on my journey of discovery. You are an amazing teacher.

Sonja
My mentor-the one that went before me and showed me the way. Your compassion, love and kindness have helped me write from a peaceful place. So much of what is written in this book is what you have given and continue to give to me.

Members of my outreach group
When I was going out of my mind with the writing, those calls kept me sane.

My fellows in recovery
Thank you for your love, support and encouragement. Breaking a project like this down to one day at a time made it manageable.

All the survivors
Thank you for helping me to find my voice.

MEDIA AND NEWS ARTICLES

SEX, LIES AND THE PLASTIC SURGEONS... - Free Online Library (nd). https://www.thefreelibrary.com/SEX%2C+LIES+AND+THE+PLASTIC+SURGEONS...- a068864697

Worcester News *Hair potion plan ended in tragedy* https://www.worcesternews.co.uk/news/7718984.hair-potion-plan-ended-in-tragedy/

Mail Online. (2006). *Anne Diamond: I finally have my body back.* https://www.dailymail.co.uk/femail/article-407733/Anne-Diamond-I-finally-body-back.html.

Newshopper.co.uk (2003). *Celebrity doctor cleared of charge of sex with patient:* https://www.newsshopper.co.uk/news/6262381.celebrity-doctor-cleared-of-charge-of-sex-with-patient/

Daily Mail.(2011). *TV psychiatrist who took £1.2 million inheritance from anorexic actress, 66, is struck off for 'appalling behaviour'.* https://www.dailymail.co.uk/news/article 1347040/TV-psychiatrist-Dr-Peter-Rowan-struck-taking-1-2m-inheritance-anorexic actress.html.

Barney Calman for The Daily Mail. (2015). *The woman who can NEVER close her eyes: Mother fears she may go blind after 'botched' nip-tuck operation... but hospital chiefs do NOTHING* https://www.dailymail.co.uk/health/article-3122786/The-woman-NEVER-close-eyes Mother-fears-blind-botched-nip-tuck-operation-hospital-chiefs-NOTHING.html.

The Times. (2009). *Stephen McNerlin and family.* https://www.thetimes.co.uk/article/stephen-McNerlin-and-family-qsz3j2vnr6h.

Anna Menin. (2021). *Hope for Women in 35 Million Faulty Breast Implant Case* https://www.thetimes.co.uk/article/hope-for-women-in-35m-faulty-breast-implant-case cmd959xks.

Adam Lusher. (2016). *Women left in pain by 'botched cosmetic surgery' fear losing compensation as firms fold* https://www.independent.co.uk/life-style/health-and-families/health-news/cosmetic surgery-gone-wrong-plastic-surgery-disasters-the-hospital-group-in-administration compensation-battles-bankrupt-transf.

Texas Department of Insurance. (2021). *Houston and Dallas-area attorneys charged with fraud.* https://www.tdi.texas.gov/news/2021/dwc03262021.html.

N/A. (2015). *State Bar of California Roger Arash Farahmand Denied Petition For Review Attorney Fail State Bar Moral Character Minimother Requirements.*
State Bar of California Roger Arash Farahmand Denied Petition For Review Attorney Fail State Bar Moral Character Minimother Requirements.

The FDA Requests Allergan Voluntarily Recall Natrelle BIOCELL Textured Breast Implants and Tissue Expanders from the Market to Protect Patients: FDA Safety Communication 06/01/2020
https://www.fda.gov/medical-devices/safety-communications/fda-requests-allergan voluntarily-recall-natrelle-biocell-textured-breast-implants-and-tissue

Channel 4. (2019). *Britain's breast implant scandal: Channel 4 Dispatches.*
https://www.channel4.com/press/news/britains-breast-implant-scandal-channel- 4- dispatches-0.

BC LEGAL. (2019). *First Letters of Claim Issued in UK Breast Enlargement-Related Cancer Litigation.*
https://www.bc-legal.co.uk/bcdn/926-279-first-letters-of-claim-issued-in-uk-breast-enlargement-related cancer-litigation.

Tingle, R. (2021) *So much for DRY January! Alcohol sales soar during first month of 2021*, *Mail Online.*

Simons N & Simons R . (2021). *Davina McCall, 53, likens going through the menopause to kicking her heroin addiction and admits her symptoms made her believe she was suffering with dementia.*
https://www.dailymail.co.uk/tvshowbiz/article-9556551/Davina-McCall-53-likens-going menopause-kicking-heroin-addiction.html.
Last accessed 18/01/2022

Dispatch .(2019). *Is menopause to blame for painkiller addiction amongst Women?*
https://wp.nyu.edu/dispatch/2019/02/01/is-menopause-to-blame-for-painkiller-addiction amongst-women/

Baker, S. (2021) *Cosmetic surgery booms during lockdowns, Mail Online.*
https://www.dailymail.co.uk/news/article-9109607/Cosmetic-surgery-booms-lockdowns.html

The Guardian Domestic abuse surged in lockdown, *Panorama investigation finds (2020)*
http://www.theguardian.com/society/2020/aug/17/domestic-abuse-surged-in-lockdownpanorama-investigation-finds-coronavirus

Emma Hatley appears on Sky News to explain why divorce rates have increased during 2020 (ND) Stewarts. https://www.stewartslaw.com/news/emma-hatley-appears-on-sky-news-to-explain-why divorce-rates-have-increased-during-2020/

Grierson J. *Domestic abuse killings 'more than double' amid covid-19 lockdown.* Guardian. 2020 Apr 15. https://www.theguardian.com/society/2020/apr/15/domestic-abuse-killings-more-than double-amid-covid-19-lockdown

Stephen Adams for the Mail Online. (2022). *Addiction to painkillers has soared during the pandemic as GPs hand out longer prescriptions, experts warn.* https://www.dailymail.co.uk/news/article-10407061/Addiction-painkillers-soared-amid pandemic-GPs-hand-prescriptions-experts-warn.html.

The Economist (2020) *'Pornography is booming during the covid-19 lockdowns'*, 10 May. https://www.economist.com/international/2020/05/10/pornography-is-booming-during the-covid-19-lockdowns

https://www.dailymail.co.uk/news/article-9146183/So-DRY-January-Alcohol-sales-soar month-2021.html

FMI: *Online grocery sales jumped 300% early in pandemic* (2020) Supermarket News.
https://www.supermarketnews.com/issues-trends/fmi-online-grocery-sales-jumped- 300- early-pandemic

Hangover From Alcohol Boom Could Last Long After Pandemic Ends (no date) NPR.org.
https://www.npr.org/2020/09/11/908773533/hangover-from-alcohol-boom-could-last long-after-pandemic-ends

Kropshofer, K. (ND) *'The pandemic has triggered a British online gambling crisis'*, *Wired U*
https://www.wired.co.uk/article/gambling-uk-online-sites-addiction

Pandemic Lockdowns Tied to More Eating Disorder Symptoms (2021) Consumer Health News | Health Day.
https://consumer.healthday.com/pandemic-lockdowns-tied-to-more-eating-disorder symptoms-2651053976.html

Khazan, O (2015) *Sexual abuse and obesity*
https://www.theatlantic.com/health/archive/2015/12/sexual-abuse-victims obesity/420186/

Professor James Goodwin. (2022). *What Covid does to the brain –and what you can do to prevent it.*
https://www.telegraph.co.uk/healthfitness/body/covid-does-brain-can-do-prevent

Professor Guy Leschziner. (2022). *How to beat the insomnia epidemic caused by Covid anxiety, leading British neurologist PROFESSOR GUY LESCHZINER writes* https://www.dailymail.co.uk/health/article-10404795/How-beat-insomnia-epidemic_caused-Covid-anxiety-PROFESSOR-GUY-LESCHZINER-writes.html.

ACADEMIC REFERENCES

Bellis M., Hughes K., Leckenby N., Jones L., Baban A., Kachaeva M. *Adverse Childhood Experiences and Associations with Health-Harming Behaviour's in Young Adults: Surveys in Eight European Countries.* vol. 92. Bulletin of the World Health Organization; 2014. [PMC free article] [PubMed] [Google Scholar]

Callaghan B., Tottenham N. *The stress acceleration hypothesis: effects of early-life adversity on emotion circuits and behaviour.* Curr. Opin. Behav. Sci. 2016;7:76–81. https://sciencedirect.com/sciencearticle/pii/S2352154615001588 [PMC free article] [PubMed] [Google Scholar]

Carver JM, Ph.D., Clinical Psychologist. (ND). *Love and Stockholm Syndrome: The Mystery of Loving an Abuser* . Available: https://drjoecarver.makeswebsites.com/clients/49355/File/love_and_stockholm_syndr o me.html. Last accessed 22/01/2022

Champagne F. *Epigenetic legacy of parental experience: dynamic and interacting pathways of inheritance.* Dev. Psychopathol. 2016;28:1219–1228. [PubMed] [Google Scholar]

Clemmensen, C, Petersen, M. B., & Sørensen, T. I. (2020). *Will the COVID-19 pandemic worsen the obesity epidemic?* Nature Reviews Endocrinology, 1-2. Obese and hungry: two faces of a nation *BMJ* 2020; 370 doi: https://doi.org/10.1136/bmj.m3084 (Published 06 August 2020)

Kershner J. R. (2020). *Dyslexia as an adaptation to cortico-limbic stress system reactivity.* Neurobiology of stress, *12*, 100223. https://doi.org/10.1016/j.ynstr.2020.100223

Liberatore S. (2022). *Terror of 1994 Rwanda genocide chemically modified DNA of Tutsi women and their offspring | Daily Mail Online.* Available: https://www.dailymail.co.uk/sciencetech/article-10418987/Terror-1994-Rwanda-genocide chemically-modified-DNA-Tutsi-women-offspring.html.

Mickelle N. Emanuel-Frith, Mona, Kingston 7 (2020) *'The pandemic intensifying the obesity epidemic'* (August, 2020), BMJ p. m3084

Mun CJ, Campbell CM, McGill LS, Aaron RV. *The Early Impact of COVID-19 on Chronic Pain: A Cross-Sectional Investigation of a Large Online Sample of Individuals with Chronic Pain in the United States,* April to May, 2020. Pain Med. 2021;22(2):470-480. doi:10.1093/pm/pnaa446

Article examining how Covid-19 has increased chronic pain and chronic pain disorders globally and contributing to a significant increase in psychosocial distress. Also discusses the impact that the pandemic has had on access to services and medications during the pandemic which has also exacerbated some patient's symptoms.

Pfefferbaum B. *Children's Psychological Reactions to the COVID-19 Pandemic.* Curr Psychiatry Rep. 2021 Oct 6;23(11):75. doi: 10.1007/s11920-021-01289-x. PMID: 34613515; PMCID: PMC8493767.

Pfefferbaum B. *Challenges for Child Mental Health Raised by School Closure and Home Confinement During the COVID-19 Pandemic.* Curr Psychiatry Rep. 2021 Aug 16;23(10):65. doi: 10.1007/s11920-021-01279-z. PMID: 34398310; PMCID: PMC8366164.

Public Health England. *Excess weight can increase risk of serious illness and death from covid-19.* Public Health England 25 July2020.
https://www.gov.uk/government/news/excess-weight-can-increase-risk-of-serious illness-and-death-from-covid-19
See also for further links from BMJ between Covid-19 and obesity to explain how Covid-19 and obesity are an extreme health risk

Roesch, Amin A, Gupta J, GarcAa Moreno C. *Violence against women during covid-19 pandemic Restrictions.* BMJ 2020; 368:m1712 doi:10.1136/bmj.m1712

Samaritans. (June 2021). *Coronavirus, young people, and self-harm.* Available:
https://www.samaritans.org/about-samaritans/research-policy/coronavirus-and suicide/one-year-on-data-on-covid-19/coronavirus-young-people-and-self-harm/
Last accessed 04/01/2022.

Will Lawn W and Skumlien, M. (2020). *How is the COVID-19 pandemic changing our use of illegal drugs? An overview of ongoing research.*

World Obesity Federation. Obesity and covid-19: policy statement.
https://www.worldobesity.org/news/obesity-and-covid-19-policy-statement

https://www.addiction-ssa.org/how-is-the-covid-19-pandemic-changing-our-use-of-illegal drugs-an-overview-of-ongoing-research/.

Wise J. *Covid-19: Highest death rates seen in countries with most overweight populations.* BMJ2021;372:n623.

Zattoni, F. et al. (2020) *'The impact of COVID-19 pandemic on pornography habits: a global analysis of Google Trends'*, International Journal of Impotence Research, pp. 1–8. doi: 10.1038/s41443-020-00380-w.

DATA SUMMARY

Addictions and mental health crises have a marked increase during the period of the pandemic and lockdown 2020-2021. Domestic violence has increased globally with particular increase against women and children. Adult women and child killings have also increased during the pandemic.

Alcohol Sales

Alcohol addictions have soared during the pandemic. **Waitrose beer sales up 49% and wine sales by 27% over first week of lockdown in 2020.** A separate YouGov survey found 28% of 'Dry January' participants had given up (Tingle, 2021).

Pornography

There has been a significant increase in users watching online porn with many people 'stuck at home and looking for an outlet". Reporting a 22% rise from February 2020- March 2020 when the lockdown hit (2020) also Zattoni (2020) argues that environments of social isolation, loneliness, and stress can alter the consumption of pornography habits.

Suicides

Although data suggests there has not been a marked increase, this could change at any time and healthcare workers must remain cautious. Calls were up to charities such as the Samaritans have expressed worries of the way Covid has affected suicidal tendencies. They explain 8% of individuals were experiencing suicidal thoughts at the beginning of the first national lockdown, increasing to nearly 10% by mid-May. Also, that women, young people (18-29 years), those from more socially disadvantaged backgrounds, and those with pre existing mental health problems had worse outcomes across nearly all psychological outcomes. Also, an early suggestion from the centre of disease and prevention explain evidence suggesting that significantly more people have thought about ending their lives during the pandemic than in recent years. The darkness, cold, isolation and economic downturn all contributing to these factors (Tingley, 2021).

Plastic Surgery

Pall Mall Cosmetics have reported lipo-suction has doubled since before the pandemic. Tummy tucks have increased by 40%. They have also seen a 520 per cent increase in breast reduction inquiries and a 110 per cent jump for breast augmentation. Men have also been looking into cosmetic procedures to try and eliminate 'breast tissue or 'man boobs', with inquiries into gynaecomastia surgery, up 115 per cent. One surgeon sights the main reason for this is that people can recuperate at home, they don't have to take sick leave, and no one has to know (Baker, 2021).

Eating Disorders

Lockdowns are now associated with an increase in self-reported eating disorder symptoms, according to a study published in the April issue of *Psychiatry Research.* Although the data is not confirmed they do know that people often use food as a coping mechanism for stress,

and clearly many people have been impacted by stressful events and significant changes over the last 12 months (Consumer health News, 2021).

Relationships

Divorce enquiries which rose by 122% from July to October 2020 during the national Covid Lockdown, compared to the same period in 2019 (Stewarts, 2021).

Domestic Abuse

Domestic violence rose in the first UK national lockdown with frightening statistics. Reporting one call made to police every 30 seconds relating to domestic abuse in the first seven weeks of the national lockdown (Guardian, 2020).

Gambling

Data collected from the Gambling Commission (the British body responsible for gambling regulation) showed that in March 2020 when the first lockdown hit, online virtual sports betting increased by 88 per cent and online poker by 53 per cent compared to the same month in 2019 .

Childhood Sexual Abuse Statistics

1 in 3 girls are sexually abused before the age of 18.

1 in 5 boys are sexually abused before the age of 18. (The Advocacy Center, 2021) More than 90% of individuals with a developmental delay or disability will be sexually assaulted at least once in their lifetime." (Valenti-Heim, D.M Schwartz L.)

Childhood Sexual Abuse and Obesity

One analysis of 57,000 women found that those who experienced physical or sexual abuse as children were twice as likely to be addicted to food. Research suggests childhood sexual abuse increases the odds of adult obesity by between 31 and 100 percent (Kahaz, 2015).

HELPFUL ORGANISATIONS

ALCOHOL & SUBSTANCE MISUSE

Adult Children of Alcoholics® & Dysfunctional Families

A programme for people grew up in dysfunctional homes.

https://adultchildren.org/

Al-Anon

Al-Anon is a free self-help "12 step" group for anyone whose life is or has been affected by someone else's drinking.

Telephone: **0800 0086 811** (daily, 10am to 10pm)

https://www.al-anonuk.org.uk

Alcoholics Anonymous

A free self-help group. Its "12 step" programme involves getting sober with the help of regular face-to-face and online support groups.

Telephone: **0800 917 7650** (24-hour helpline)

https://www.alcoholics-anonymous.org.uk

Drinkline

A free confidential helpline for people worried about their own or someone else's drinking.

Telephone: **0300 123 1110** (weekdays 9am to 8pm, weekends 11am to 4pm)

Gay and Sober

Gay & Sober's mission is simple – to provide a safe, fun, and enriching experience to the sober LGBTQ community.

https://www.gayandsober.org/england

Narcotics Anonymous (NA)

Help and advice, recovery groups support and literature for all adults recovering from drug abuse.

https://na.org/

National Association for Children of Alcoholics

Telephone: **0800 358 3456**

https://www.nacoa.org.uk

Narcotics Anonymous (NA)

Help and advice, recovery groups support and literature for all adults recovering from drug abuse.

https://na.org/

National Association for Children of Alcoholics

Telephone: **0800 358 3456**

https://www.nacoa.org.uk

MENTAL HEALTH

Anxiety UK

Charity providing support if you have been diagnosed with an anxiety condition.

Telephone: **03444 775 774** (Monday to Friday, 9.30am to 5.30pm)

https://www.anxietyuk.org.uk

Bipolar UK

A charity helping people living with manic depression or bipolar disorder.

https://www.bipolaruk.org.uk

Black, Asian and Minority Ethnic (BAME) Mental Health

https://www.rethink.org/advice-and-information/living-with-mental-illness/wellbeing physical-health/black-asian-and-minority-ethnic-mental-health/

CALM

CALM is the Campaign Against Living Miserably, for men aged 15 to 35.

Telephone: **0800 58 58 58** (daily, 5pm to midnight)

https://www.thecalmzone.net

Mental Health Foundation

Provides information and support for anyone with mental health problems or learning disabilities.

https://www.mentalhealth.org.uk

Mind

Promotes the views and needs of people with mental health problems.

Telephone: **0300 123 3393** (Monday to Friday, 9am to 6pm)

https://www.mind.org.uk

No Panic

Voluntary charity offering support for sufferers of panic attacks and obsessive-compulsive disorder (OCD). Offers a course to help overcome your phobia or OCD.

Telephone: **0844 967 4848** (daily, 10am to 10pm)

Obsessive Compulsive Anonymous UK

OCA holds regular meetings to help people with OCD.

https://www.obsessivecompulsiveanonymous.org.uk/

Over Eaters Anonymous

12 Step recovery programme for people struggling with eating and food addictions.

https://www.oagb.org.uk/

PAPYRUS

Young suicide prevention society.

Telephone: HOPElineUK **0800 068 4141** (9am to midnight, every day of the year)

https://www.papyrus-uk.org

Samaritans

Confidential support for people experiencing feelings of distress or despair.

Telephone: **116 123** (free 24-hour helpline)

https://www.samaritans.org/

SANE

Emotional support, information and guidance for people affected by mental illness, their families and carers.

https://www.sane.org.uk/support

SLAA

Sex and love addicts anonymous confidential advice and group meetings

https://www.slaauk.org/

Workaholics Anonymous

https://workaholics-anonymous.org/

OBESITY

Association for the Study of Obesity (ASO)

The ASO aims to develop an understanding of obesity through the pursuit of excellence in research and education, the facilitation of contact between individuals and organisations, and the promotion of action to prevent and treat obesity.

https://aso.org.uk

European Coalition for People Living with Obesity (ECPO)

Work collaboratively across Europe to improve the lives of people who are living with and are affected by the chronic disease of obesity through advocacy, policy and education.

https://eurobesity.org/

Obesity Empowerment Network (OEN)

Obesity Empowerment Network UK is a non-profit, user led, advocacy organisation, dedicated to empowering people affected by obesity by giving them a public voice.

https://oen.org.uk/

Obesity UK

Obesity UK is a registered charity to represent the voice of people with obesity.

https://www.obesityuk.org.uk/

Over Eaters Anonymous

12 Step recovery programme for people struggling with eating and food addictions.

https://www.oagb.org.uk/

ABUSE (CHILD, DOMESTIC, HATE-CRIME, SEXUAL)

HEAL FOR LIFE FOUNDATION

Residential healing programmes for survivors of childhood trauma and abuse.

Telephone: **01233 813884**

admin@healforlife.org.uk

NSPCC

Children's charity dedicated to ending child abuse and child cruelty.

Telephone: **0800 1111** for Childline for children (24-hour helpline) **0808 800 5000** for adults concerned about a child (24-hour helpline)

https://www.nspcc.org.uk

Proud Mistletoe/Stonewall

Supporting the LGBTQ + community in solidarity against hate crimes and creating more inclusive workspaces.

https://www.stonewall.org.uk/ourwork/campaigns/proud-mistletoe

Rape Crisis

To find your local services phone: **0808 802 9999** (daily, 12pm to 2.30pm and 7pm to 9.30pm)

https://www.rapecrisis.org.uk

Refuge

Advice on dealing with domestic violence.

Telephone: **0808 2000 247** (24-hour helpline)

https://www.refuge.org.uk

Survivors of Incest Anonymous

Is for men and women, 18 years and older, who were sexually abused as children

https://siawso.org/

Thar
you
sho
at
Am

Pac
You
Ord

Qty

1

0/UC

amazon.co.uk

A gift from **Shirley Henderson**

Happy Easter Aunty Betty, Love Shirley xxxxx From Shirley Henderson

Gift note included with **The Cost Of Life - Recovering from an Epidemic of Addictions, Anxiety, Depression and Obesity**

THE NEXT CHAPTER

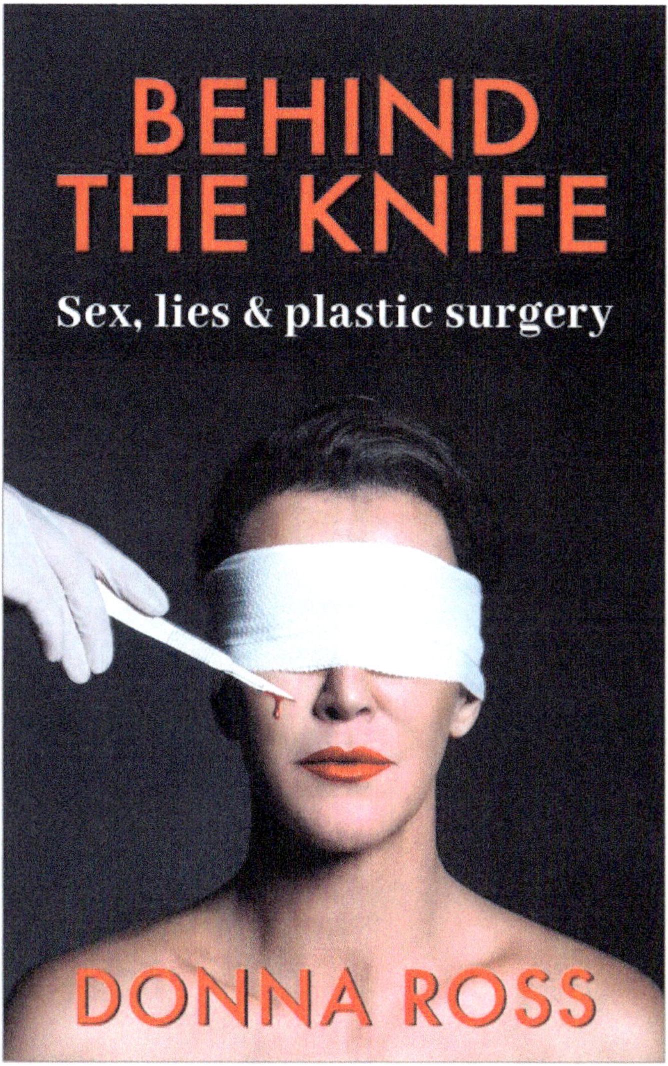

Printed in Great Britain
by Amazon

19648631R00242